ALL ABOUT

INCLUDES ACCESS TO OVER 50 TRACKS FEATURING LOTS OF GREAT SONGS!

GUITAR

A FUN AND SIMPLE GUIDE TO PLAYING GUITAR

by Tom Kolb

PLAYBACK
Speed • Pitch • Balance • Loop

To access audio visit:
www.halleonard.com/mylibrary

Enter Code
6961-7327-1479-3680

ISBN 978-1-4234-0815-4

HAL•LEONARD®
7777 W. Bluemound Rd. P.O. Box 13819 Milwaukee, WI 53213

Visit Hal Leonard Online at **www.halleonard.com**

FUNNY STUFF

Q: How do you get a guitar player to turn down?
A: Put sheet music in front of him.

Q: How many guitar players does it take to change a light bulb?
A: Ten. One to change the bulb, and nine to say, "I could have done that better!"

Q: What's the difference between a guitarist and a mutual fund?
A: One matures.

Q: What do you call a guitar player without a girlfriend?
A: Homeless.

Q: How many guitar players does it take to cover a Stevie Ray Vaughan tune?
A: Evidently all of them.

Q: What did the guitar say to the guitarist?
A: Pick on someone your own size!

Q: How many lead guitarists does it take to change a light bulb?
A: None... they just steal somebody else's light

Q: What do you say to a guitar player in a three-piece suit?
A: "Will the defendant please rise..."

Q: Did you hear about the guitarist who was in tune?
A: Neither have I.

Q: How does a lead guitarist change a light bulb?
A: He holds it and the world revolves around him.

Q: What's the difference between a guitar and a tuna fish?
A: You can tune a guitar but you can't tune a fish.

Q: What's the range for an electric guitar?
A: About 20 yards if you have a good arm.

Q: What's black and blue and laying in a ditch?
A: A guitarist who's told too many drummer jokes.

Q: What's the difference between a fiddle and a violin?
A: Who cares, neither one's a guitar.

Q: How do you get a guitar player off of your front porch?
A: Pay for the pizza.

BRIEF CONTENTS

FULL CONTENTS

INTRODUCTION

The world would be a strange place without the guitar. Think about it—who would accompany all those campfire sing-alongs at the beach? Ever try to drag a baby-grand piano across the sand? What would John, Paul, and George have strapped on their shoulders on the "Ed Sullivan Show?" Accordions? What instrument would be casually propped in a corner of your living room, or lovingly tucked away in a case under your bed? A tuba? Well, maybe. Thankfully, we don't have to worry about those scenarios because the guitar is a reality. In actuality, it's the most popular instrument in the world.

The mere fact that you are holding this book in your hands proves that you're at least casually interested in the guitar. Or, maybe you really want to learn how to play. Perhaps you simply want to purchase a guitar for a friend or loved one. Or you're a professional guitarist who's looking for source material with which to teach beginners or intermediates. If you fit any of these descriptions, then there's something in *All About Guitar* for you.

I truly hope you enjoy this book and find it useful. Good luck, and may music always be a part of your life. –Tom Kolb

ABOUT THIS BOOK

From a general viewpoint, *All About Guitar* is geared toward the beginning to intermediate guitarist who wishes to learn and improve his or her playing. More importantly, it's an easy-to-follow manual to guide him or her through various guitar-related subjects, such as purchasing a guitar; changing strings; buying gear (amplifiers, effects, cords, etc.); famous players; and essential listening. *AAG* is also an entertaining read for those who are simply interested in the guitar and its role in music.

Furthermore, *AAG*, unlike similar publications, uses copyrighted (read: popular) songs, selected riffs and solos, and five full-blown songs (see Section 5) to demonstrate key factors of guitar playing in various styles.

Do I Need To Read Music?

Good news! You don't need to read a fly-spec of music to benefit from *AAG*. Although traditional music notation appears throughout the book, it's accompanied by a user-friendly brand of guitar notation known as tablature. Tablature is a logical, visual system that tells you what string to play and what fret to press down on. Very simple! Also, there are pictures and diagrams that show you how to form chords. And don't forget the accompanying audio. All of the examples in the book are performed, so you can learn by simply listening.

Here's a guideline you can follow to help take in the information in the book:

- **Look at the pictures and diagrams.** Much can be learned by simply copying the hand positions shown in the photos, or the fingerings depicted in the diagrams.
- **Follow the guitar tablature.** This easy-to-follow system tells you exactly which strings to pluck and what frets to press down on.
- **Listen to the audio for reference.** Some people learn just by listening. Use the audio to aurally reinforce the visual information in the book.
- **Gradually rely on the music staff as you improve.** This is not absolutely necessary. As a matter of fact, many great guitarists can't read music. But if you're interested in learning to read traditional music notation, it's located right above the tablature examples in the book.

Do I Need an Electric or Acoustic Guitar?

It makes no difference if you own an electric or acoustic guitar. If your guitar has six strings (instead of four or 12), it's a standard guitar and, if set up and tuned properly, behaves like any other six-string guitar. All of the examples in this book are playable on either an electric or acoustic guitar. If, for example, you don't own a guitar, this book will help you find the right instrument that will fill your needs and fit your budget (see Chapter 22).

ABOUT THE AUDIO

The majority of the music examples found in *AAG* are performed on the accompanying audio. To locate the appropriate audio example, simply match the audio-icon number (located in the left margin) with the track number. Some tracks include two or more performances. In these cases, "minutes and seconds" information is given, which indicates where each example is located within the track.

In most cases, the featured guitar is mixed hard right (right side of your stereo system), with the backing instruments mixed hard left. This allows you to isolate the guitar example by dialing your balance knob to the right, eliminating (or diminishing) the volume level of the backing instruments. You can also dial out the featured guitar by spinning the balance to the left. In this way, you can play along to the rhythm track without the interference of the featured guitar. (If your system doesn't have a balance control, you can isolate either side by disconnecting one of the speakers. If you're using headphones or earphones, simply remove either the left or right side from your ear.)

Each audio example is preceded by the sound of clicking drumsticks performing a "count off." The count off is an aural warning that sets the tempo (speed) of the example and tells you when to begin. Think of it as having your very own instructor saying, "One-two-ready-begin." If the example is in 4/4 time (see "Playing a Chord Progression," Chapter 7), the sticks will click four times. Examples in 3/4 time have three clicks up front.

COMMON TERMS USED IN THIS BOOK

There are several descriptive terms that you'll occasionally encounter as you work your way through the book. Here is a list of these terms and their definitions:

Higher: Generally, this means higher in pitch (see "A Crash Course on the Music Staff," Chapter 8), or "up" the neck (fretboard), toward the body of the guitar.

Lower: This is the opposite of higher, and translates to "down" the neck (fretboard), or toward the guitar's headstock (where the tuning pegs are located).

Right hand/left hand: We know that not everyone is right-handed, but for the sake of continuity the direction "right hand" will correspond to the picking/strumming hand (the hand that strikes the strings), with "left hand" referring to the fretting hand (the hand that presses the strings to the fretboard). If you choose to play the guitar left-handed, think of the right hand as your left, and vice-versa.

Guitar: When the word "guitar" is used in this book, it refers to a standard six-string guitar—not a 12-string, seven-string, or any such derivative.

ICON LEGEND

Throughout the book, you'll encounter various icons located in the left margins. These icons are designed to draw your attention to specific topics and to help you navigate through the book. Here's a list and a description of these icons:

AUDIO

This icon symbol accompanies each music example. The number on the icon corresponds to the audio track.

TRY THIS

This includes helpful advice about various aspects of guitar playing.

EXTRAS

Here, you'll find additional information on a variety of topics that you may find interesting and useful, but not necessarily essential.

Don't Forget

This book includes a wealth of information that may prove difficult to remember. This icon marks short refresher lessons that will help you stay the course.

DANGER!

The guitar can be a physically demanding instrument. Here, you'll learn what to avoid to stay healthy and in shape. Also included are helpful tips to keep your equipment from going on the fritz.

Origins

Here, you'll find interesting and fun historical blurbs.

Nuts & Bolts

Included with this icon are tidbits on the fundamentals or building blocks of music.

SECTION 1

Preparation

CHAPTER 1
GUITAR ANATOMY

What's Ahead:
- Electric vs. acoustic
- Parts of the guitar
- How guitars work
- How guitars are played

In this introductory section, you'll find out everything you ever wanted to know about the guitar. Well, almost. You'll learn how the guitar is constructed, how it's held, how it's played, and how it's tuned. We'll also cover some basic equipment needs, along with some warm-up suggestions and practice tips.

If you haven't purchased a guitar yet, go immediately to Section 6 before speaking to any fast-talking salesmen. However, if you have your brand-new (or beat-up) instrument with you, then we can proceed.

ELECTRIC VS. ACOUSTIC

Essentially, there are two types of guitars: electric and acoustic. Although they look radically different, from a playing perspective they're essentially the same. Both have a neck, body, and headstock, with six strings attached. The main difference is that acoustic guitars are loud enough to be played without the aid of amplification, while electric guitars need to be plugged into an amplifier. Before we get into the inner workings of each, let's first take an overall look at the physical aspects of both instruments.

PARTS OF THE GUITAR

The following photos show the parts of the acoustic and electric guitar. As you can see, there are quite a number of extra doohickeys on the electric guitar. Follow the legend below the illustrations for a brief explanation of the various parts.

Acoustic Guitar

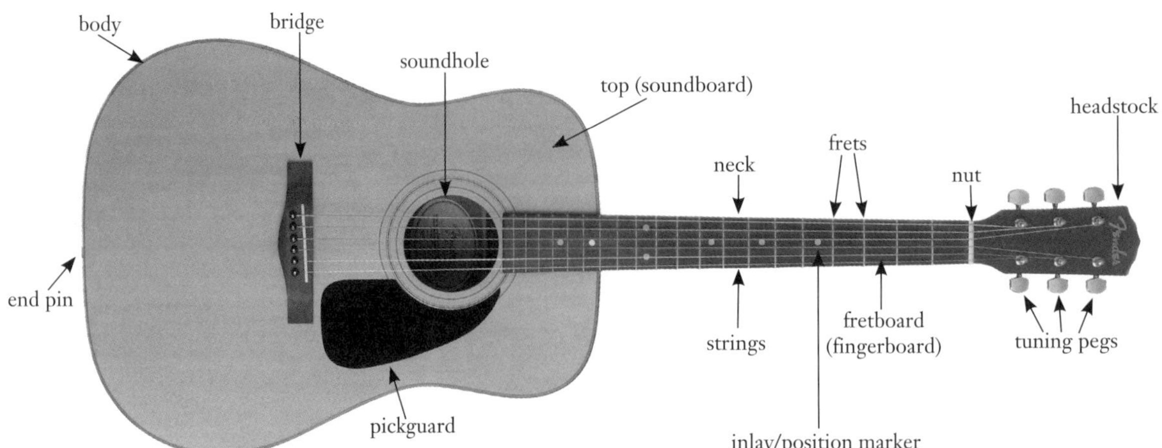

Electric Guitar

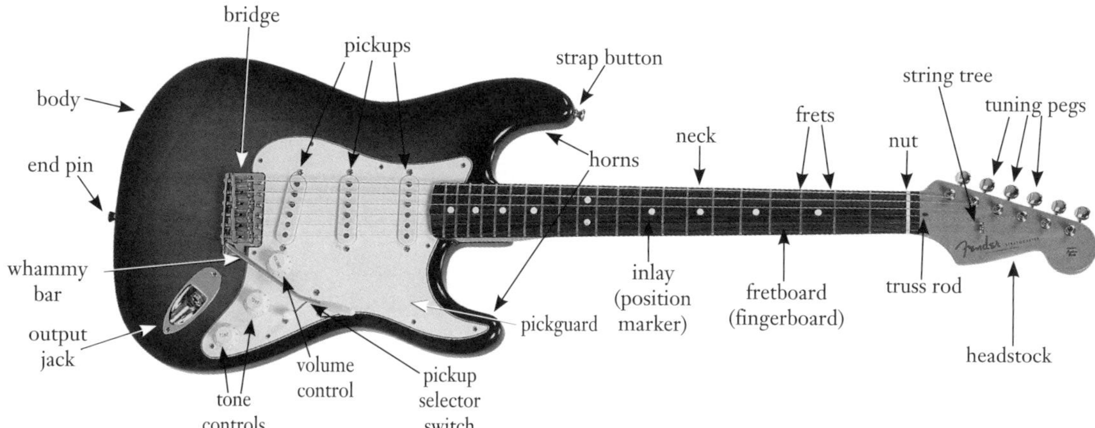

Back (acoustic only): Back part of the body that holds the sides in place.

Bridge: Wooden plate (metal on electrics) that anchors the strings to the body of the guitar.

Body (acoustic): Houses the amplifying sound chamber that produces the guitar's tone.

Body (electric): Houses the bridge assembly and the electronics.

End pin: Metal or plastic post to which one end of the shoulder strap attaches.

Fretboard: A wooden slab that sits atop the neck (also called a fingerboard), upon which the frets are embedded.

Frets: Metal wires embedded in the fretboard that run perpendicular to the strings. Pressing a string down on a fret shortens the length of the string, thus raising its pitch.

Headstock: Contains the tuning pegs to which the strings are attached.

Horns (electric only): Hornlike shapes cut into the upper body of the guitar. This design creates "cutaways," which provide easier access to the higher frets.

Inlays: Also called position or fret markers, inlays are placed at strategic areas along the fretboard to aid the player in visually locating specific frets.

Nut: A grooved strip of plastic (or other synthetic material) through which the strings pass on their way from the bridge to the tuning pegs.

Neck: Often called the backbone of the guitar, the neck attaches the headstock to the body.

Output jack (electric only): This is the electrical output of the guitar from which a guitar cable is connected to an amplifier or other sound-making device.

Pickguard: Slab of material glued to the top of the guitar to protect it from pick scratches.

Pickup selector (electric only): A switch that can be used to activate different pickup combinations.

Pickups (electric only): Bar-shaped magnets housed in plastic or metal casings that sit on the face of the guitar, underneath the strings. Wrapped in coils of wire, they create an electrical current, which is sent to an amplifier. You can think of them as little microphones that "pick up" the sound of the strings.

Sides (acoustic only): Curved strips of wood that connect the top to the back of the guitar.

Soundhole (acoustic only): Round or oval opening on the top of the guitar from which the sound escapes the body cavity.

Strap button: Metal or plastic post to which one end of the shoulder strap attaches. Many acoustics aren't equipped with this pin. In such cases, you can tie the top of the shoulder strap to the headstock.

Strings: Six wires made of steel, bronze, or nylon that, when properly tuned, produce the fundamental notes of the guitar.

String tree (electric only): Metal hook attached to the headstock of some guitars. The string tree creates a downward pressure for a designated string, thus affording a better angle for the string to pass over the nut.

Top (acoustic only): Also called the soundboard. Many soundboards are made of spruce.

Truss rod: Metal rod fitted into the neck to correct bending caused by string tension.

Tuning pegs: Also called tuning machines, tuning keys, or machine heads, they are used to tune the strings to pitch.

Volume and tone controls (electric only): Control knobs that are located on the body of the guitar, and used to adjust the volume and tone of the pickups.

Whammy bar (electric only): Also called a tremolo bar, the whammy bar is attached to a specially designed bridge mechanism on the front of the guitar. Moving the bar up or down rocks the bridge back and forth, thus changing the pitch of the strings.

HOW ACOUSTIC GUITARS WORK

Acoustic guitars are made up of three main components: the headstock, which holds the tuning pegs that tune the strings; the neck, which contains the frets; and the body, which anchors the strings and amplifies the sound. The most important part of the body is the *soundboard*, or top of the guitar. Its main job is to make the guitar loud enough to hear. That is, when a string is struck, its vibrations travel through the bridge and onto the soundboard. Now the entire top of the guitar is vibrating. The sound then resonates in the hollow cavity of the body before projecting through the soundhole and into the ears of the listener.

Although the origins of the guitar can be traced back over a thousand years to its distant cousins the ud and lute, many historians agree that the 16th-century Spanish Vihuela is the closest precursor to the modern acoustic guitar. A 12-string instrument consisting of six pairs of strings called "courses," the Vihuela inspired other guitar-like inventions. These mostly consisted of four or five courses. It wasn't until late in the 18th century that the guitar evolved into the six-string form we know today.

HOW ELECTRIC GUITARS WORK

The main physical difference between electric and acoustic guitars is that most electrics have a solid (as opposed to hollow) body. The same string-vibration theory applies to the electric guitar, but since there is no hollow chamber for the sound to resonate, the instrument is whisper quiet when played acoustically. Therefore, a pickup (or pickups) is needed to "amplify" the sound.

Electric guitars come with various combinations of pickups; some have one, while others have two or more. These pickups are located on top of the body of the guitar, just beneath the strings.

A basic *pickup* consists of a single magnet, which is wrapped with several thousand coils of thin copper wire. This combination of magnet and wires creates a magnetic field, which is disturbed when the strings vibrate. This disturbance creates small pulses of electrical energy, which are passed through a guitar cord to an amplifier. The *amplifier* converts the signal and then passes it through a loudspeaker.

The Origin of the Electric Guitar

In the history of the electric guitar's evolution, four names loom large: Adolph Rickenbacker, Les Paul, Leo Fender, and Lloyd Loar. The first three names you may recognize, but who's Lloyd Loar? Well, he's the man who, in 1924, invented the most integral part of the electric guitar—the pickup. In the 1930s, Adolph Rickenbacker picked up the ball and developed the first pickup-equipped guitar, dubbed the "Frying Pan." Although the Frying Pan was technically a lap-steel guitar (an instrument positioned on the lap and played with a steel bar laid across the strings), it qualifies as the first mass-produced electric.

In the mid-'30s, the Gibson Guitar Company took Rickenbacker's idea and ran with it. Essentially slapping a pickup on a hollowbodied "archtop" guitar, the L-150 was born. Now guitarists could be heard above the din of the horn sections in the big-band era. However, there was one drawback—feedback; an annoying howling sound caused by the body of the guitar vibrating at loud volumes.

To alleviate the feedback dilemma, guitar experimenters began tinkering with guitar bodies made from a solid piece of wood rather than the traditional soundboard glued onto a hollow chamber. One such experimenter was popular guitarist/part-time inventor Les Paul. His solidbody prototype (known as "The Log") consisted of a standard guitar neck fitted onto a 4x4 inch solid block of pine, which contained two pickups. To give the strange-looking instrument a more conventional appearance, he glued on the two halves of a traditional archtop guitar. In the mid-'40s, the Gibson Guitar Company passed on this early prototype, but did go on to work with Les Paul and use his name on its first line of solidbody guitars in the 1950s.

Working feverishly throughout the '40s and essentially beating Gibson (and Les) to the punch, Leo Fender got credit for inventing and distributing the first mass-produced electric guitar—the Fender Broadcaster. Issued in 1950, it was renamed the Telecaster two years later and has since become the longest-running solidbody electric guitar in history.

HOW THE GUITAR IS PLAYED

String Length and Pitch

The guitar is played by picking, plucking, or strumming the six strings one at a time or simultaneously. Each of the strings is tuned to a different pitch—that is, each is tuned to a different tension. The higher the tension of a string, the higher in pitch it sounds; the lower the tension, the lower the pitch.

Fretting the Instrument

The guitar would be a ridiculously difficult instrument to play if you had to madly adjust the tuning of each string every time you wanted a different pitch. That's why there are frets located along the fretboard. Pressing a string down on a fret shortens the vibrating length of that string, thus raising its pitch. By fretting (pushing the string down on a certain fret) up and down the neck, many different pitches can be played along a single string. Incidentally, each fret represents a half-step interval, the equivalency of the distance between two adjacent notes on the piano keyboard.

Using Both Hands

The guitar is a two-handed instrument. In other words, it requires that both hands work in tandem to produce music. Generally, the right hand creates the rhythms by strumming or picking the strings, while the left hand locates and produces the pitches by fretting the notes. Picking a designated string with the right hand while the left hand pushes down on the appropriate frets produces a melody. Similarly, strumming the strings with the right hand while the left hand either frets notes or allows open strings to ring produces chords and rhythm.

- Acoustic and electric guitars are played in much the same way.
- The three basic parts of the guitar are the body, the neck, and the headstock.
- The higher (or tighter) the string tension, the higher the pitch. The lower (or less taught) the tension, the lower the pitch.
- The skinny strings are higher in pitch; the fatter ones are lower in pitch.
- The right hand plucks or strums the strings; the left hand frets the notes.

CHAPTER 2
TUNE UP OR TUNE OUT

What's Ahead:
- Names of the open strings
- Tuning the guitar to the audio
- Tuning the guitar to a piano
- Tuning the guitar to itself
- Other tuning methods

In the hands of a good player, the guitar is a beautiful-sounding instrument. However, if the guitar is out of tune it can sound like your neighbor's cat at 2:00am, even in the hands of a professional. Unlike the piano, which only needs occasional tuning (performed by a qualified professional), the guitar needs constant tuning attention. Unfortunately, learning how to tune the guitar can be the most frustrating task as a beginner guitarist. But, until you become a successful rock star and can afford to have a roadie do all of your tuning, you'll want to learn to tune your instrument. Consider this a good thing, though, as the more "in tune" your guitar is, the better you will sound.

NAMES AND PITCHES OF THE STRINGS

String Numbering System
The strings of the guitar are numbered sequentially, 1 through 6. String 1, or the first string, is the skinniest and located closest to the floor when the guitar is held in playing position. The second string is just above the first string, and so on all the way to the sixth string, which is the fattest and located closest to the ceiling.

Names of the Strings
The strings also have letter names, which correspond to the pitch to which they are tuned. Here are the letter names as they correspond to each string number:

First string: high E string (skinniest string)
Second string: B string
Third string: G string
Fourth string: D string
Fifth string: A string
Sixth string: low E string (fattest string)

Do yourself a favor—commit the names of the strings to memory as quickly as possible. Therefore, you won't always have to refer to them by number.

TUNING THE GUITAR TO THE AUDIO
The very first track provides reference notes to help you tune your guitar. It's almost like having a private teacher sitting right there with you, guiding you through the tuning process! On the track, each open string is not only played once, but three times. With a little practice, this should allow you ample time to get each string in tune. Here's a rundown of how to use this tuning track.

The first string that's played is the high E. When you hear the note being played, strike your high E string with your right-hand thumb, index finger, or a pick. If your string doesn't sound the same as the one recorded, it's probably out of tune. This means it's either flat (tension of the string is too slack) or sharp (tension of the string is too taught). If it seems flat (too low) you'll need to increase the tension of that string by turning its tuning peg in the proper direction (counterclockwise on most guitars). If the string seems sharp (too high) you'll need to decrease the tension by turning the tuning peg in the other direction (clockwise on most guitars). If you can't tell if the string is in tune or not, tune it flat intentionally, then bring the string up to pitch.

Tuning
high E, B, G, D, A, low E

While you're tuning you'll hear the high E string played a total of three times on the track. If you don't have your string in tune by the time the track goes on to the B string, simply pause the track or skip back to the beginning. Repeat this process as many times as needed until you've tuned all of your strings. When you're finished you may want to go back and repeat the entire process just to be sure you're fully in tune. Believe it or not, sometimes it's necessary to tune the guitar several times in a row. It all depends on how out of tune it was from the start. (Note: If you have successfully tuned your guitar from the track, feel free to go directly to Chapter 3.)

TUNING THE GUITAR TO A PIANO

If you have access to a piano or electronic keyboard, you can tune your guitar by matching pitches to the corresponding notes on the keyboard. The following example shows a section of a piano keyboard and the names of its white keys. (Notice that the note names repeat themselves every seven keys.)

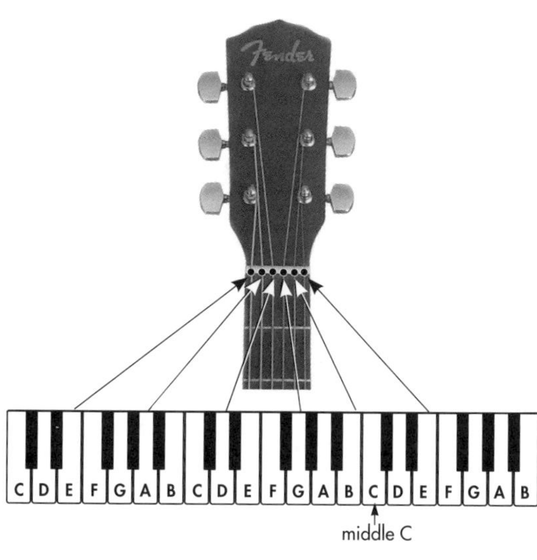

Begin by locating the E key that is to the right of middle C. (Middle C is the C key located in the middle of the keyboard.) Pressing down on this key produces the pitch to which your first, or high E, string should be tuned. Go back and forth repeatedly between the E key on the piano and your first string until the pitches match. Then, go to the B string and repeat the process with the corresponding key on the piano. (The B, G, and D string pitches are located below middle C. The A and low E strings are in the second octave below middle C.)

After striking the piano key, hold down the sustain pedal (far right foot pedal located under the piano keyboard) and then let go of the key. This will allow the note to ring so you can use both hands to tune your guitar.

TUNING THE GUITAR TO ITSELF

To check or correct your tuning when no other pitch source is available, you'll need to learn how to tune the guitar to itself. This is known as *relative tuning.*

The Fifth-Fret Tuning Process

The fifth-fret tuning process involves fretting a string at the fifth fret (fourth fret on the G string) and tuning the higher, adjacent open string to that pitch. The drawback with this system is that your low E string needs to be in tune. Here's how it works:

1. With the tip of your left-hand index (first) finger, press down on the low E string at the fifth fret—not on the fret itself, but in the "fret area" behind it, toward the nut. Now play the open

A string, allowing the two notes to ring together. (Arch your index finger so that it doesn't rub against the A string.) If the two pitches don't match, then the A string is out of tune and needs to be adjusted accordingly. Repeat the process until the strings match in pitch.

2. Now play the A string at the fifth fret. Let that note ring while you play the open D string. Tune the D string until the two pitches match.
3. Play the D string at the fifth fret and tune the open G string to that pitch.
4. Play the G string at the fourth fret (the G string is the only exception to the fifth-fret tuning process) and tune the open B string to that pitch.
5. Finally, play the B string at the fifth fret and tune the high E string to that pitch. When you're finished tuning the high E, your guitar should be in tune with itself. It's always a good idea to go back and double-check, though.

Here's a way to keep both strings ringing while you tune: Keep your left-hand finger on the fretted note and reach over with your right hand to adjust the tuning peg.

The above scenario works great if your low E string is already in tune, but it can also work if you need to start the process from a different string. Let's say you know your D string is in tune but you think the others are out of whack. In this case, start with step 3 (tuning the open G to the D string at the fifth fret), and then proceed with steps 4 and 5.

Now the top four strings are in tune (D, G, B, and high E), but what about the bottom two (A and low E)? You'll need to tune the A string first. Just like in step 2, you play the open D string while you fret the A string at the fifth fret, but instead of tuning the D string, you need to adjust the pitch of the A string. When those pitches match, go to step 1 and adjust the pitch of the low E.

When you use relative tuning, you may or may not be in tune with other instruments. When playing with other musicians it's best to use a master-tuning source such as a piano or electronic tuner. You could be in for an unpleasant surprise if you launch into a song before making sure you're in tune with each other!

Tuning With Harmonics

Another popular relative-tuning method involves natural harmonics. A *natural harmonic* is a bell-like tone produced when an open string is plucked, while a fret-hand finger lightly touches the same string above a designated fret wire. As with the fifth-fret method, you'll need to be certain that your starting-point string is in tune. Here's a step-by-step scenario using the low E string as the starting point:

1. Lightly touch the low E string directly above the fifth fret *wire* (not the fret area) with a finger of your left hand, while you simultaneously pluck the string with your right hand. Let that note ring while you play the harmonic at the seventh fret of the A string. If the harmonics are not in tune with each other you should hear a pulsation. The faster the beat of the pulse, the more the strings are out of tune. Adjust the tuning of the A string (either up or down) until the pulsation slows and eventually stops.
2. Next, compare the fifth-fret harmonic of the A string with the seventh-fret harmonic of the D string. Adjust the pitch of the D string.
3. Compare the fifth-fret harmonic of the D string with the seventh-fret harmonic of the G string, and tune the G string accordingly.

4. This next one is a little different. Compare the seventh-fret harmonic of the low E string with the open B string, and tune the B string accordingly.
5. Finally, compare the fifth-fret harmonic of the B string with the seventh-fret harmonic of the high E string, and tune the high E string accordingly.

TUNING WITH AN ELECTRONIC TUNER

The easiest and most accurate way to tune is to use an electronic tuner. Usually battery-powered, this marvelous little device is quick, easy to use, and the perfect solution for tuning up in a noisy atmosphere.

All electronic tuners have a selection of tuning notes from which to choose. Some have only the open strings (low to high: E–A–D–G–B–E), while others will automatically detect and indicate any note. There's also an indicator (either a needle meter or a light meter), which tells you if the note is sharp, flat, or in tune.

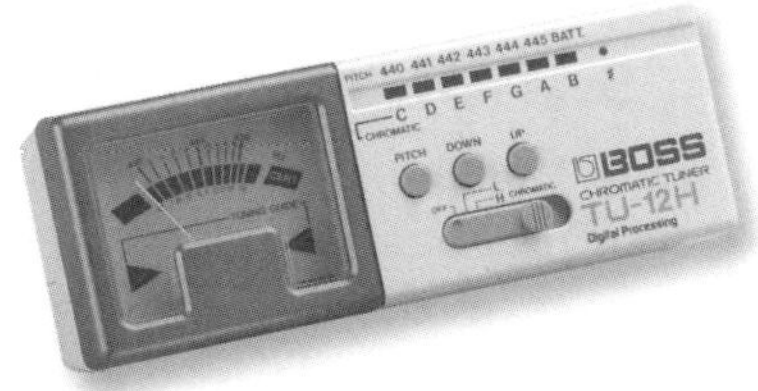

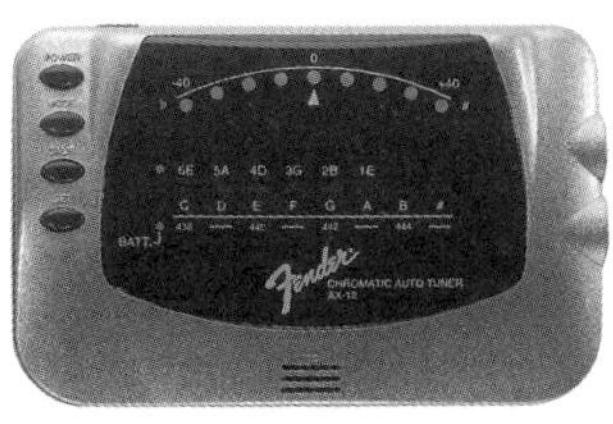

To use an electronic tuner, simply plug in your guitar (or, if you're tuning an acoustic guitar, use the built-in microphone); play the string you wish to tune; watch the pitch meter; and tune the string until the meter reads dead center, telling you the string is in tune.

Be careful—if your string is way out of tune it may register as another note entirely. Make sure that the note indicator matches the string you are playing. For example, if you play the A string, make sure the indicator reads A, not G#, A#, or some other note. (Note: Some older units require that you move a dial to the note to which you want to tune.)

OTHER TUNING METHODS

Guitar *pitch pipes* come in a set of six (attached as one small unit), with each pipe tuned to an open-string pitch, albeit an octave higher. With this handy device you can hold the pipes firmly in your mouth while blowing, keeping your hands free to tune the guitar.

A *tuning fork* is a metal instrument with a handle and two forked tines. It resonates at a specific pitch (usually "A") when struck against a surface or an object. Most guitarists who use an "A" tuning fork to tune their open A string then use that string as the pitch source to tune the other strings (as explained earlier in the "Fifth-Fret Tuning Process").

The tuning fork is convenient because it's so compact, but it's tricky to use. One method is to play the open A string, and then strike the fork on your knee with your right hand. Next, hold the fork to your ear while you tune the string with your left hand. Many acoustic guitarists amplify the sound of the fork by holding the tip of the fork's handle to the playing surface of their guitar. Some even hold the handle between their clenched teeth. This may look goofy but you can really hear the pitch that way!

- The names of the strings from lowest (fattest) to highest (skinniest) are: E–A–D–G–B–E. The sixth string is referred to as low E; the first string is called high E.
- If the string is "flat" you need to increase the tension by tuning it *up*. If it's "sharp" you need to decrease the tension by tuning it *down*.
- If you tune the guitar to itself you may not be in tune with other instruments.
- To assure concert pitch (standard pitch), you must use a true pitch source such as a piano, pitch pipe, tuning fork, or electronic tuner.

CHAPTER 3
NECESSARY EQUIPMENT

What's Ahead:

- Acoustic guitar pros and cons
- Electric guitar pros and cons
- Equipment and accessories

SHOULD I LEARN ON AN ACOUSTIC OR AN ELECTRIC GUITAR?

At this point, it makes little difference if you start out on an acoustic or an electric. The learning process for beginners is transferable to either instrument. The most sensible thing to do is to start on the type of instrument that you already own, be it acoustic or electric. However, if you don't own a guitar you'll need to ask yourself a few questions. First, do you intend to buy, rent, or borrow a guitar? Second, are you more interested in the electric guitar or an acoustic?

If you're going to purchase a guitar, remember—you don't need an expensive instrument to get started. Actually, that's often an unwise decision, especially if you're not sure how interested you really are in learning to play. A good student-level guitar is all you need. There are many reasonably priced guitars that are of excellent quality (see Chapter 22). You could also rent one. Many music stores offer monthly rates for new and used instruments. Also, check with your family and friends. Maybe someone has a guitar that's been packed away in the closet, forgotten and abandoned for many years. That guitar is just crying out to be played by someone!

If you're pondering whether to go acoustic or electric, it sometimes comes down to what type of music you like. If you're a rocker or a bluesman, you'll need an electric. If you love folk music and singer/songwriters, perhaps the acoustic guitar is the answer. If you love all types of music, you may want to consider this list of pros and cons:

Acoustic Guitar

Pros:

- You can take it anywhere: beach, mountains, etc.
- You don't need to purchase extra equipment.
- Acoustics are generally much lighter than electrics.

Cons

- It's not loud enough to be heard over the drums.
- The strings are sometimes harder to press down compared to an electric guitar.

Electric Guitar

Pros

- Electrics are generally easier to play than acoustics.
- You can practice without disturbing the neighbors.
- With an amplifier, you can practice loud enough to disturb your parents (or your spouse).
- You can join a rock band!

Cons

- You need an amplifier to be heard.
- You can't take it to the beach or the mountains (unless you have a battery-powered amplifier).
- Electrics are generally much heavier than acoustics.

ACCESSORIES

Guitar Case

If you're planning to take your guitar out of the house, you may want to invest in a carrying case. A *gig bag*—a cushioned, light-weight zipper bag—offers protection from scratches and the like, but it affords little defense if you drop it or place something heavy on top of it in transit. A hard-shell guitar case offers the best protection, especially if you're somewhat clumsy. (See Chapter 24 for more information on cases.)

Picks

You may choose to play with a pick instead of with your fingers. Although picks come in a variety of shapes and sizes, it's a good idea to start with a standard, medium-size pick such as a Fender medium gauge. You'll want to have a few on hand just in case you misplace them. (See Chapter 24 for more information on picks.)

Shoulder Strap

If you choose to stay seated while playing, you don't need to worry about a strap. But if you want to stand up and stretch your legs, you'll need a strap to hold up your guitar. Shoulder straps come in all kinds of styles, materials, and colors. The most important thing is to find one that is adjustable and is comfortable for your shoulder. (See Chapter 24 for more information on guitar straps.)

Extra Strings

Believe it or not, breaking a string is a common occurrence for guitar players. The first time it happens it's quite startling, but don't worry—you'll get used to it! For this reason, you'll always want to have an extra set of strings packed away in your case or gig bag. (See Chapter 24 for information on the different types of guitar strings.)

Guitar Cloth

Get in the habit of wiping off your guitar after you're finished playing (a cheap cotton cloth will do just fine). As you play, the oils and sweat from your fingers and hands build up on the strings, behind the neck, and the top of the body. If you don't wipe off your instrument these body oils can corrode the strings and mar your guitar's finish. You'll need to pay special attention to these problem areas but it's a good idea to wipe off the entire instrument.

DO I NEED AN AMPLIFIER?

You don't necessarily need an amplifier to play an electric guitar. Unplugged, the acoustic volume of an electric guitar is whisper soft, but in a quiet atmosphere this poses no problem. Eventually, you'll want to purchase one. When that time comes, you can refer to Chapter 23 for buying tips.

- Acoustic guitars can be taken and played anywhere.
- Electric guitars require amplification to be heard.
- A guitar bag (gig bag) will protect your instrument from scratches.
- A guitar case will protect your instrument from being crushed.
- Always carry an extra set of strings.

CHAPTER 4
PROPER POSTURE

What's Ahead:

- Sitting while playing
- Standing while playing
- Proper hand position
- Using a pick
- Picking with your fingers

In this chapter, we'll discuss proper posture and how to hold your hands while playing the guitar.

Correct way to hold the guitar

Photo by FG/LFI

Incorrect way to hold the guitar

PLAYING WHILE SEATED

Choose a chair without armrests that is the right height for your stature. Ideally, when your feet are flat on the floor, your thighs should be parallel to the floor. Now, with feet slightly apart, place the guitar in your lap with the back resting against your stomach and chest and nestle the waist (indented section of the lower body) onto your right leg. Balance the guitar in your lap by bringing your right arm over the body and applying a little pressure with your forearm to the bass bout (widest section of the guitar body).

Your left hand holds the neck, palm upward. For now, just place your thumb behind the neck and rest your fingers on the strings. Remember to tilt the neck of the guitar slightly upward—never down.

PLAYING WHILE STANDING

Playing the guitar while standing requires the use of a shoulder strap. The two ends of a shoulder strap attach to the strap buttons (pins), which are usually located at the bottom of the guitar's body and at the top horn or shoulder. (Some acoustics don't include a top strap button. In such cases, the strap is tied to the headstock.) The guitar is supported by the strap, which is placed over the left shoulder. While you can adjust the strap's length so that the guitar is at the same level as when seated, many players (particularly in rock) prefer to hold their guitars lower while standing. This is more for looking "cool" than it is for comfort.

Let your body make the natural transition from holding the guitar while seated to letting it hang from your shoulder while standing. Similar to sitting, bring your right arm up and over the body of the guitar and your left hand under the neck when standing.

Old, worn-out straps have a nasty habit of slipping off strap buttons while you're playing. This is not only embarrassing; it can cause great damage to your instrument if you're not quick enough to break its fall. Make sure your strap fits nice and snug over both end pins.

RIGHT-HAND POSITION

Proper right-hand positioning varies, depending on whether you're using a pick or playing with your fingers. Although there are exceptions, when playing an electric guitar you'll want to use a pick. Acoustic guitars can be played with a pick or with the fingers.

Playing With a Pick

A *pick* is a thin, flat piece of plastic, shaped like a triangle. Held between the thumb and index finger of the right hand, it's used to strum and pick the strings. Picks come in various sizes, shapes, and gauges. The gauge measures the thickness of the pick and, thus, its flexibility. Gauges generally run thin, medium, and heavy. Thinner picks are better for strumming, while heavier picks work well for soloing. Consider the medium-gauge pick the middle-of-the-road choice, equally at home strumming or picking.

To hold a pick, first bend your index finger and place your thumb on the side of the first knuckle, much the same way as when you're holding the key to open the front door. Now, grab the pointy end of the pick with your left hand and slide the opposite end between your positioned thumb and index finger. Shove the pick in far enough so only the tip is showing—about 1/4 inch or so. Don't squeeze too hard; just enough so you don't drop the pick when you hit the strings. You can keep your other three fingers either tucked into your palm, fanned out, or at rest on the body of the guitar.

Now bring your right hand up and over the guitar's body, and position your hand so that the flat side of the pick is resting on the A string, as shown here. When you're ready, pick down on the string, allowing the pick to come to rest on the neighboring D string. Congratulations! You've just played your first note on the guitar!

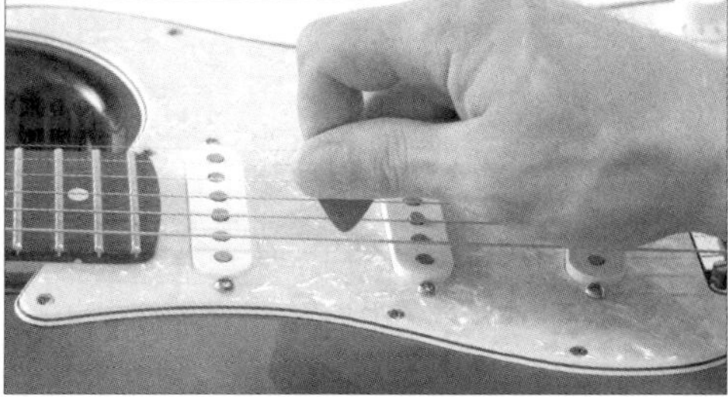

Fingerpicking (a.k.a. Fingerstyle)

You don't need a pick to play the guitar. (But what will you toss to your adoring fans?) Instead, you can employ a fingerpicking technique called *fingerstyle*. Fingerstyle is when you pluck the strings with your right-hand thumb and fingers. The most common fingerstyle technique involves picking down on the lower strings with your thumb, and picking up on the higher strings with your first (index), second (middle), and third (ring) fingers.

The adjacent photo shows proper hand position for fingerstyle. The hand is placed over the soundhole; there is a slight arch to the wrist; the tips of the fingers are perpendicular to the strings; and the thumb plucks the strings at a slight angle.

Here's a simple exercise to help you get the feel of fingerpicking: Start by planting your first, second, and third fingers under the G, B, and high E strings, respectively. Holding your fingers in that position, individually pick down on the low E, A, and D strings with your thumb. As you do this, let your thumb come to rest on the adjacent string.

Now play the top three strings: Pluck up on the G string with your first finger, up on the B string with your second finger, and up on the high E with your third finger. Try to keep the volume of all the notes consistent by applying the same amount of plucking pressure. Chapter 16 (Folk/Country) contains more information on fingerpicking styles.

LEFT-HAND POSITION

Although your left hand will be in perpetual motion while playing the guitar, let's get started with a general "home base" position.

Home-base Position

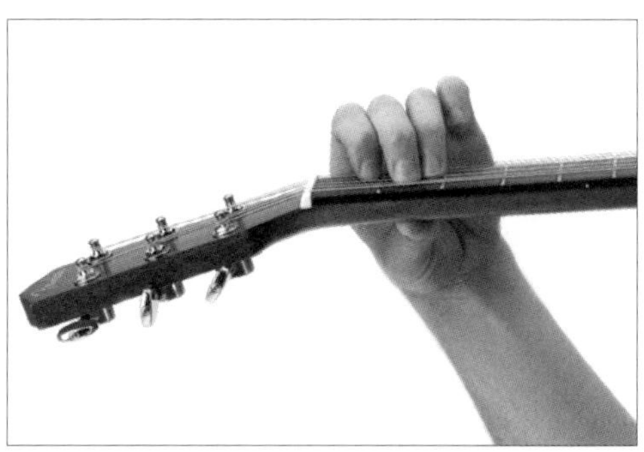

Get into the proper sitting position with your guitar, as previously illustrated. Now drop your left hand and let it relax by your side. Once you're relaxed, slowly bring your hand up, pointing your thumb and fingers skyward. Then, with your fingers still in mid-air, press the fleshy pad of your thumb (just above the joint) against the neck, behind the second-fret area. Tilt your thumb, ever so slightly, so that the fleshy pad that's closest to the index finger comes into contact with the neck. Now, with your fingers arched, let the fingertips come to rest along the D string. Keep your second finger lined up with the thumb, at the second fret, allowing the other fingers to fall into place around it. Looking at your hand, your palm should not be touching the bottom of the fretboard, and it should be cupped (as if it were holding a baseball), with your fingers curved. Your wrist should have a slight arch to it.

- Try to keep your thumb perpendicular to the neck.
- Keep your fingers arched.
- The palm should be cupped.
- Keep a slight arch in your wrist.

There will be times when the perpendicular-thumb rule becomes an exception. For instance, blues and rock guitar involves a technique known as string bending. String bending requires that you actually wrap your thumb around the top of the neck in order to achieve the required leverage.

Fretting Notes

To fret a note, press down on a string until it makes firm contact with the fret. (This changes the length of the string, altering its pitch.) Keep your finger arched, and come straight down onto the fretboard, pressing the string with the top part of your fingertip. From its position behind the neck, squeeze with your thumb for added leverage.

Don't press down directly on the fret wire; press down on the fret "area" directly behind the fret. For example, to play the G string at the third fret, place your finger in the square area between the third and second fret—not in the center of the square, but closer to the higher (third) fret wire. This affords the clearest sound with no string buzz, or fret rattle. If the note still doesn't sound, check to make sure your other fingers aren't touching the upper part of the string (toward the body). It's okay if they're touching the string behind the fretted note (toward the headstock).

If you've followed all of the aforementioned rules and you still can't get a clear sound out of a fretted note, then perhaps your fingernails are too long. Try bringing each finger down vertically on a hard surface like a tabletop. If the nail hits the surface before the pad of your finger, then your fingernail is probably too long.

- Electric guitarists usually use a pick.
- Acoustic guitars can be played fingerstyle or with a pick.
- Never use an old, worn-out strap.
- From a playing perspective, "fret" means the fret area, not the fret wire.
- Right hand: Whether picking or playing fingerstyle, remember to keep your wrist slightly arched.
- Left hand: Try to keep your second finger (on the fretboard) directly opposite your thumb (behind the neck).

CHAPTER 5
PRACTICE HABITS

What's Ahead:

- How to practice
- What to practice
- Maintaining a practice schedule
- Warming up
- Practicing away from the guitar

You've probably heard the saying, "Practice makes perfect." But have you ever heard this one: "The better your practice habits, the quicker you'll improve?" It's true. The most accomplished guitarists got to their levels not by merely practicing but by knowing *how* to practice—in other words, making the most of their practice time. Whether you're a beginner, intermediate, or advanced player, you'll reach your goals much quicker if you organize your practice time.

PREPARING TO PRACTICE

There are three fundamental factors that are often responsible for making or breaking a practice session:

1. Location
2. Materials
3. Time allotment

Location

Where you practice can be just as important as what you practice. Find a room in which you'll have the fewest distractions, such as telephones, the television, clutter, and conversation. If it's impossible to isolate yourself, you might try plugging your guitar into a set of powered headphones (see Chapter 24). If you play acoustic, you might want to take it outdoors. With a little ingenuity, you'll be able to find some privacy.

Materials

Make sure all of your equipment (guitar, amp, cord, metronome, tape recorder, CD player, etc.) and materials (method books, CDs, videos, paper, pencil, etc.) are within reach of your practice spot. Nothing is as frustrating as having to get up and hunt for your supplies.

Time Allotment

The guitar can be so much fun to play that it's easy to get carried away and lose track of time. Before you sit down to practice, make a list of what you want to accomplish, set a time limit for each topic, and stick to it! The last thing you want to do is waste all of your time on the first item on your list. Use a kitchen timer or some type of alarm to remind you when it's time to move on.

CREATING A PRACTICE SCHEDULE (POWER PRACTICING)

How Much Should I Practice?

The amount of practice time varies from player to player. Segovia (the father of modern classical guitar) was known to practice three to four hours a day, while Steve Vai (veteran rock instrumentalist) once had a ten-hour daily routine! How much you should practice depends on how interested you are in learning and how much time you have to spare. Thirty minutes a day is a reasonable goal for a beginner. You'll often get better results if you split those thirty minutes into two or three smaller segments. For instance, you could practice ten minutes in the morning, ten minutes in the afternoon, and ten minutes in the evening. The important thing is consistency. You'll see more progress if you practice 30 minutes daily rather than cramming for four hours once a week.

What Should I Practice?

Often the hardest part of practicing is deciding what to practice. In those times of indecision, it's extremely helpful to have a set routine to follow. A good private teacher can help you here, but with a little forethought and organization you can customize your own personal practice schedule.

Although it can be broken down to many sub-categories, a good practice routine should include the following wide-ranging topics:

- Warm ups
- Technical practice for muscle development and maintenance
- Work on new material
- Perform existing repertoire

Warming Up

Warming up for a practice session or a performance will not only make you play better, it will help guard against injuries such as simple muscle strain, or more serious problems such as tendonitis (inflammation of the tendon caused by repetitive motion and overexertion). The first step is to get the blood flowing to your hands. Some common techniques include: repeatedly making a fist, and then relaxing the hands; clapping the hands together; running warm water over your hands; swinging your arms in the air; virtually anything to simply get your hands warm and ready to play.

A warm-up routine on the guitar can be as basic as randomly playing notes, very slowly, around the fretboard; simply getting acquainted with the instrument. After that you could play a few simple chords and rhythms. Then you might play some scale exercises. The main thing to remember is to start slowly and precisely. This will help to get your hands "in sync," thus establishing a precedent of precision that should carry on through the practice session. Think of it like patting your head while rubbing your stomach. Get the picture?

> Make sure you warm up before you practice or perform. This will help ward off hand and arm injuries such as muscle strain and tendonitis.

Technique

This wide-ranging topic helps to improve and maintain your mechanical skills. More technical than it is musical, technique practice helps you develop speed, dexterity, and precision in your right (picking and strumming) and left (fretting) hands. Typical picking routines involve playing scale patterns, scale sequences, arpeggios, and short chord progressions in various styles.

New Material

This is the learning section in which you work on brand-new material. It could be a new set of chords you're trying to get down, or a new scale, lick, riff, or an entire song.

Repertoire

Believe it or not, there are many technically impressive guitarists who can't play an entire song. If asked to play something, the best they could offer is some isolated pieces of songs or solos they've been working on. We don't want you to become one of those types of players, and neither do you. In this book, we'll help you build your repertoire. Think of your repertoire as being your musical catalog, or the songs that you've memorized and feel comfortable playing. For many, the repertoire portion of a practice session is the most fun. It's where all the nuts and bolts of your technique practice come together to actually make music with your instrument.

A *chord* is a group of three or more notes sounded simultaneously. Chords are the basic building blocks of songs. Chord progressions (a sequence of chords played one after another) supply the *harmony* from which songs are structured. Harmony occurs when two or more notes are played at the same time.

A *scale* is a series of notes arranged in a specific order of intervals (the distance between two notes), from its tonic (root, or central note) to its octave. Scales are used to create the melodies of songs.

PUTTING IT ALL TOGETHER

Dividing Your Time

Let's say you have an hour to practice. You might start with a five-minute warm up, followed by a ten-minute scale workout, taking one-minute breaks here and there to rest your muscles and tendons. (Be sure to use a timer or alarm to remind you to move on.) You could then practice some chords and rhythms for ten minutes. The next 15 minutes could be spent learning a new scale and a couple of chords, before finishing the hour by playing through a few songs in your repertoire.

You may want to spread out this session over the course of the day. For example, if you wanted to practice 30 minutes in the morning and 30 minutes in the afternoon, you could follow the same routine simply by spending half as much time on each topic. Or you could do your scale workout and repertoire practice in the morning, leaving the chord drill and new material segment for the evening. Then there may be days when you only have 20 minutes to practice, in which case you could get through everything by spending five minutes on each topic. The main thing is that you consistently touch on all four subjects.

Setting Goals

In creating a practice schedule, it's helpful to have a set of goals for which to aim. Whether you make them weekly, monthly, or bi-annual goals, they will give you a focus and help you track your progress. For instance, you might set a goal to learn three new chords and one new scale pattern a week. Or you may be determined to learn two new songs a month. Then again, you may set a six-month goal for learning how to improvise over a 12-bar blues progression (see "The 12-bar Blues Form," Chapter 15). Whatever your desires, it's helpful to put them down on paper so that you can structure reasonable time frames in which to achieve them.

PRACTICING AWAY FROM THE GUITAR

The more you get into the guitar, the more you'll hate being parted from it. But don't worry—there are many ways to practice guitar technique when you don't have it with you. Here are some tips:

- Lay your hands on a table and tap your fingers in sync. For example, tap both index fingers at the same time; now tap your middle fingers, etc. Try other combinations. This strengthens coordination between the hands. You can even do this on the steering wheel if you're driving a car.

- Press your left-hand fingers to your thumb, one at a time. This simulates the act of fretting notes.
- Here's an air-guitar trick that will strengthen your sense of time: Simply swing your right hand (as if strumming the guitar) to the rhythm of the music on the radio, iPod, etc.
- Here's a visualization exercise: While pretending to hold the neck of your guitar, practice playing chord shapes and scales. It may feel a little weird at first, but you'll catch on.

Ear Training

It's been said that the most important asset a musician can have is a good ear. Some guitarists have such a good ear that they can instantly play what they hear in their head or on a recording. How did they get that way? Well, some lucky people are born with *perfect pitch*, the ability to recognize any note with no pitch reference, but most musicians develop *relative pitch*, a sense of pitch based on comparisons, through ear-training exercises. When you tune your guitar, you're "training" your ear to detect the correct pitch of your string. Likewise, there are standard music drills that are used to develop the ears to be able to discern any pitch.

Ear training doesn't have to be a formal set of drills. Actually, the most important type of ear training is listening to music, preferably as many styles as possible. It makes sense, doesn't it? If you want to be a writer, you should read voraciously. If you want to learn another language, you should communicate with people who speak it profusely, or, better yet, visit the country of its origin. If you want to play guitar, listening to music will give you an endless source of inspiration. Here's a list of things you can do away from your instrument to help train your ear:

- Listen to music on the FM dial of your radio. Be sure to switch back-and-forth between stations (i.e., rock, pop, country, blues, jazz, R&B, Latin, classical). In all cases, try to cue in on what the guitar player is doing.
- When you're at the movies or watching television, listen to the background music.
- Watching music being played is also helpful to the ear. Go to concerts, clubs, town festivals—anywhere music is being played—and watch the guitar player.
- Ear training is not just about pitches, it's also applied to rhythms. Pretend you're a drummer and pound out the beat on your thighs, or, at the very least, tap your foot.

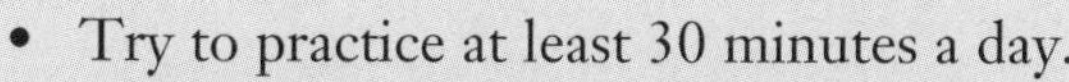

- Try to practice at least 30 minutes a day.
- The better your practice habits, the quicker you'll improve.
- Always warm up before you play.
- It's important to build a repertoire.
- You can get a lot of practicing done without your guitar in hand.
- Be aware of the music around you.

SECTION 2

Playing 101

CHAPTER 6
GUITAR NOTATION

What's Ahead:

- Tablature explanation
- Chord frames
- What's a chord?
- Box scale patterns

Now the fun starts! In this section, you'll actually start to make music on the guitar. After a brief chapter on the explanation of tablature (a special guitar-notation system) and music notation, we'll move ahead with basic chords, scale patterns, and arpeggios, and we'll even play several songs.

TABLATURE

Tablature (or "tab" for short) is the easiest way to notate guitar music. The advantage of using tab in place of conventional music notation is that it tells you exactly where to place your fingers on the fretboard. This is especially handy considering that it's possible to play the same note in several different places on the guitar.

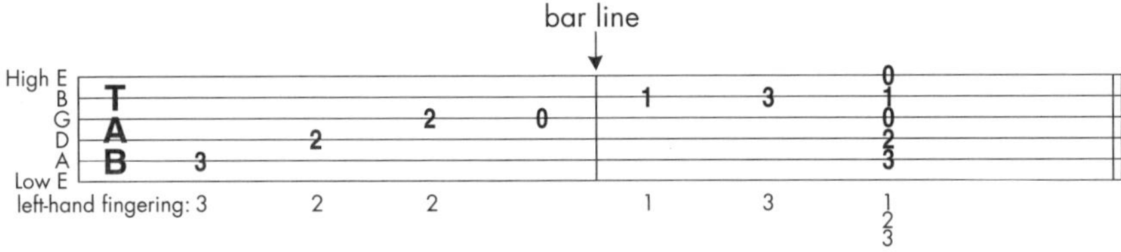

- The word "tab" is placed at the beginning of the system, or "tab staff." The tab staff consists of six horizontal lines, representing the strings of the guitar. The top line represents the high E string; the bottom is the low E. The other lines are the other four strings of the guitar. For example, the second line from the bottom is the A string, and so on.
- The numbers written on the lines indicate which fret to play on which string. "0" represents an open string, which means you play that string without fretting it.
- Numbers stacked on top of each other should be played simultaneously, or strummed like a chord.
- Sometimes, but not always, left-hand fingerings are notated under the tab staff. This tells you which fingers to use to fret the notes. 1=index; 2=middle; 3=ring; and 4=pinky.
- The vertical line has nothing to do with the guitar fretboard. It represents the bar line, which divides the measures, as in conventional music notation.

If you're still confused about the tab staff, try laying your guitar on the table, face up, with the headstock to your left. Now look down on the fretboard. Essentially, that's what the tab staff is: a visual snapshot of the guitar fretboard without the frets.

CHORD FRAMES

Although they can be notated on a tab staff, the easiest way to notate guitar chords (three or more notes played simultaneously) is to use diagrams known as chord frames. You'll often find these little frames located along the top of the staff in standard sheet music and play-along songbooks.

A chord frame is virtually a "snapshot" of an isolated part of the fretboard. If you hold your guitar out in front of you, with the fretboard facing you and the headstock toward the ceiling, you'll understand how chord frames align with the fretboard.

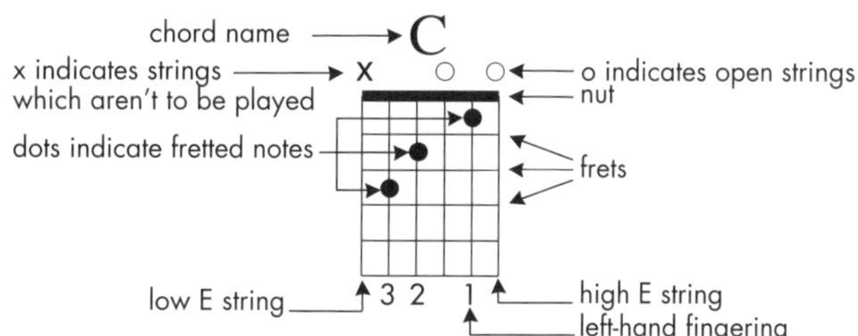

- The six vertical lines represent the strings. From left to right they are: low E–A–D–G–B–high E. The horizontal lines are the frets, with the thick one at the top representing the nut.
- The dots that appear on the string lines indicate fretted notes. The numerals located below the chord frame represent the fingers that should be used to fret each string (1 = index; 2 = middle; 3 = ring; and 4 = pinky).
- If an "X" appears at the top of a string, the string is not to be played. An "O" indicates that the string is to be played open, or without fretting it.
- The letter C at the top of the chord frame is the actual chord name.

If a chord is to be played further up the neck, a numeral appears to the right of the chord frame indicating the starting fret, or the lowest fret in the chord.

What's a Chord?

In general terms, a *chord* is three or more notes played at the same time. A chord voicing is the shape in which you arrange those notes on the fretboard. The most fundamental chord is the *major chord.* Major chords contain three specific notes. For instance, the C major chord contains the notes C, E, and G. To play a C major chord on the guitar, you have to locate and play all three notes simultaneously. The previous chord frame arranges those three notes in what is called open position. You may be saying, "But there are five notes in that chord." You're correct! That's because two of the notes (C and E) are included twice. Doubling the notes of a chord is common practice on the guitar.

BOX PATTERNS

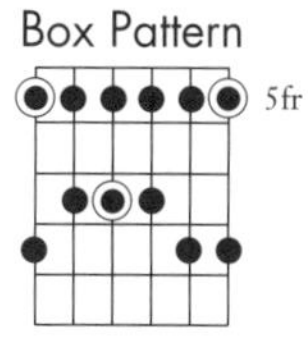

Still another form of guitar notation is the *box pattern.* Box patterns are generally reserved for *scales,* a series of notes arranged in specific order. Scales are usually played on the guitar in patterns that loosely resemble a box, thus the term "box pattern." Shown here is a popular scale pattern played in the middle of the neck.

Similar to a chord frame, a box pattern is a visual snapshot of an isolated section of the fretboard. Again, the vertical lines are the strings and the horizontal lines are the frets. The notation "5fr," located to the right of the diagram, indicates that the box is to be positioned at the fifth fret. The dots tell you where to fret the strings, while the circled dots indicate the root notes of the scale. All this information tells you that the notes of this particular scale pattern are located on the fifth and eighth frets of the low E string; the fifth and seventh frets of the A, D, and G strings; and the fifth and eighth frets of the B and high E strings. Left-hand fingering is at the discretion of the player.

CHAPTER 7
BASIC CHORDS

What's Ahead:

- Playing your first chord
- Chord families (A, D, G, and C)
- Open-position major and minor chords
- Chord progressions
- Classic progressions
- Play-along songs

You are about to enter the all-important chord section of the book. Chords are at the very heart of guitar playing. Armed with just a few, you can accompany yourself while you sing many of your favorite songs. If you don't sing, you can accompany someone who does. You could even play rhythm guitar in a band simply by playing chords. As a matter of fact, many famous guitar players rarely, if ever, play a lick of lead (single-note melodies). Some famous guitarists who are best known for their rhythm roles are Malcolm Young (AC/DC), John Lennon, Freddie Greene (Count Basie Orchestra), Tom Fogerty (Creedence Clearwater Revival), and James Hetfield (Metallica). That said, let's start playing some chords.

PLAYING YOUR FIRST CHORD

As we learned earlier, chords are groups of three or more notes sounded simultaneously. On the guitar, this translates to three or more strings being played at once. This is achieved by rapidly strumming the strings with either a pick, the side of your thumb, or the backs of your fingernails. Chords can also be played by plucking the strings simultaneously with your fingertips. To form a chord, you can't just strum any set of strings willy-nilly; you need to form a musical relationship with the group of notes you choose. Therefore, you need to start by learning chord forms, or chord voicings, on the fretboard.

Most guitar chords incorporate four, five, or all six strings. The easiest chords to play are *open-position* chords, or open chords. Open-position chords are played on the first few frets of the guitar. They're called "open" because they include at least one open string; the other strings are fretted on either the first, second, third, or fourth fret. We're going to start with the "king daddy" of all open-position chords—the E major chord.

The E Major Chord

If you take a gander at the chord frame below, you'll see that it illustrates an open-position E chord. Notice that the low E, B, and high E strings are open, while the A, D, and G strings are fretted at the second and first frets. Once you get a handle on playing chords, you'll be able to place your fingers on the frets simultaneously. For now, we'll fret the strings one at a time.

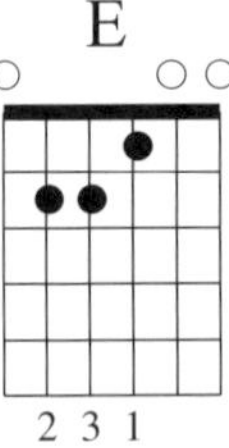

1. Place your first (index) finger (fingertip) on the first fret of the G string—not on the fret wire itself, but just behind it, toward the nut. There's no need to press down too hard yet; wait until you have your other fingers in place. Apply just enough pressure so that your finger doesn't move out of position.
2. Skipping over the D string, place your second (middle) finger on the second fret of the A string.

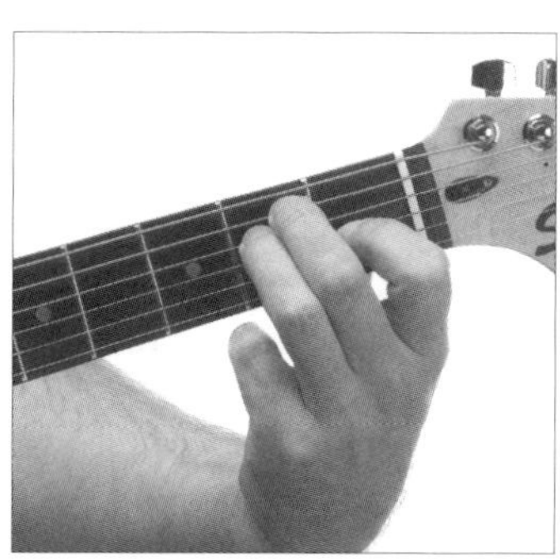

3. Place your third (ring) finger on the second fret of the D string. You'll notice that you'll have to move your second finger toward the nut in order to squeeze your third finger into place.
4. Now, press down firmly on the three fretted strings with the top parts of your fingertips, making sure your fingers are arched and coming straight down on the fretboard. Remember to use your thumb for leverage by squeezing the back of the neck.

Although the ideal fretting position is just behind the fret wire, some chord voicings require that you place some of your fingers in the middle of the fret area. For instance, the E chord requires the second finger to fret the A string in the middle of the second fret area.

Now that you have all three fingers in place, strum all of the strings in rapid succession from the low E string to the high E string. Congratulations! You've just played your first chord. Doesn't that sound glorious?

Yuck—That Doesn't Sound Right!

If your chord sounds less than spectacular, here are some troubleshooting tips to consult:

- **Is your guitar in tune?**
  This is the number-one reason why guitar chords don't sound pleasant.
- **Are you fretting down hard enough on the strings?**
  If you're not pressing down hard enough, your fretted notes will either buzz (commonly known as "fret rattle") or not sound at all. Make sure you're applying consistent pressure to all of your fretted notes. Lift your fingers off the fretboard and inspect your fingertips. If there isn't a little groove on the fleshy pad, you aren't pressing hard enough. We know it's painful at first (see "Building Calluses" sidebar), but once you've built up some calluses, your chords will ring out loud and clear.
- **Are you bending the strings out of place?**
  Make sure you aren't pushing the strings out of place (toward the ceiling or the floor) when you fret them. When playing a chord, all of the strings should remain parallel.
- **Are you accidentally muting the strings?**
  Make sure none of your fretting fingers are touching any surrounding strings. Touching the strings with your fingers will keep them from ringing out, causing a *muted*, or dampened, tone.

Building Calluses

In case we didn't warn you, learning to play the guitar can be a little painful at first. In the beginning, the pain will emanate from your left hand fingertips. This, of course, is the result of fretting the strings. Playing the guitar comfortably requires that you build up *calluses* (layers of dead skin) on your left-hand fingertips. Practic-ing the chords in this chapter repeatedly will do the trick. How quickly you build up those calluses depends on how much and how often you practice. Just remember, as with any new physical activity, you should take a break when your fingers start to feel sore.

CHORD FAMILIES

You can play hundreds of songs simply by knowing a few basic chords. As a matter of fact, many songs are entirely based on only three or four chords. Most of these types of songs use chords that belong to the same family. A chord family is a group of related chords. In musical terms, it means that they all belong to the same key. For instance, the Beatles' "Twist and Shout" uses D-family chords, therefore it is in the key of D.

The Rolling Stones' "Start Me Up" is based on F-family chords, placing it in the key of F. For now, don't worry too much about it; just think of chord families as a system for organizing chords.

A-FAMILY CHORDS

The chords in the A family all revolve around three central chords: A, D, and E. By the way, when a chord is named by a letter name alone, it means it's a *major chord*. Therefore, A, D, and E are all major chords. A good description for the sound of a major chord is "happy" or "stable." The rock 'n' roll classic "Peggy Sue," by Buddy Holly, is a great example of a song that uses A-family chords.

Buddy Holly is considered by many to be the first "hero" of the Fender Stratocaster—a guitar made even more famous by Jimi Hendrix.

A and D Major

You already know how to play an E chord, so all you need to do is learn A and D to have the three main A-family chords under your fingers. Check out the fingerings for both the A and D chords below. Use the chord frame as a reference for where to place your fingers and which strings to play. The picture will help you with correct hand position.

For the A chord, place your first finger at the second fret of the D string; your second finger at the second fret of the G string; and your third finger at the second fret of the B string. (Allow the A and high E strings to ring open, but don't strike the low E string.) Notice how, in the picture, the fingers are staggered in the second-fret area: the third finger is in the ideal spot (just behind the fret), while the second finger is roughly center-fret and the first finger is tucked slightly behind it. This method of compromise is necessary with many chords.

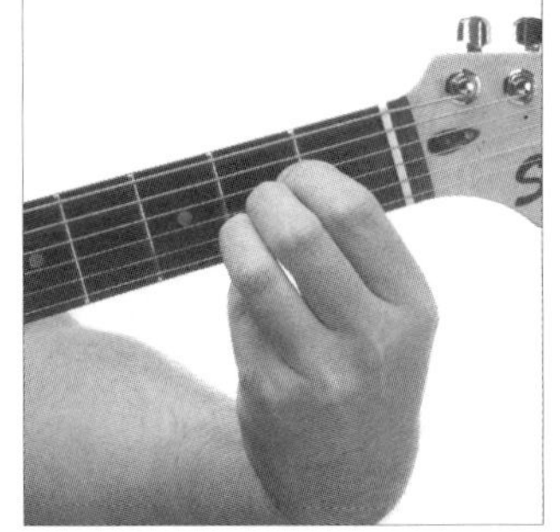

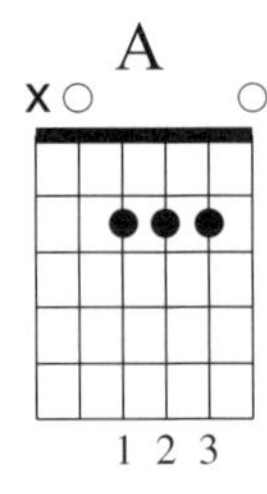

For the D chord, place your first finger at the second fret of the G string; your second finger at the second fret of the high E; and your third finger at the third fret of the B string. (With the D chord, it's possible to have all three of your fingers in the ideal spot, just behind the fret.) The D string is played open, but don't strike the low E and A strings.

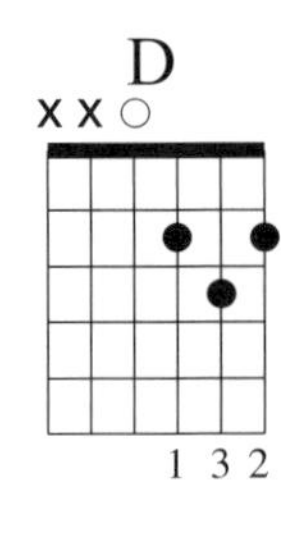

Don't play any strings marked with an "X" above the chord frame. The "O" indicates that the string should be played open.

Strumming and Changing

Now that you have the A-family chords under your fingers, practice changing from chord to chord, starting with A and D. Get your fingers in place for the A chord and, using a pick, your thumb, or the backs of your fingernails, slowly and evenly strum down from the A string to the high E, four times in succession. (Remember, don't pick the strings individually; instead, rapidly strum across the strings so that they all blur together.) After the fourth strum, get your fingers in place to play the D chord. When you're ready, strum that chord four times. Try to make your movement from A to D as smooth and quick as possible so that there's no hesitation between chords. Be patient with yourself and try not to get frustrated. Making chord changes is one of the most difficult tasks when learning to play guitar.

Try to move as few fingers as possible off of the strings when you change chords. For instance, when changing from an A to a D chord, you have to lift your first and second fingers off of the strings but you don't have to lift your third finger. You can keep it pressed lightly on the B string, dragging it up from the second to the third fret. This economy of movement affords a smoother transition from chord to chord. You can also keep your third finger on the B string when changing back to the A chord.

Here's a pro's tip for developing speed when making chord changes: Before you play the next chord, visualize the shape in your mind's eye. That is, see your hand in position, fingering the chord before you even make a move to play it. This may sound like a magic trick, but the world's finest athletes use similar techniques. It's actually nothing more than visualizing a positive outcome.

After strumming the D chord four times, go back to the A chord and repeat the process until you can change chords smoothly and evenly. When you're satisfied with your progress, practice changing from an A chord to an E chord.

Playing a Chord Progression

A *chord progression* is a series of chords played in succession. Many songs are constructed from a series of repeating chord progressions. Some are short, some are medium in length, and some are long. Chord progressions can be notated on a musical staff (not to be confused with a tab staff). The example below features a short chord progression that uses the A-family chords you've just learned. Incidentally, this means the progression is in the key of A.

The Musical Staff

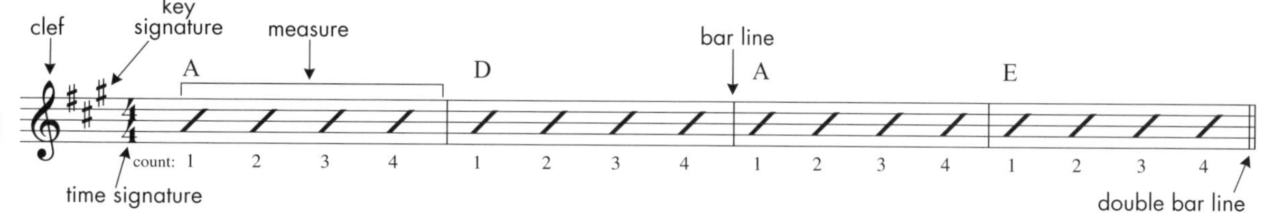

Without getting into too much music theory (yet), here's a brief description of the symbols used in the notation:

- The *musical staff* is a grid consisting of five horizontal lines and four spaces. As with the tab staff, you read left to right.
- The vertical lines are called *bar lines*, which separate the staff into small segments called *measures*, or *bars*. A *double bar line* is used to mark the end of a section of music.
- The funny, curved symbol at the beginning of the staff is called a *clef*, also called the *treble clef*, or *G clef*.
- The 4/4 symbol is the *time signature*. The top number represents the number of beats (counts) per measure; the bottom number indicates the type of note that receives the beat.

- The three "♯" symbols are the *key signature*. This indicates that the music is in the key of A.
- The slashes that appear in the measures are called *hash marks*, which are used to notate when and where chords are to be played.

The chord progression is four measures in length, and a new chord is played in each measure. The hash marks indicate that you are to play each chord four times. As you play along, count "1–2–3–4; 1–2–3–4," etc. Use all downstrokes (strum down, toward the floor), and don't forget to change chords at the beginning of each measure. Practice as slowly as necessary to keep the beat steady. When you're ready, you can play along to the audio example. Wait until you hear four clicks of the metronome before you begin.

When you come to the end of the progression (or any piece of music for that matter) you'll want to stop your guitar from sounding—similar to stepping on the brakes when you're driving. You can do this by resting the heel of your right hand (fleshy part between your pinky and wrist) on all six strings of the guitar a couple of inches above the bridge. This mutes the strings and stops them from sounding. You can also lift your fretting fingers off the strings for added insurance.

Playing and Singing a Song in the Key of A

Now let's use the A-family chords to play the famous gospel hymn "When the Saints Go Marching In." The song appears below in double-staff notation. The lyrics and melody are notated in the top staff with chord symbols above; the guitar rhythms are notated in the lower staff. This uses the same four-strums-to-the-bar rhythm we used in the previous figure. On the track, you'll hear five clicks of the metronome followed by three melody notes on the piano ("Oh, when the…"). Come in on the fourth note ("saints…"). Once you have the song down, try singing along while you play. At first, you may be tempted to strum to the rhythm of the melody, but in time you'll be able to keep a steady strumming pattern while you sing. In the final measure, hold the A chord for four counts and then dampen the strings with the heel of your right hand to stop them from sounding.

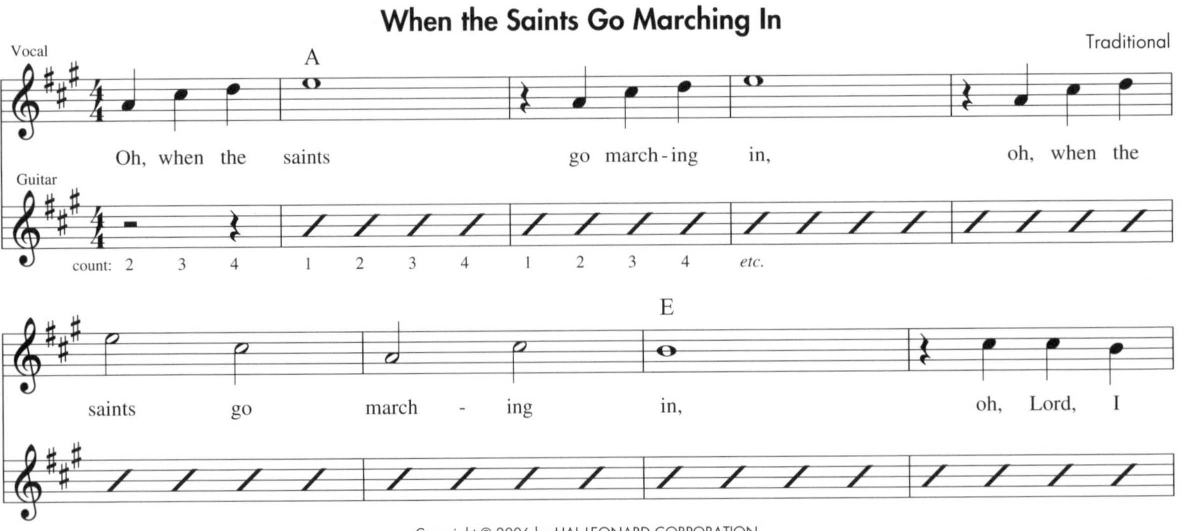

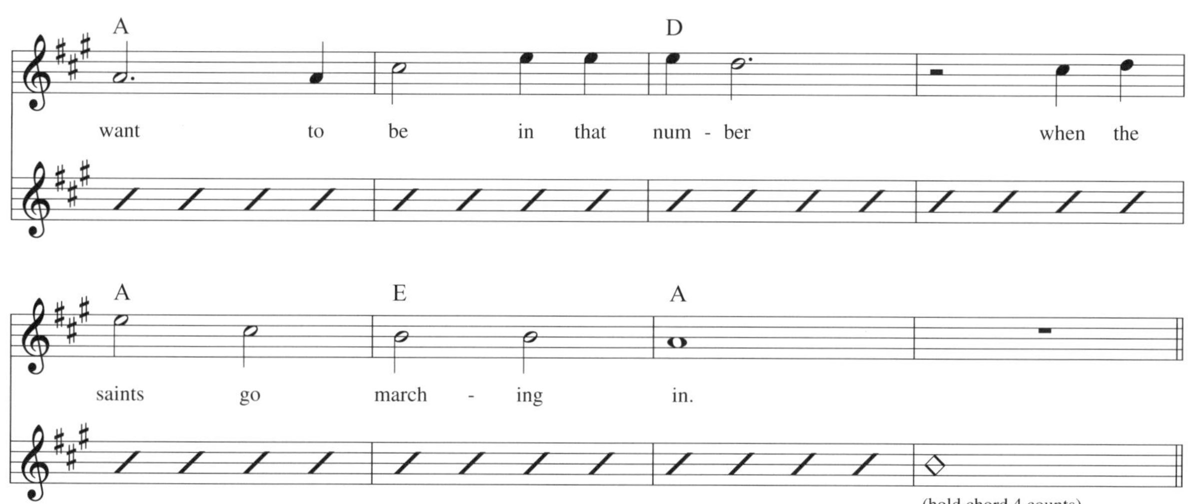

Every chord family is made up of seven basic chords. The A family contains A, Bm, C♯m, D, E, F♯m, and G♯° (G♯ diminished). The G♯° chord is rarely used, but you'll encounter the other chords in many songs in the key of A. "A Summer Song," by Chad and Jeremy; "Tears in Heaven," by Eric Clapton; "Again," by Lenny Kravitz; and "Come Monday," by Jimmy Buffett all use a wide variety of A-family chords.

D-FAMILY CHORDS

The basic chords that make up the D family are D, G, and A. As you can see, the D family shares two chords with the A family (D and A). As a matter of fact, many chord families share common chords. Thus, all you have to do is learn one chord (G), and you'll have the main chords in the D-family down.

The G Major Chord

The following chord frames illustrate two ways to finger an open G chord. Because the pinky is usually the weakest finger, you'd be wise to learn the first voicing before moving on to the second. The reason we give you two choices is that, depending on what chord you're transitioning from or going to, one voicing works better than the other.

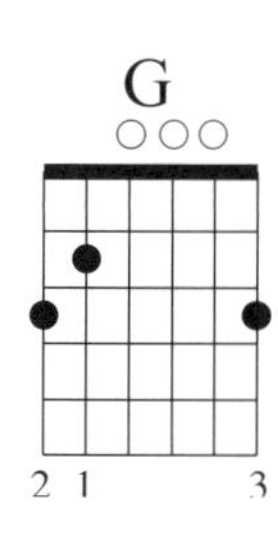

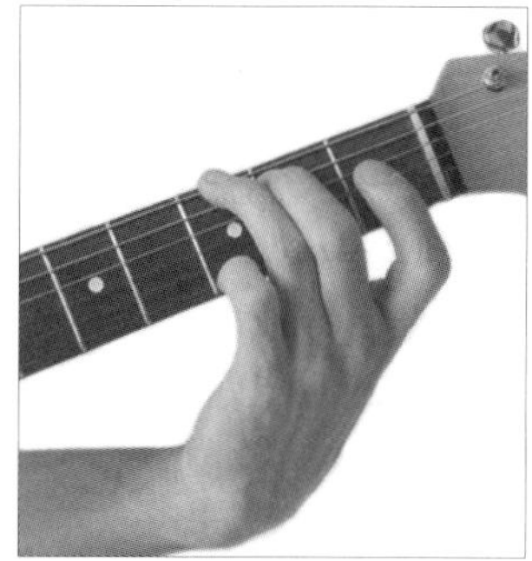

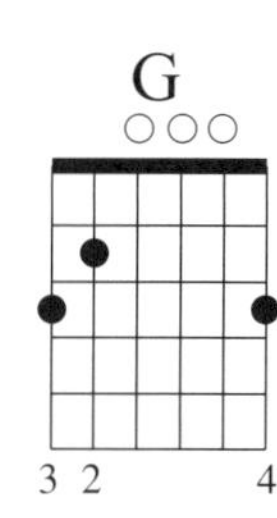

A New Strumming Pattern

Now that you've learned to play chord progressions using all downstrokes, it's time to add a little rhythmic pizzazz to your playing. This example demonstrates a slight variation on our "all downstroke" approach.

Notice that there are downward *stems* attached to the hash marks. When combined they form a musical code used to decipher rhythms. The hash marks on beats 1, 3, and 4 all have one stem attached to them. These symbols signify one beat, or *quarter note*, and receive one downstroke apiece. The second beat has two hash marks, with their stems linked by a beam. These symbols represent two *eighth notes*, which means that the beat is divided into two. In other words, you need to squeeze two strums into the space of one. This is achieved by strumming down and up in a single motion.

Confused? Well, take a look at the funny-looking figures located on top of the staff, above each hash mark. These symbols indicate strumming directions. The ones that look like two-legged tabletops (⊓) represent downstrokes. The ones that look like the letter "V" (V) represent upstrokes. This all translates to a down/down-up/down/down strumming pattern for each measure. The abbreviation "*sim.*" above the third measure stands for the Italian word "*simile*." This means to continue playing in similar fashion.

To play an upstroke with a pick, simply drag it across the strings from the highest to the lowest, or toward the ceiling. (You don't need to adjust your right-hand position; simply come back up the strings using the opposite side of the pick. Remember not to hold it too tightly.) Keep your right wrist loose and allow it to swing, much like the motion you use to shake water off your hands when you get out of the swimming pool. If you're strumming with your fingernails, use your thumbnail for upstrokes.

To stay in rhythm while you're playing through the example, count "One, two-and, three, four." (Be careful not to strike the low E and A strings.) While you're counting, tap your foot on counts 1, 2, 3, and 4.

If you're having a hard time understanding upstrokes, try looking at them this way: When you strum only downstrokes, you're actually performing upstrokes between each one; it's just that they're in mid-air, away from the strings. To perform upstrokes, simply bring your hand in toward the strings when you come back up.

A Classic Progression

Let's put our D-family chords to task in a progression that utilizes the strumming pattern we just learned. The following example contains a D–G–A progression. In the industry, this is called a I–IV–V (pronounced "one–four–five") progression in the key of D. (In music notation, Roman numerals are often used to represent chords.) Technically, a *I–IV–V progression* is based on the harmony of the first, fourth, and fifth scale tones of the major scale, but we don't need to go into that. For now, let's just say that there are thousands of songs that are based upon I–IV–V progressions, including "Wild Thing," by the Troggs; "Twist and Shout," by the Beatles; "La Bamba," by Ritchie Valens; and "Like a Rolling Stone," by Bob Dylan. Although these songs are in different keys, they still use the same I–IV–V structure. By the way, the double bar line with the two dots in front of it is called a *repeat sign*, which means to go back to the beginning of the progression (where the backward repeat sign is located) and play it again.

Track 4
(0:15)

Strumming upstrokes doubles the chances of hitting unwanted strings (e.g., the open A and low E strings in a D chord). Concentrate on hitting the higher strings in a chord on which you strum up to avoid this unfortunate experience.

Other D-family chords include Em, F♯m, and Bm. "The Long and Winding Road," by the Beatles; "Wherever You Will Go," by the Calling; and "Teach Your Children," by Crosby, Stills, Nash & Young all use a full array of D-family chords.

G-FAMILY CHORDS

The basic chords that make up the G family are G, C, D, and Am (pronounced "A minor"). You can think of *minor chords* as being major-chord counterparts. Compared to major chords, minor chords sound "sad" or "bittersweet." We already know the G and D chords, so let's have a look at C and Am.

C and Am Chords

The adjacent chord frames demonstrate the fingerings for C and Am chords. Notice that you only need to lift your third finger off the A string and put it on the second fret of the G string to change from the C to the Am chord. Practice these chords back-and-forth, one measure at a time.

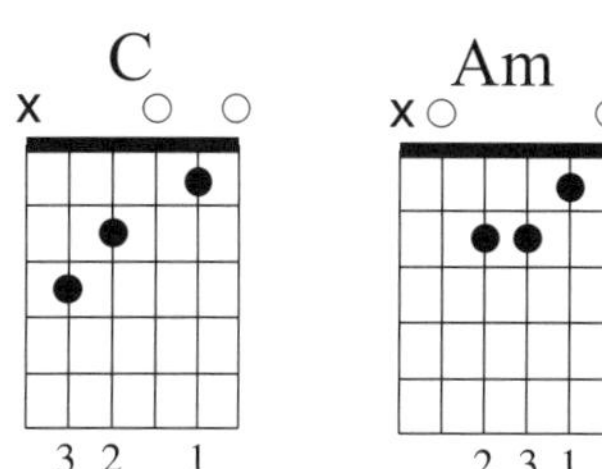

A Hands-on Lesson on Chord Qualities

Just as there are many different types of shoes, there are many different types of chords: A major, A minor, etc. The term *chord quality* means "chord type." For example, an A major chord (A) is major in quality; an A minor (Am) is minor in quality. Chord qualities are defined by the relationship of the notes that make up that chord. Pretty technical stuff! For now, let's concentrate on the sound of some basic chord qualities.

In these chord frames, you'll notice voicings for five different chord qualities, all in the key of A; meaning that the lowest note is A, the root. Play the A major chord. Notice that it sounds stable and happy. Now play the Am chord. By comparison, it has a softer, bittersweet sound. (The alternate fingering for the A chord allows easy access between voicings.) Next, play the A7, also referred to as A *dominant seventh*. An active-sounding chord, the A7 has a bluesy, funky quality. The Am7 chord is very similar to Am, except it has an added jazzy texture. You'll find *minor-seventh* chords in jazz, funk, and Latin music styles. Last, we have the Amaj7 (A *major-seventh*) chord. It has a vibrant, jazzy quality. You'll encounter major-seventh chords galore in jazz, but they also pop up in country, rock, soul, and folk styles. (See Chapter 9 for more on seventh chords.)

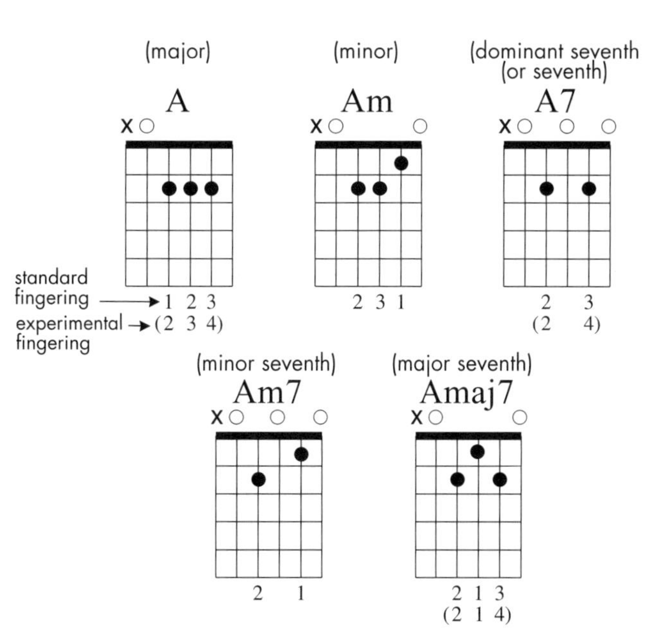

Playing a Progression in the Key of G

The progression below is in the style of a '70s atmospheric folk-rock ballad. The rhythm notation indicates that you play a down-up strum on beats 2 and 3. Remember to tap your foot on each beat (not on the "ands"). Don't forget—you can listen to the track to hear how the example is to be played.

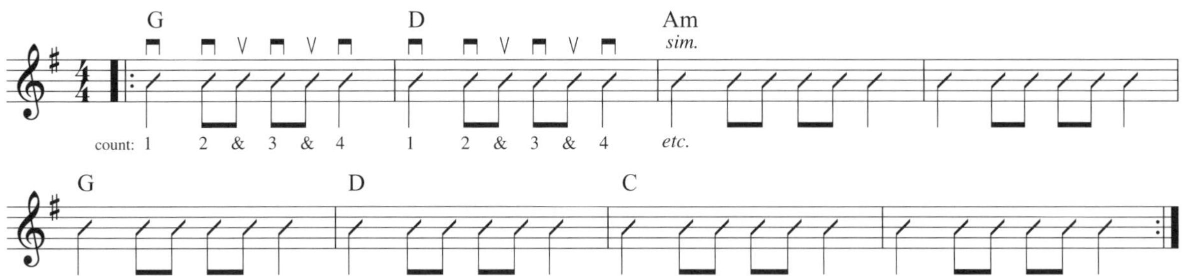

Playing a Cowboy Song in the Key of G

Speaking of soul-wrenching ballads in the key of G, here's one that's guaranteed to bring a tear to an old cowboy's one good eye: "Streets of Laredo" (see below). Notice that the time signature reads 3/4. This means that there are three beats, or counts, per bar. To keep time in 3/4, count "one, two, three" in each measure. The notation indicates a down/down-up/down strum pattern. Wait until you hear six clicks of the metronome (signifying two measures of time) before you begin.

Other G-family chords include Em and Bm. "The Time of Your Life," by Green Day; "Take It Easy," by the Eagles; "Breathe," by Faith Hill; and "You Shook Me All Night Long," by AC/DC all use a boatload of G-family chords.

C-FAMILY CHORDS

The last chord family you're going to learn is C. C is a very important and popular key, so the more C-family chords you know, the better. You already know three C-family chords: C, G, and Am. That leaves Dm, Em, F, and B°. B° is seldom used so we can skip it for now. That means we only have to learn Dm, Em, and F.

Em, Dm, and F Chords

The next chord frames contain the fingerings for Em, Dm, and F. Em is very similar to E, which you've already learned. In fact, if you finger an E chord, all you have to do is lift your first finger off of the G string and—*voila!*—you have an Em chord.

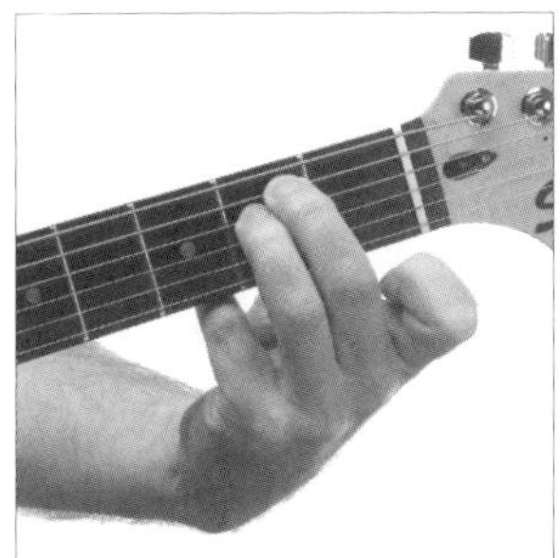

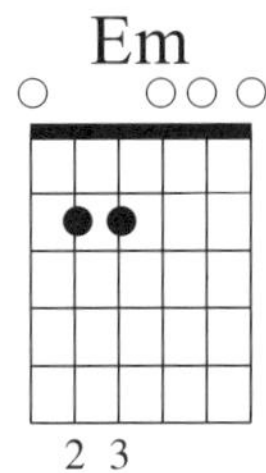

Although the fingering is entirely different, only one note (and fret) separates the Dm chord from the D chord we've been playing: the note on the top string is at the first fret instead of the second.

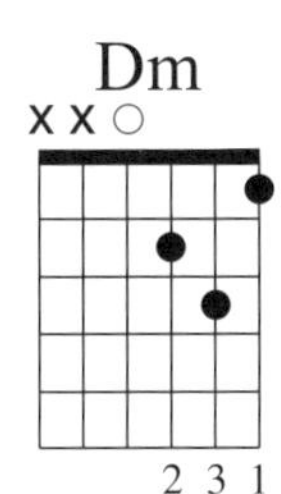

All of this is good news, but the F chord opens a brand-new can of worms. In fact, the F chord is the most difficult chord we've covered so far. That's because it requires you to press down on two strings with the same finger; specifically, the high E and B strings at the first fret. A chord that requires you to fret two or more strings with the same finger is called a *barre chord*. To play an F chord, barre the high E and B strings at the first fret with your first (index) finger. The trick is to get your third and second fingers in

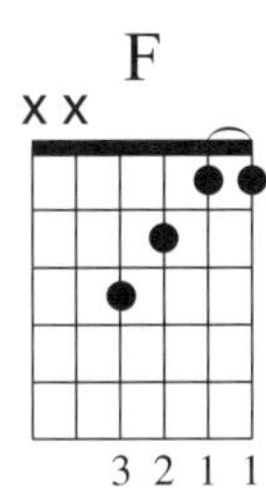

position at the third fret of the D string and the second fret of the G string, respectively. Now, touch the bottom part of the G string, at the first fret, with the very tip of your first finger. This will put your finger in a good position for the barre. Finally, bring your fingerpad down to make contact with both the B and high E strings, pressing down *hard*. Hurts, right? Don't worry—in time you'll build up calluses, and playing an F chord will be like visiting an old friend.

When you first play the F chord it might sound muffled, or you may hear some string buzz. Try fretting only the barre portion of the chord, wiggling your finger around from side-to-side until the notes ring clearly when you strum the two strings. Position your thumb behind the second-fret area and apply extra pressure for added leverage. When you're satisfied with the sound of the notes, fret the rest of the chord.

Putting C-family Chords to Good Use

The following example is in the style of the guitar/piano rock ballads of the '60s and '70s. As you can see, there are a lot of chords in this progression. For this reason, we've kept the strumming pattern to a simple quarter-note rhythm (four downstrokes for each measure). Piece this example together, chord by chord, going very slowly at first. For example, practice changing back-and-forth between the C chord and the G chord. When you've got that down, move on to the next two chords (Am and F) and practice them in the same way. Little-by-little you'll get to the end of the progression. By then, you should be able to play along with the track.

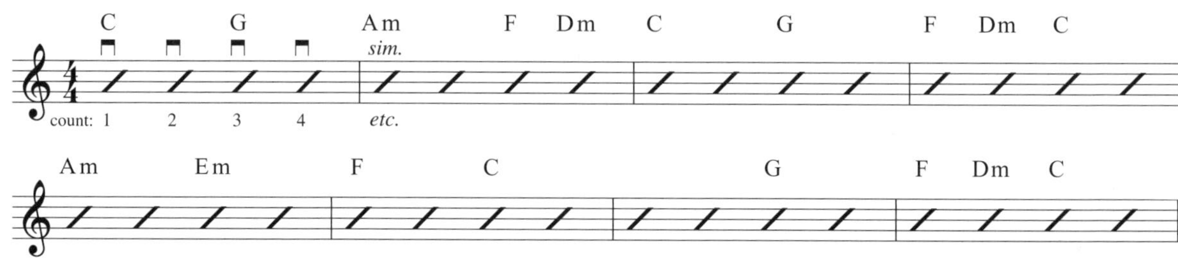

The songs "Whiter Shade of Pale," by Procol Harum; "Drops of Jupiter," by Train; "The Boxer," by Simon and Garfunkel; and "Chattahoochee," by Alan Jackson are all chock full of C-family chords.

Using C-family Chords in a Minor Way

The traditional English folk song "Scarborough Fair" (see next page) is based on chords from the C family (with one exception: D). But instead of using C as the central chord, the progression keeps coming back to Am. Like the chord itself, this gives the song a sad, wistful quality. This example is in 3/4 time. Count "one, two, three" and use a down/down-up/down strum pattern. Hold the last Am chord for three counts.

audio tracks 8

Scarborough Fair

Traditional English

Vocal

Am G Am

Are you go - ing to Scar - bor - ough Fair?

Guitar

sim.

count: 1 2 3 1 2 3 etc.

C Am D Am

Pars - ley, sage, rose - ma - ry, and thyme. Re -

F C G

mem - ber me to one who lives there, for

Am D G Am

once she was a true love of mine.

(hold chord for 3 counts)

In "Scarborough Fair" you learned that a C-family progression could revolve around another chord besides C. In that case it was Am. Using an alternate chord as the centerpiece in a progression is common practice in many styles of music, especially rock. One prime example is the E–A–D progression. You'll recognize these as being the three main chords of the A family. However, rock tunesmiths love to combine these three chords into progressions that feature E (instead of A) as the central chord. Some famous examples include "What I Like About You," by the Romantics; "R.O.C.K. in the U.S.A.," by John Cougar Mellencamp; "Satisfaction," by the Rolling Stones, "Back in Black," by AC/DC; and "Communication Breakdown," by Led Zeppelin. The placement of the D and A chords vary, but E is always the starting and ending chord.

ICE CREAM CHANGES

Ice cream changes refers to a specific chord progression that was often used in "oldies" ('50s and early '60s) songs such as "In the Still of the Night," "You Send Me," and "Duke of Earl." The name sprang from the fact that kids in those days used to hang out in malt shops (ice cream parlors) and dance to records on the jukebox.

In music-theory terms, ice cream changes translate to a I–VI–IV–V (pronounced: "one–six–four–five") progression. Ice cream changes in the key of C are C–Am–F–G. In the key of G they are G–Em–C–D. Below, you'll find an extensive list of oldies tunes that use ice cream changes. Simply pick a key (either C or G), strum each chord the indicated amount of times, and sing away to your heart's content. For example, to play "26 Miles (Santa Catalina)" in the key of C, strum a C chord two times; an Am two times; an F two times; and a G chord two times. Then, go back to the C chord and repeat.

For these songs, play each chord for two beats:

"26 Miles (Santa Catalina)" by the Four Preps
"All I Have to Do Is Dream" by the Everly Brothers
"Blue Moon" by the Marcels
"Book of Love" by the Monotones
"Breaking Up Is Hard to Do" by Neil Sedaka
"Cherry Pie" by Skip and Flip
"Come Go With Me" by the Del Vikings
"Daddy's Home" by Shep and the Limelites
"Earth Angel" by the Penguins
"Hey Paula" by Paul and Paula
"Lollipop" by the Chordettes
"Sherry" by Franki Valli and the Four Seasons
"Silhouettes" by the Rays
"Tears on My Pillow" by Little Anthony and the Imperials
"This Boy" by the Beatles
"We Go Together" from *Grease*
"Why Do Fools Fall in Love" by Frankie Lymon and the Teenagers
"You Send Me" by Sam Cooke

For these songs, play each chord for four beats:

"Diana" by Paul Anka
"Duke of Earl" by Gene Chandler
"In the Still of the Night" by the Five Satins
"Little Star" by the Elegants
"Poor Little Fool" by Ricky Nelson
"Unchained Melody" by the Righteous Brothers

For these songs, each chord receives eight beats:

"Little Darlin'" by the Diamonds
"Runaround Sue" by Dion

- When playing chords, keep your fingers arched so that the fingertips come straight down on the fretboard.
- Many chord families share common chords.
- Learn the main chords from the A, D, G, and C families and you'll be able to play thousands of songs.
- Playing guitar becomes more comfortable when you develop calluses.
- Many songs (although they may be in different keys) are based on identical chord progressions.
- Keep that foot tapping in time (quarter-note pulse).

CHAPTER 8
PLAYING MELODIES

What's Ahead:

- C major scale patterns
- Left-hand fingering
- Picking techniques
- Playing melodies in the key of C
- A minor scale
- Playing melodies in the key of A minor

The art of guitar playing can be broken down to two basic categories: playing chords (see Chapter 7) and playing melodies. Chords, we've learned, are groups of notes played simultaneously. Melodies are played on the guitar by picking strings individually. As with chords, sometimes the strings are picked open, but more often they're fretted.

We promised early on that we weren't going to force you to learn how to read music. We're still sticking to our oath but some of the things in this chapter are best explained using the musical staff as a reference. Don't feel like you need to become an avid sight-reader (music reader) to learn how to play melodies. On the contrary, we'll be relying on our old friend, the tablature system (see Chapter 6), as well as the two strongest musical tools you have at your disposal—your ears.

PICKING OUT YOUR FIRST SCALE

Many guitar method books bore you from the outset with endless picking exercises that sound more like a really bad horror-movie soundtrack than they do music. But here, in *All About Guitar*, everything is musical. We're going to start right away with the most important melodic device known to music: the C major scale.

The C Major Scale

If you've ever sang or heard the "do-re-mi-fa-so-la-ti-do" melody, well, that's the major scale. If it starts on a C note, it's the C major scale. The *C major scale* contains these seven notes: C–D–E–F–G–A–B.

The *musical alphabet* contains seven letters: A–B–C–D–E–F–G. These letters represent the seven natural notes (white keys on the piano). The other five notes (black keys on the piano) are named in reference to their natural-note neighbors. For example, the note between C and D is called either C♯ (C sharp) or D♭ (D flat); the note between D and E is referred to as D♯ or E♭; and so on.

It's very easy to play the C major scale on a piano. All you have to do is start at any C note (see next page) and play every white key, in order, until you arrive at the next C.

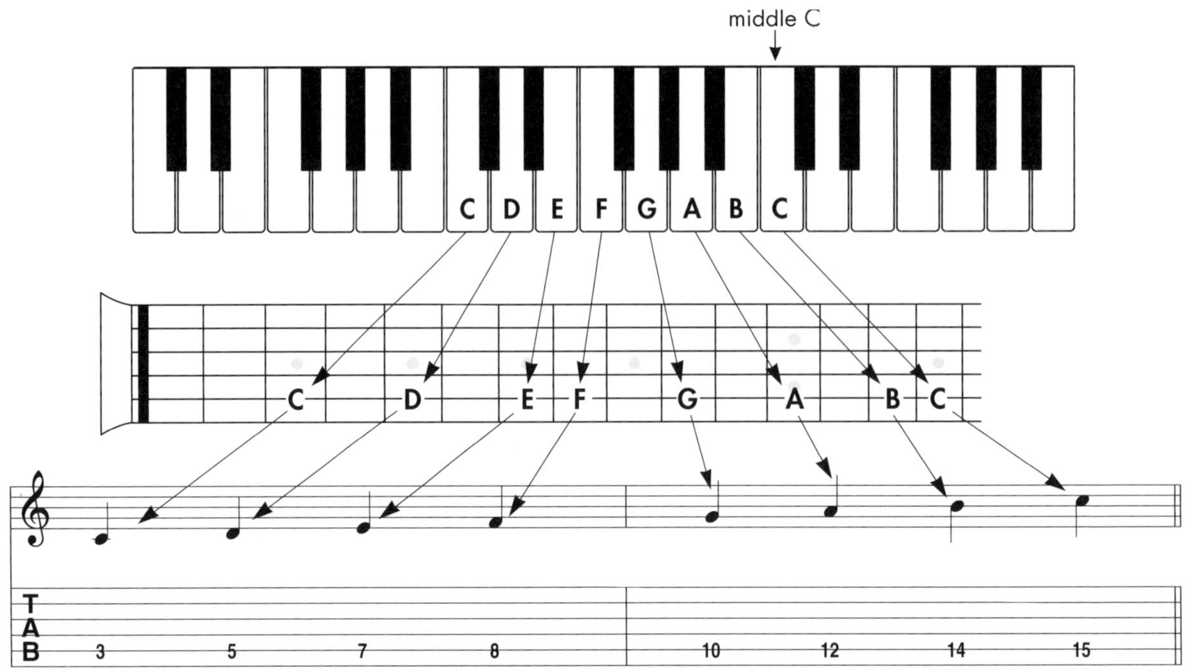

You can play the C major scale along a single string (as depicted above) but, more often than not, it's impractical. Guitarists usually play box scales in patterns that run across the fretboard, rather than along it. For example, the figure below depicts an open-position scale pattern for the C major scale in neck diagrams and in tab.

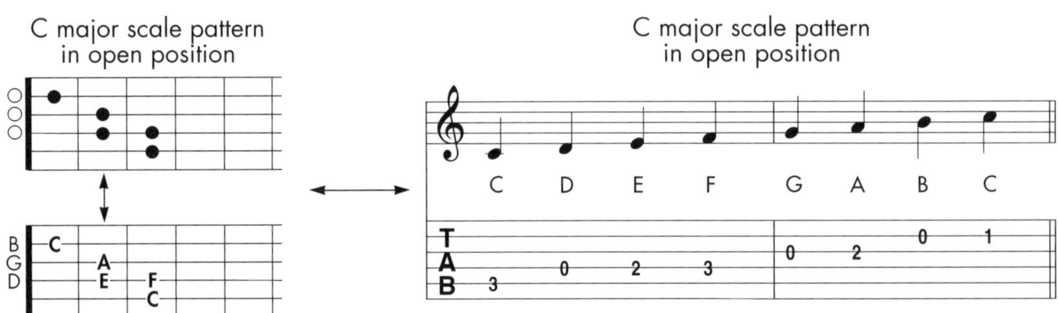

Notice that the notes you played up the A string in the previous example are now organized in a scale pattern that runs across the strings. Now that you understand what constitutes a scale pattern, practice picking through it. But before you do, let's take a quick and painless (we promise) lesson on the music staff.

A CRASH COURSE ON THE MUSIC STAFF

Standard music notation is written on a grid consisting of five lines and four spaces, called a *staff*. As illustrated below, the lines are counted from the bottom up (1–2–3–4–5), as are the spaces (1–2–3–4). At the beginning of the staff, you'll find a symbol called a *clef*. There are many different types of clefs, but guitar music is notated on the *treble clef*, or *G clef*.

The Musical Staff

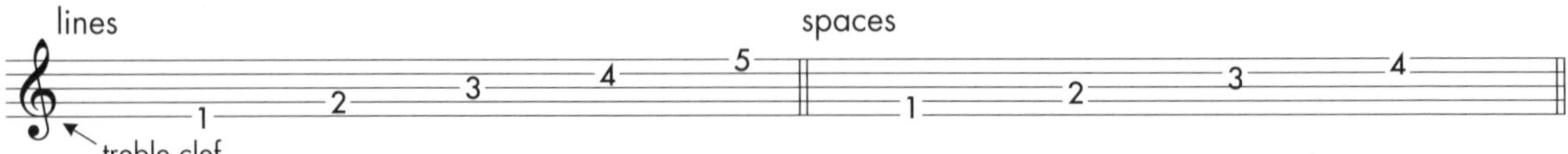

Music is written in *notes* on the staff. Where a note is written on the staff determines its *pitch* (highness or lowness). Each line and space of the staff has a letter name: The lines are, from the bottom up, E–G–B–D–F, and the spaces are F–A–C–E.

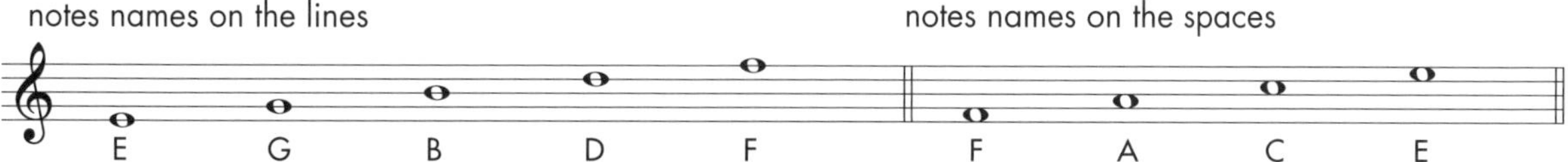

Many of the notes on the guitar extend beyond the staff. These pitches are notated on *ledger lines*, short lines that act as temporary staff extensions (see below). The only non–ledger line notes that appear outside the staff are G, directly above the staff, and D, directly below the staff.

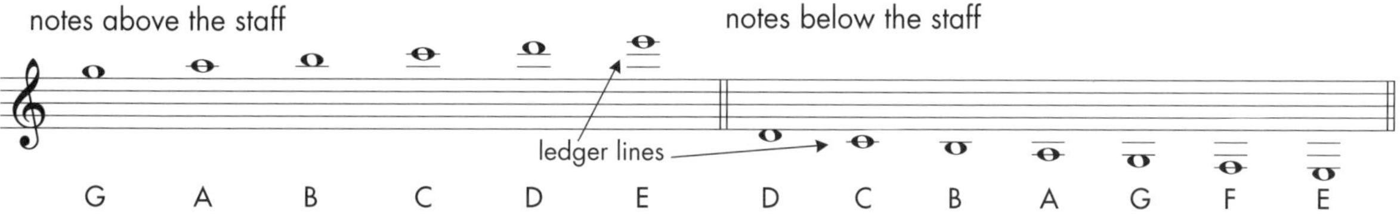

Pitches are represented in vertical fashion (up and down) on the staff. Rhythms, however, are represented in horizontal fashion (left to right) along the staff. To help keep track of these rhythms, the staff is divided into small segments called *measures*, or *bars*. Measures are separated by vertical lines called *bar lines*. (Note: A double bar line marks the end of a section of music. An end bar line marks the end of a piece of music.)

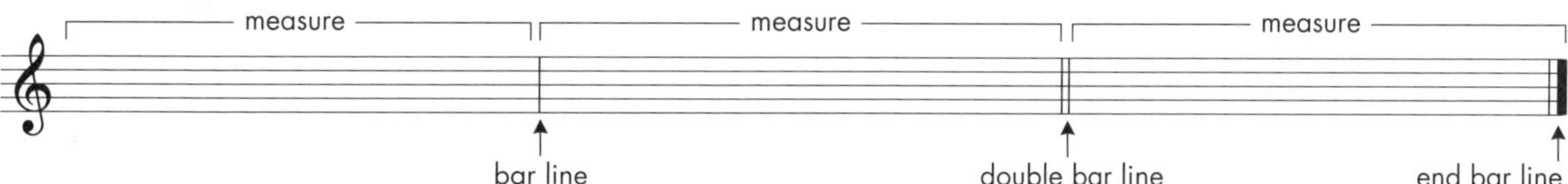

Each measure receives a certain number of *beats*, or *counts*. The number of beats per measure is determined by the *time signature*, which appears at the beginning of the staff, just right of the treble clef (see below). The time signature consists of two numbers, one on top of the other. The top number represents the number of beats per measure, and the bottom number indicates the type of note receiving one beat.

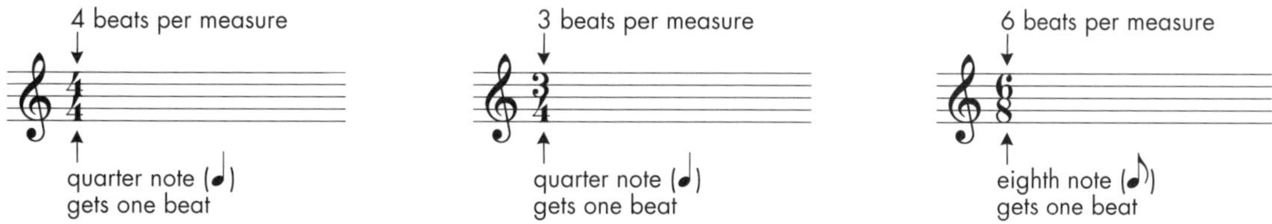

As previously stated, the location of a notehead on the staff indicates its pitch. The duration (length or value) of the note, however, is indicated by the "shape" of the note. Here's a breakdown of common note values:

In a nutshell, when different kinds of notes are placed on different lines or spaces on the staff, the information tells you the pitch of the note and how long to play it.

LEFT-HAND FINGERING

When playing scale patterns, it's important to use consistent left-hand fingering placements. This translates to assigning a specific finger to a specific fret within the pattern. As you can see below, our C major scale combines open strings with fretted ones. Notice that all of the fretted notes are located on either the first, second, or third frets. As you play through the scale, remember to play first-fret notes with your first finger, second-fret notes with your second finger, and third-fret notes with your third finger. Speed isn't the issue right now; give yourself plenty of time, counting "One, two, three, four" after you pick each note. Use all downstrokes for now, as well.

count: 1 2 3 4 1 2 3 4 *etc.*

TAB: 3 0 2 3 0 2 0 1

left-hand fingering: 3 2 3 2 1

When playing the scale, pick straight down (toward the floor) on each string, letting the underside of your pick come to rest on the adjacent string. For example, when you play the first C note on the A string, let your pick come to rest on the D string; when you play the next note (open D string), let the pick come to rest on the G string; and so on. This method will help keep your right hand in a strategic position, guiding your "aim" for each new string attack.

- Press down on each fretted string with the tip of your finger, just behind the fret wire (toward the headstock).
- Similar to playing chords, keep your fingers arched so they come straight down on the fretboard.
- Keep your fingers close to the fretboard, ready for action; don't lift them too high off of the strings when you release fretted notes.

Once you can play the scale without making any mistakes, try going down the scale from the highest note to the lowest (see below). Once you have that down, go up and down the scale without stopping.

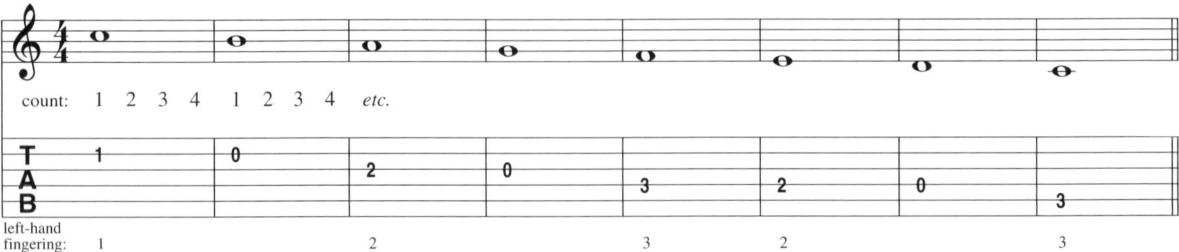

You don't want to develop any bad habits so early in the game. If you're having trouble playing notes with a pick, refer back to Chapter 4 for proper technique.

PLAYING MELODIES IN THE KEY OF C

Now that you have the C major scale under your fingers, let's move on to some melodies. Next, you'll find several examples of familiar melodies, all in the key of C, and all playable in the scale pattern you now know like the back of your hand. The tab staff tells you exactly where to fret the notes, but if you can't decipher the rhythms, you can refer to "A Crash Course on the Music Staff," which can be found earlier in this chapter, or you can use your ears and listen to the performances.

The first two melodies are nursery rhymes ("Frere Jacques" and "Twinkle, Twinkle Little Star") and contain half notes, which are played on beat 3 and held through beat 4. (Remember to keep that foot tapping in time!) The third melody is in a '60s pop-rock vein. It starts on a quarter-note rest, which signifies a beat of silence. The melody starts on beat 2. The fourth melody is a well-known Christmas carol ("Joy to the World"). The melody is quite simple (it slips straight down the scale) but the rhythm is rather tricky. On beat 3 of measure 1, the B note is held for 1-1/2 beats (dotted quarter notes receive 1-1/2 beats). This is followed by an A note played on the "and" of beat 4. The final example is slightly different from the rest. Notice that the melody keeps coming back to A instead of C. This gives it a sad, romantic quality. We'll explain why a little later.

audio tracks 10

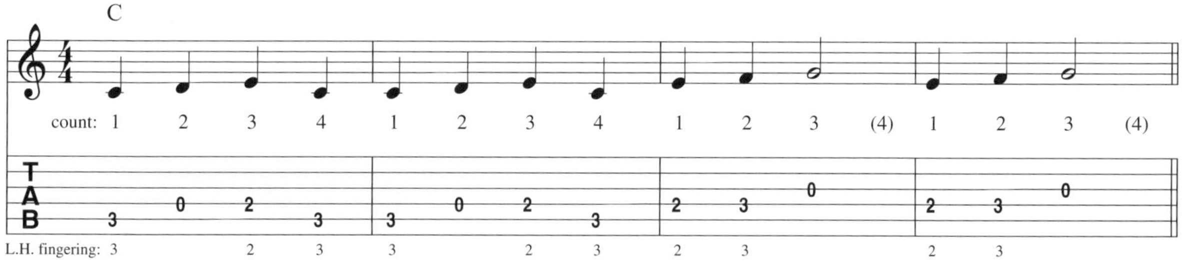

C

count: 1 2 3 4 | 1 2 3 4 | 1 2 3 (4) | 1 2 3 (4)

TAB: 3 0 2 3 | 3 0 2 3 | 2 3 0 | 2 3 0

L.H. fingering: 3 2 3 | 3 2 3 | 2 3 | 2 3

Track 10 (0:15)

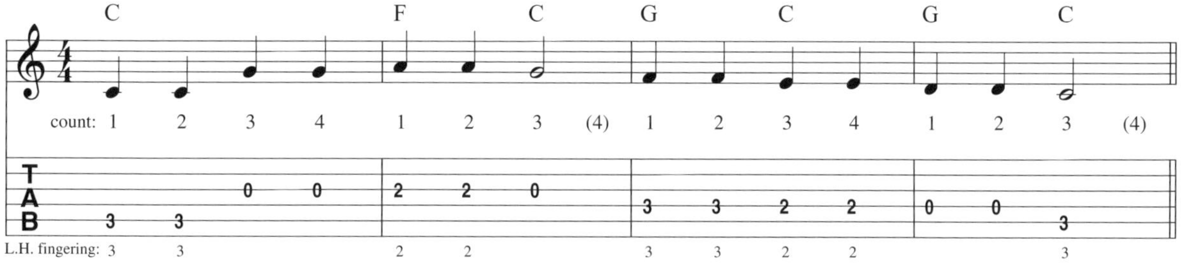

C F C G C G C

count: 1 2 3 4 | 1 2 3 (4) | 1 2 3 4 | 1 2 3 (4)

TAB: 3 3 0 0 | 2 2 0 | 3 3 2 2 | 0 0 3

L.H. fingering: 3 3 | 2 2 | 3 3 2 2 | 3

Track 10 (0:26)

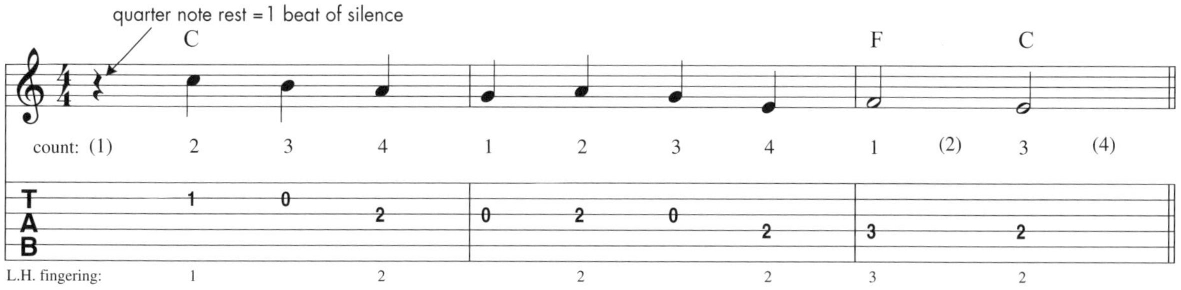

quarter note rest = 1 beat of silence

C F C

count: (1) 2 3 4 | 1 2 3 4 | 1 (2) 3 (4)

TAB: 1 0 2 | 0 2 0 2 | 3 2

L.H. fingering: 1 2 | 2 2 | 3 2

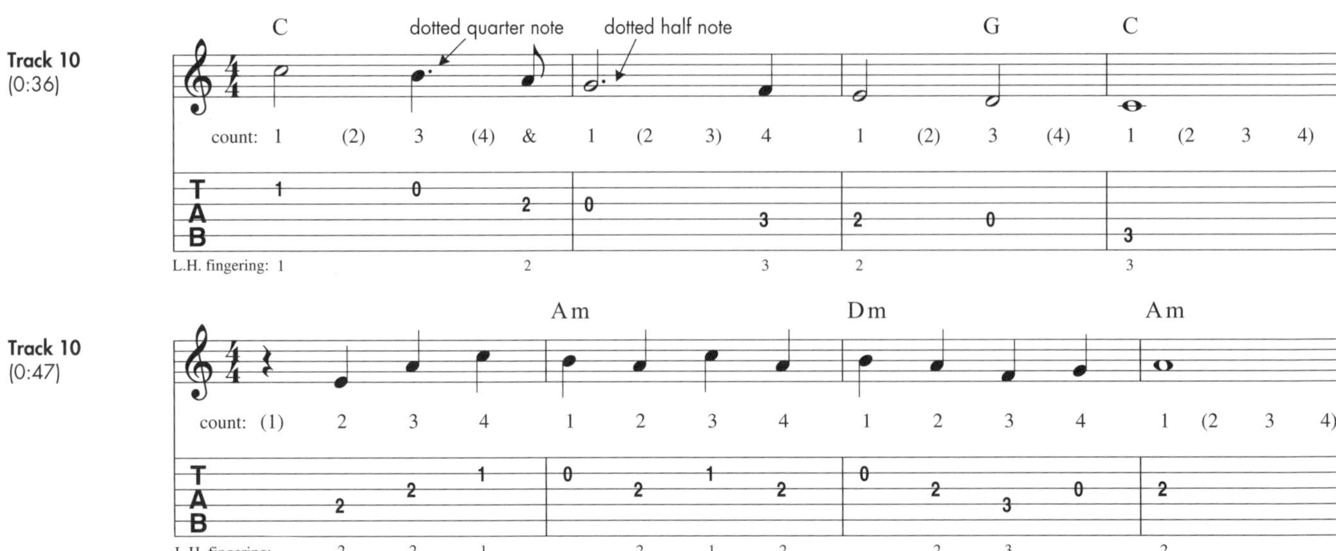

EXTENDING THE C MAJOR SCALE PATTERN

The C major scale has seven notes, C–D–E–F–G–A–B, but you'll notice the pattern we learned has eight notes. That's because the eighth note is also C. The lowest C is called the *root*, or *tonic*, and the highest C is called the *octave*. Standard scale patterns extend beyond the octave. In other words, once you reach the octave C, you start over again with the same notes (C–D–E, etc.), only an octave higher. You can also extend a scale pattern by going the other way, back down from the root (C–B–A, etc.). If this all sounds like mumbo-jumbo, don't worry—things will clear up once we apply it to the fretboard.

Below, you'll find diagrams and tablature depicting an extended form of the C major scale pattern we just learned. Notice that it passes the octave C (first fret of the B string) and continues up to G at the third fret of the high E string. It also extends below the C (third fret of the A string), going all the way down to E (open low E string). Listen to the track to hear this scale pattern performed from the lowest note (E) to the highest note (G).

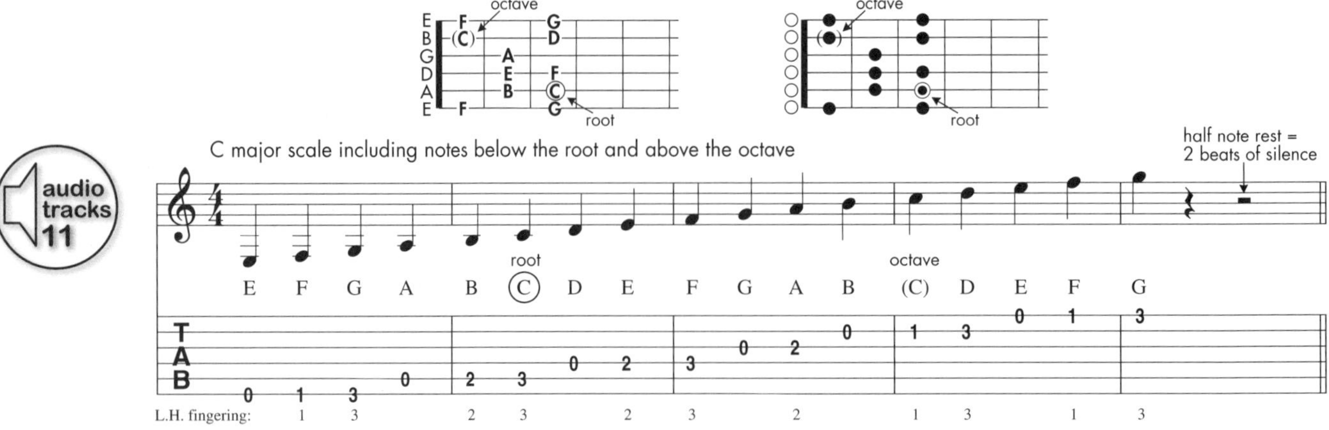

PLAYING SONGS IN THE KEY OF C

Melodies are not always confined to the space of one octave. Some extend above the octave, and some dip below the root. The following songs use "both sides" of the C major scale. Learning to play them is a fun and musical way to practice the entire range of the open-position C major scale.

- "Ode to Joy" is a great exercise for the notes on the high E and B strings. Watch those rhythms in the fourth and last measures. Count "one, two-and, three, four," picking the notes on beats 1, the "and" of 2, and 3. Remember to tap the quarter-note pulse with your foot.
- "The Birthday Song" concentrates on the top three strings (G, B, and high E). It's in 3/4 time and includes a *pickup measure*, an incomplete measure at the beginning of a song. This pickup measure leaves out beats 1 and 2. The *pickup note* (G) comes in on beat 3.
- "The Yellow Rose of Texas" has a wide-ranging melody that is played on the top four strings (D, G, B, and high E). There are two pickup notes: G and F. These are eighth notes (eighth notes receive half a beat) and should be played on beats 4 and the "and" of 4.
- "My Bonnie Lies Over the Ocean" is played on the three lowest strings (low E, A, and D). The curved symbol that connects the two low E notes across measures 3 and 4 is called a *tie*, which signifies that you don't strike the second note. Instead, you play the first one and let it ring for the value of both notes combined. In this case, you hold the low E for four beats. Measures 7 and 8 tie two D notes together. Add up the value of the two notes (dotted half note receives three beats; half note receives two beats) and you get five beats. So, you guessed it, hold the D note for five beats. (In case we didn't tell you, music is a very mathematical art form!)

audio tracks 12

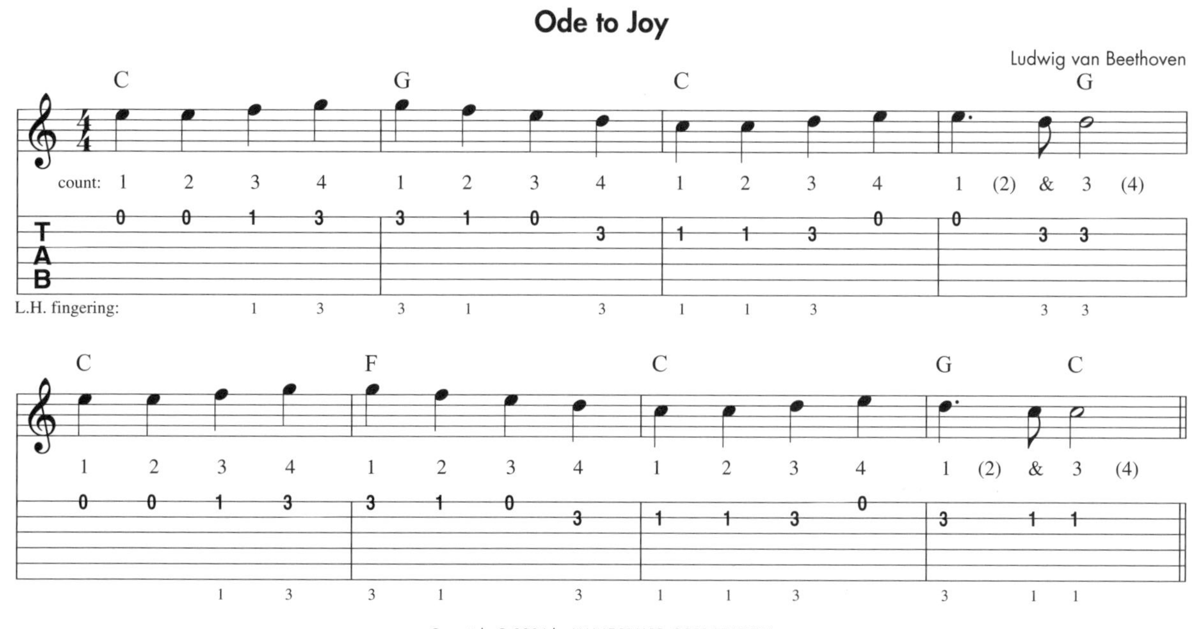

Birthday Song

Traditional

Track 12
(0:20)

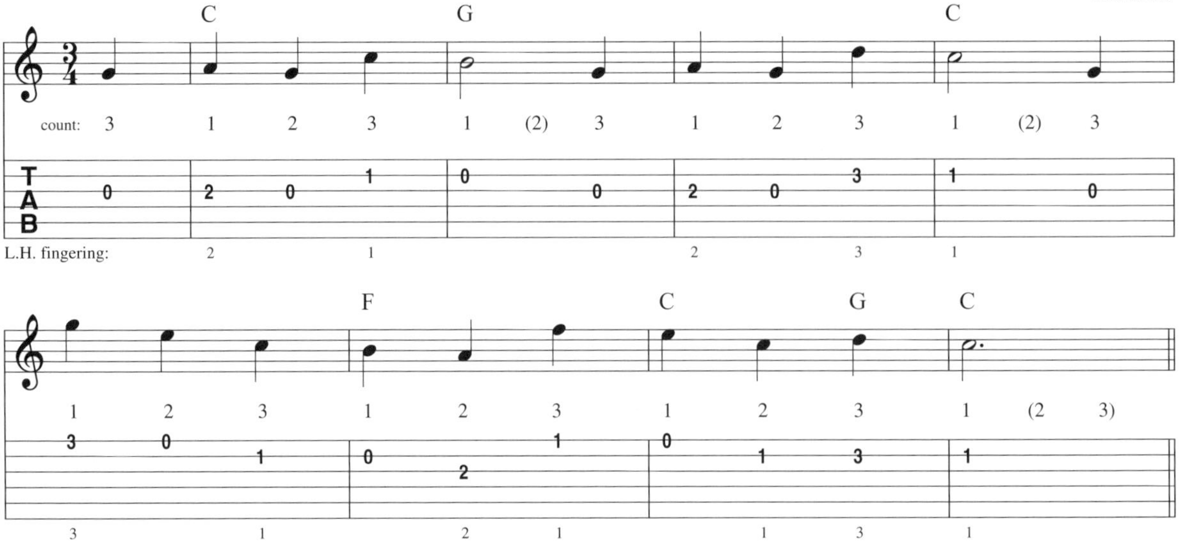
count:
L.H. fingering:

Yellow Rose of Texas

Civil War

Track 12
(0:41)

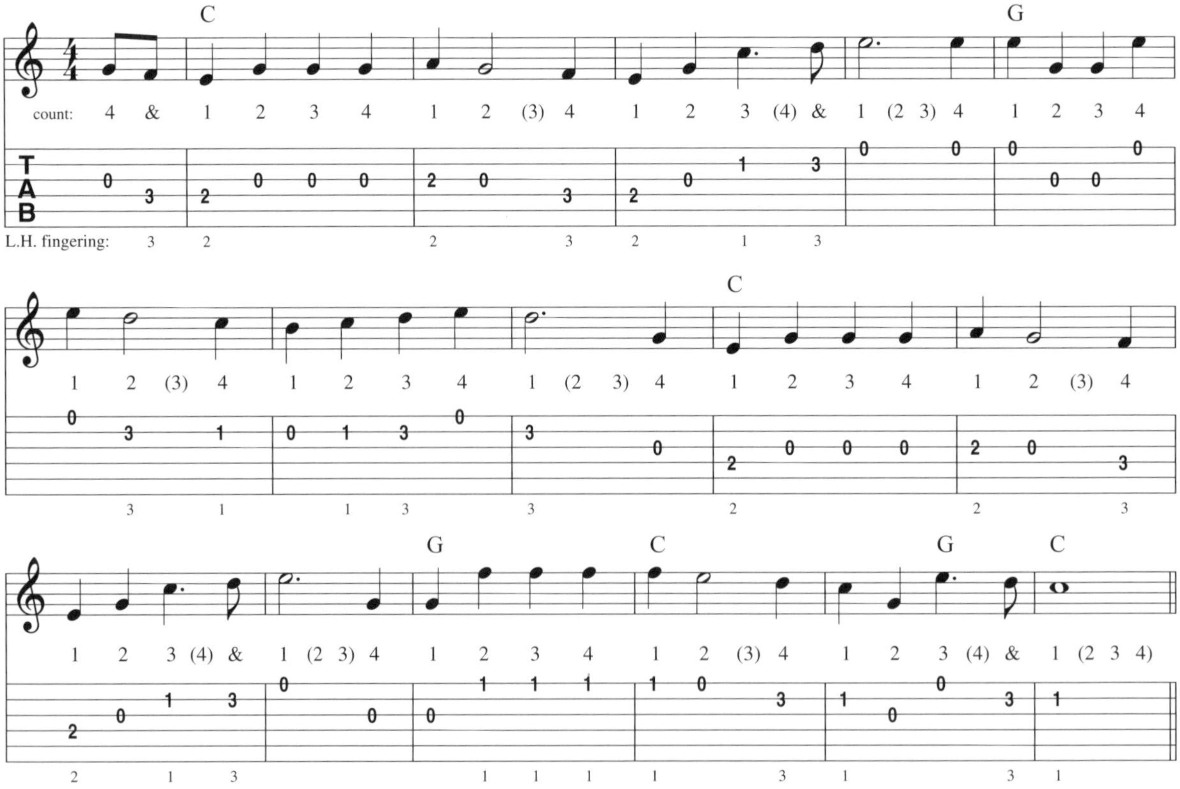
count:
L.H. fingering:

Track 12
(1:11)

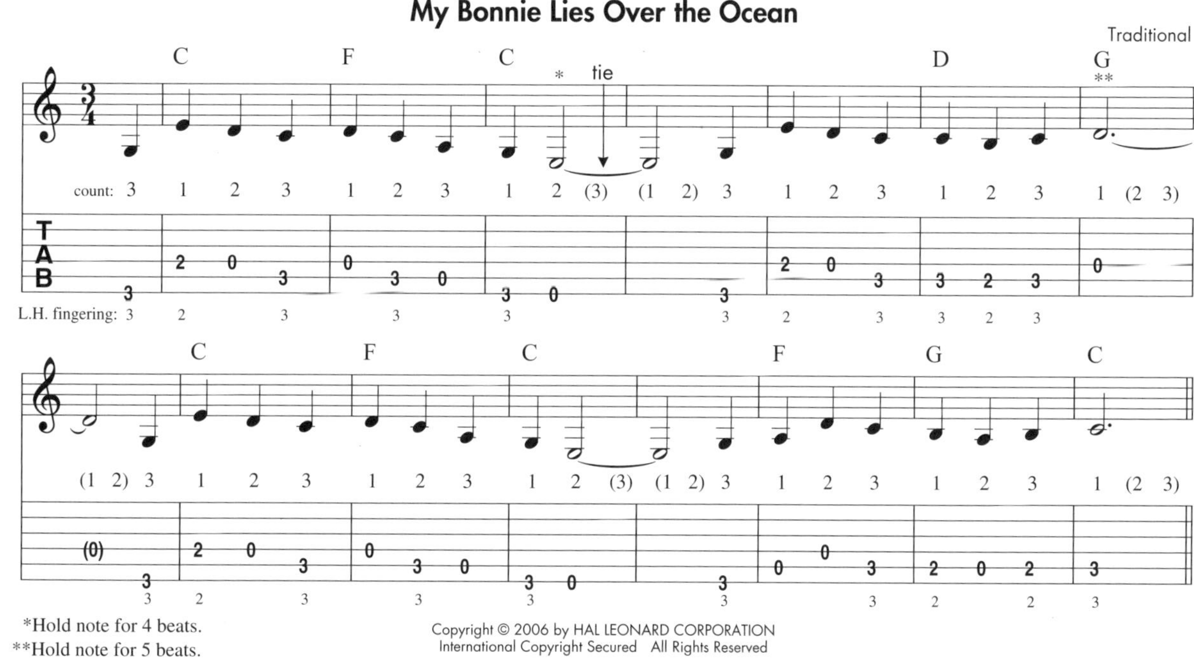

You may find that when you play these songs (even with much practice) they don't sound quite like the audio examples. First, check to make sure your guitar is in tune. (use Track 1 to tune up.) Second, make sure you are fretting the correct notes and picking the same string. If all this checks out, perhaps you're accidentally hitting surrounding open strings with your pick, or letting your fretted notes ring too long. If the latter is the case, remember to release your fretting finger from the string after you've held each note for its full value. If you're accidentally hitting open strings, you need to pay more attention to your right hand. Picking strings on target takes practice. Go slowly and be patient with yourself.

THE RELATIVE A MINOR SCALE

When you play the notes of the C major scale from the root to the octave (C–D–E–F–G–A–B–C), it has a specific sound. Some describe the sound as being "happy" or "pretty." However, if you play the notes of the C major scale starting from the note A, and play up to its octave (A–B–C–D–E–F–G–A), it sounds completely different. Try it for yourself by playing through the following examples.

(0:00)
(0:07)

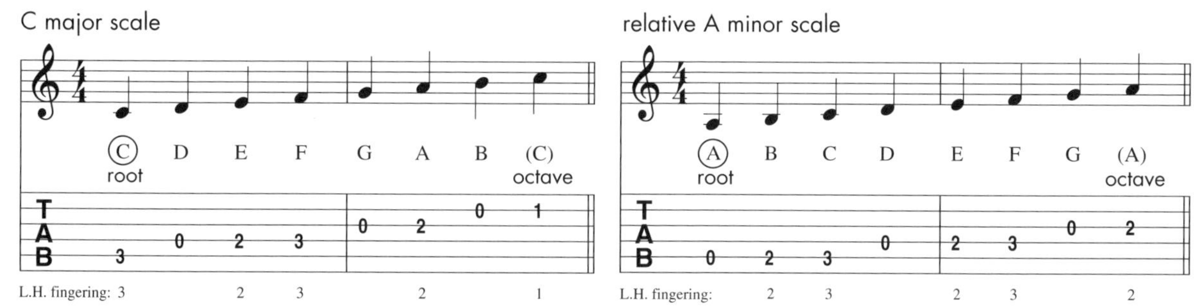

When you play the notes of the C major scale starting on A, you are playing the *relative A minor scale*. It's called the "relative" minor scale because it's related to C major, or, it shares the same notes. The figure below shows the open-position scale pattern for the A minor scale. If you look at it carefully, you'll notice it's the same as the C major scale pattern you already know. The only difference is the note A is now assigned as the root of the scale.

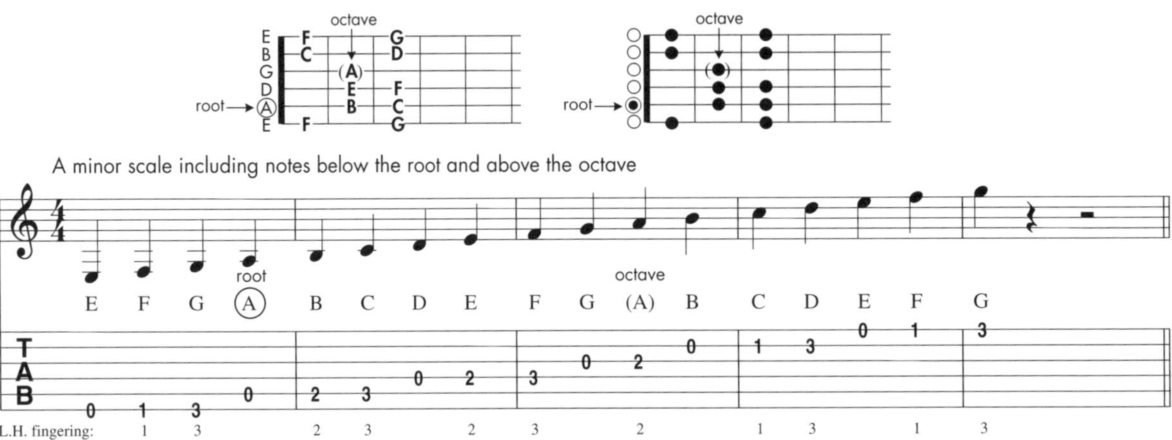

PLAYING A MINOR SCALE MELODIES

In the figures below, you'll find three familiar A minor scale melodies played in open position: "God Rest Ye Merry Gentlemen," "House of the Rising Sun," and "Volga Boat Song." As you play through them, keep in mind that all of the fingerings are the same as the open-position C major scale pattern.

GAINING SPEED WITH ALTERNATE PICKING

You don't want to go through life playing melodies using only downstrokes (unless you just want to play Ramone songs!). Similar to playing chords, which involves a combination of downstrums and upstrums, playing melodies with finesse calls for the use of both downstrokes and upstrokes.

If you pick in a down/up/down/up fashion, you're using a technique called *alternate picking*. The advantage of alternate picking is that you can play moderate-to-fast music passages in a smooth and flowing manner. Look at it this way: If you pick down on a string and then pass by the same string to come swooping in for another attack in the same direction, you've missed an opportunity to strike the string on the way back up. Makes sense, does it not? Honestly, alternate picking could double your picking speed in no time at all.

Let's try a little experiment. Watch your right hand as you pick down continuously on the open B string. Notice that you have to lift the pick up and over the B string on the way back up? Good. Now, instead of lifting the pick over the string, allow it to strike the string on its way back up. Now you're playing twice as fast as you were when you used all downstrokes. Fascinating! Of course, acclimation of this new technique will take some time. Nonetheless, here are some things to remember:

- Hold the pick firmly, letting only a little of the pointed edge peek out from under your thumb (about 1/4 inch).
- Keep your right wrist loose, allowing it to swing slightly with the picking motion. Your wrist should supply the picking motion, not the elbow.

Here are two songs designed to sharpen your alternate-picking "chops." Both use the familiar open-position C major scale pattern. Start with "Yankee Doodle," the easier of the two. Pick down/up for each series of eighth notes, and pick down for all quarter notes. This translates to picking down on all of the "downbeats" of beats 1, 2, 3, and 4; and picking up on all of the upbeats, or "ands" (notated with "&" symbols). "Sailor's Hornpipe" (Popeye's secondary theme song) is a much more challenging piece. Tackle this song only when you're comfortable with the basics of alternate picking.

Track 15
(0:18)

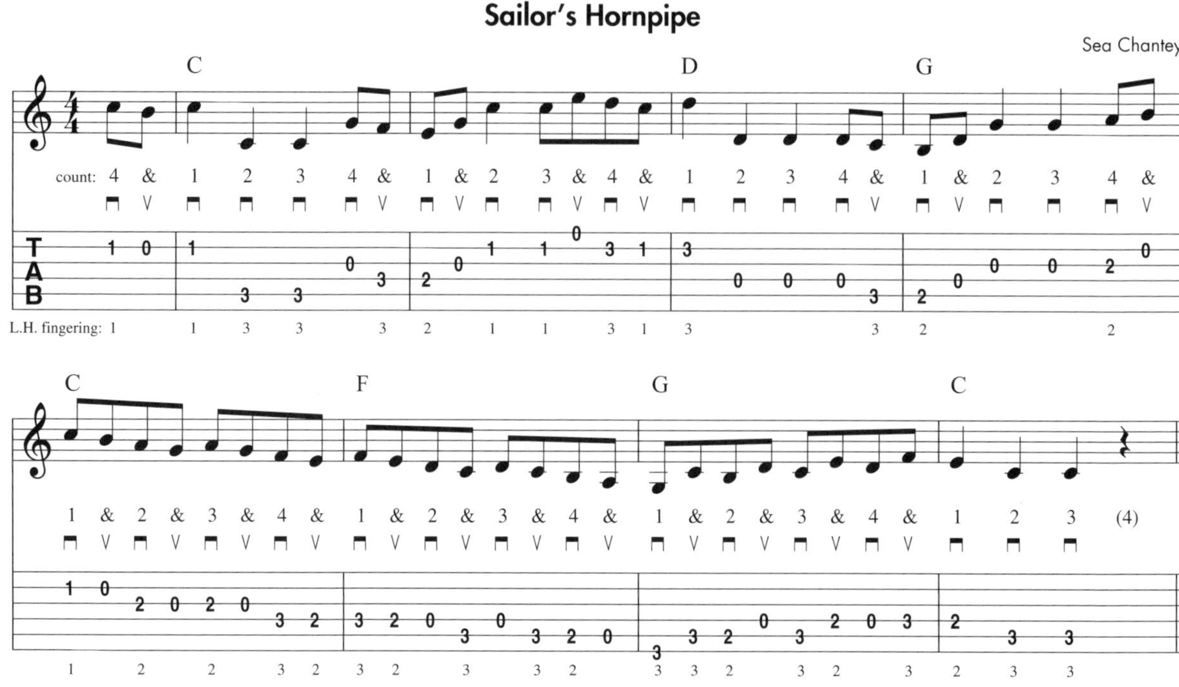

- The C major scale contains these seven notes: C–D–E–F–G–A–B
- When playing the open-position C major scale, the first finger plays all notes that fall on the first fret; the second finger plays notes on the second fret; and the third finger plays notes on the third fret.
- When playing melodies, keep your fingers arched and close to the strings, ready for fretting action.
- The A minor scale contains these seven notes: A–B–C–D–E–F–G
- Alternate picking increases your picking speed.

SECTION 3

Advanced Playing

CHAPTER 9
SEVENTH CHORDS

What's Ahead:

- Open-position seventh chords
- Playing seventh-chord progressions
- Advanced rhythms
- The secret strum

Now that we've covered the basics, it's time to rub shoulders with the big guys. In this section, you'll learn advanced chords and rhythms, new scales, and techniques you can use to sound like a pro.

In this chapter, you'll learn seventh chords, the colorful alternatives to the basic major and minor chords you learned in Chapter 7. There are three types of seventh chords: major seventh, minor seventh, and dominant seventh. The first stop in our seventh-chord journey will be major-seventh chords.

MAJOR-SEVENTH HEAVEN

Major-seventh chords are really basic major chords in disguise. The only difference between a major-seventh chord and its major-chord counterpart is the addition of one particular note. What note? Don't worry—we'll get to that momentarily. But, first, some background on the major-seventh chord.

Major-seventh chords have a bright, slightly jazzy quality. For this reason they are fixtures in jazz music (you'd be hard pressed to find a jazz tune in a major key that doesn't include at least one major-seventh chord), but they're also used in other styles, particularly light-rock, ballads, and country rock. Some notable songs include "Something," by the Beatles; "Ventura Highway," by America; "Color My World," by Chicago; "I Can't Tell You Why," by the Eagles; "Under the Bridge," by the Red Hot Chili Peppers; "Every Morning," by Sugar Ray; and "Sunday Morning," by Maroon 5.

Cmaj7, Fmaj7, Dmaj7, Amaj7, Gmaj7, and Emaj7 Chords

On the following page, you'll find six major-seventh chords depicted on chord frames and in pictures (maj7 is the chord symbol for major seventh; the letter name indicates the root of the chord). Most of the fingerings speak for themselves, but the Dmaj7 chord involves a technique we haven't yet covered. This chord requires you to bar across the top three strings with your index finger. This is easier than it looks because you don't have to worry about fretting additional notes.

Once you get the fingerings down for the major-seventh chords, practice them in concert with their major counterparts (located to the left of each major-seventh chord frame) to hear the difference in sound.

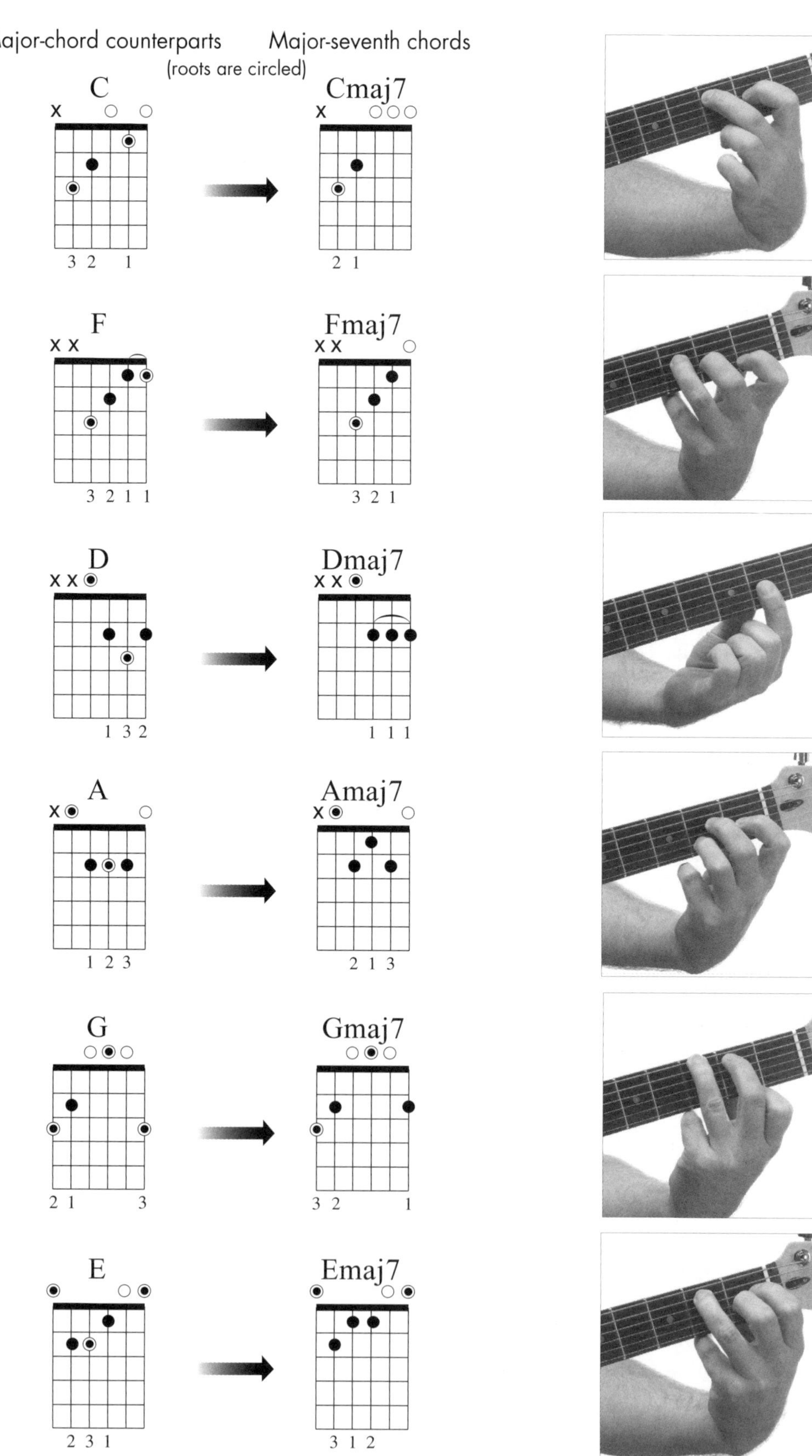
Major-chord counterparts
Major-seventh chords
(roots are circled)
C
Cmaj7
F
Fmaj7
D
Dmaj7
A
Amaj7
G
Gmaj7
E
Emaj7

If you study the major-chord counterparts for each respective major-seventh chord, you'll notice the similarities of the two chords. Although the fingerings are different, they are essentially the same chord. The exception is that the upper roots (octave notes) have been omitted and replaced with another note. Notice that these "other notes" are located a half step (the distance of one fret) below the upper root. The note that is a half step below the upper root of a chord is called a *major seventh*. Hence, the name: major-seventh chord.

Major-seventh chords are constructed from the root, third, fifth, and seventh scale tones of the major scale. For example, a Cmaj7 chord consists of the root, third, fifth, and seventh scale tones of the C major scale: C, E, G, and B.

MAJOR-SEVENTH CHORD PROGRESSIONS AND ADVANCED RHYTHMS

The purpose of the chord-progression exercises below is twofold: to drill your new major-seventh chords and to introduce some advanced rhythm patterns.

The first progression pairs Cmaj7 with Fmaj7, the easiest of the bunch. Notice the curved line connecting the second half of beat 2 to beat 3 in each measure. This curved line is called a *tie*, which tells you not to strike the second note (or chord, in this case). In this example, strum the Cmaj7 chord on the "and" of beat 2 with an upstroke, pass over the strings without hitting them on the count of "three," and strum the chord again on the "and" of beat 3 with another upstroke. It's a bit tricky at first, but if you practice it slowly and follow the strumming directions, it will become second nature in no time. The Amaj7–Dmaj7 progression uses a similar tied rhythm.

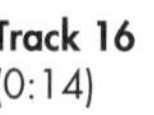

From time to time, you'll see funny-looking symbols that resemble lopsided tic-tac-toe boxes placed next to the clef sign. These symbols are called *sharps*, and when they're grouped together they form the *key signature*. Sometimes the key signature comprises a group of *flats* (symbols that look like a lower-case "b"). The key signature signifies the music's key. For example, three sharps indicate the key of A; three flats represent the key of E♭.

The Dmaj7–Gmaj7 and the Amaj7–Emaj7 progressions feature a two-measure rhythm pattern. In the following examples, the tie crosses the bar line, connecting the "and" of beat 4 with the downbeat of beat 1 in the next measure. Again, follow the strumming directions and go slowly at first. Perhaps work on one chord at a time until you get the strumming down. And don't forget—you can listen to the track to hear how it's done.

Track 16 (0:28)

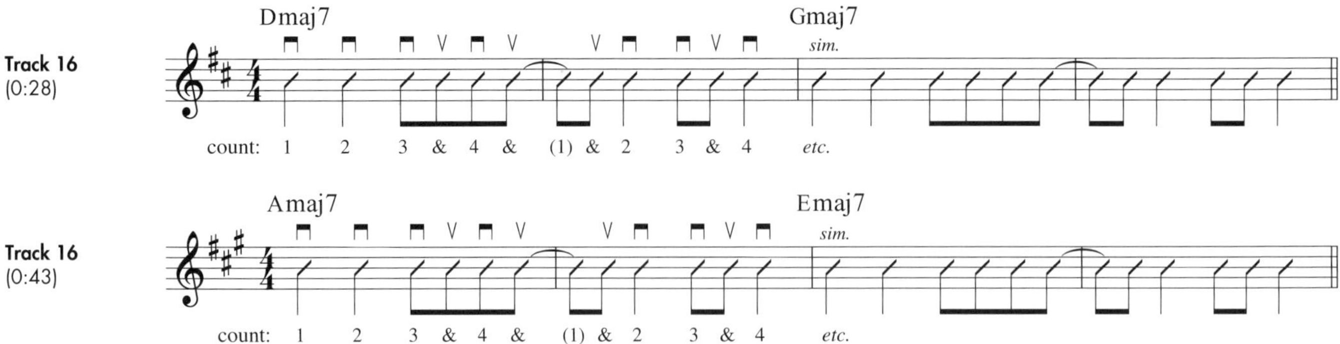

Track 16 (0:43)

The ties in the previous examples create subtle variations on otherwise steady rhythm patterns, temporarily disrupting the normal flow of the beat. This element of rhythmic "surprise" is called *syncopation.*

DOMINANT-SEVENTH CHORDS

Like major-seventh chords, dominant-seventh chords can be considered major chords in disguise. Whereas a major-seventh chord is essentially a major chord with an added major seventh (half step below the upper root), a dominant-seventh chord contains an added flat seventh (two half steps below the root). Dominant-seventh chords have a funky, bluesy sound and appear in virtually all types of music. You'll hear dominant-seventh chords featured in songs such as "Born on the Bayou" and "Suzie Q," by Creedence Clearwater Revival; "She's a Woman," by the Beatles; "Wooly Bully," by Sam the Sham and the Pharaohs; "Mustang Sally," by Wilson Pickett; "Papa's Got a Brand New Bag," by James Brown; and "Pride and Joy," by Stevie Ray Vaughan.

G7, E7, A7, D7, C7, and B7 Chords

Dominant-seventh chords are notated with the symbol "7" located to the right of the letter name. For example, G dominant seventh is written as "G7." Following are open-position dominant-seventh chords. (Their major-chord counterparts appear to the left.) Practice getting them under your fingers, and then we'll put them to practical use in a few progressions.

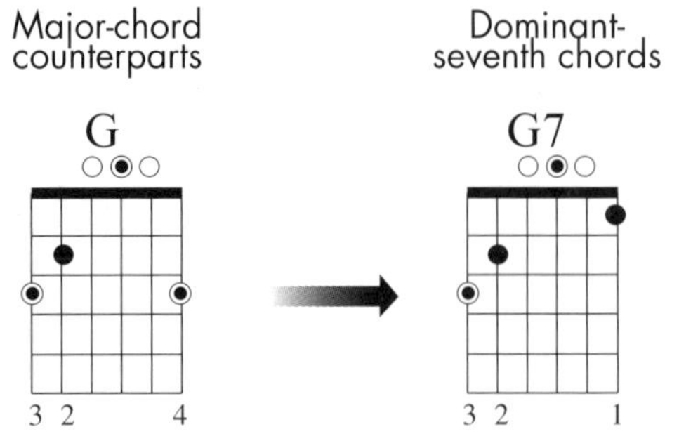

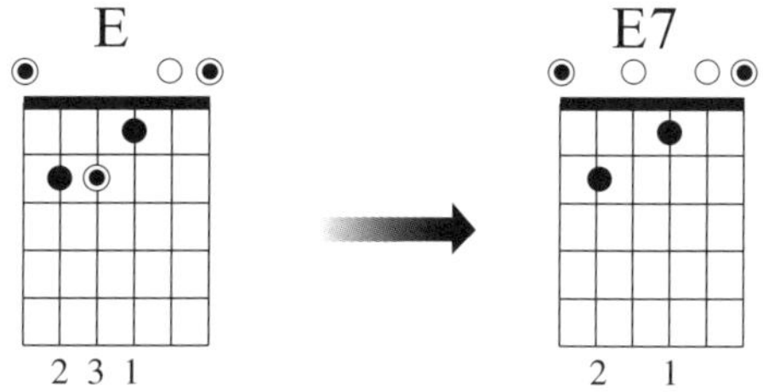

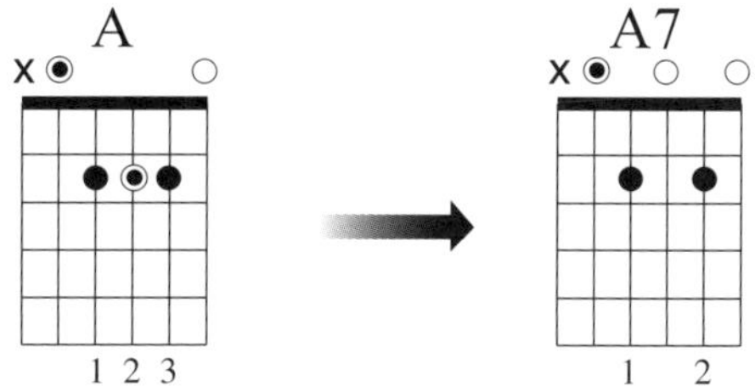

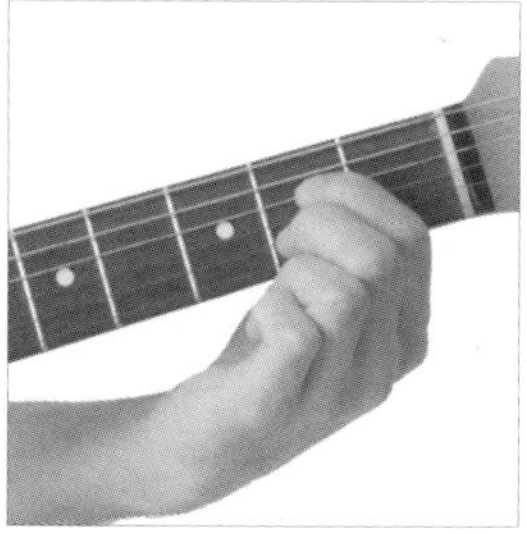

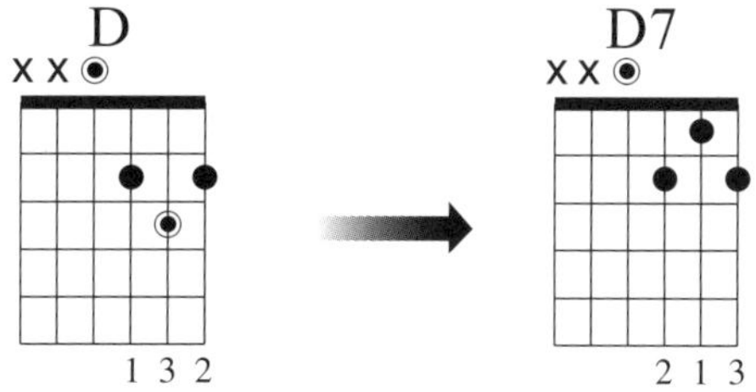

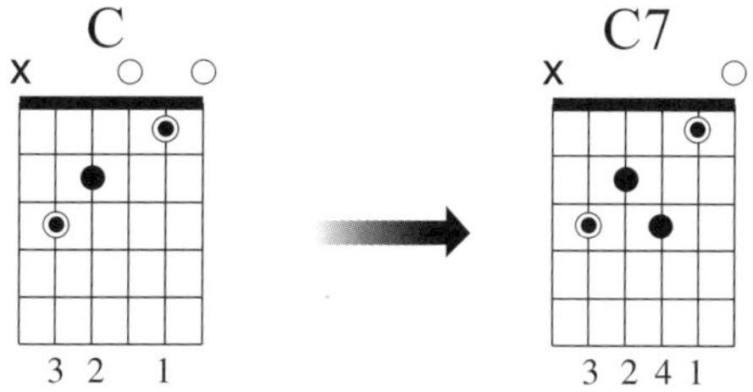

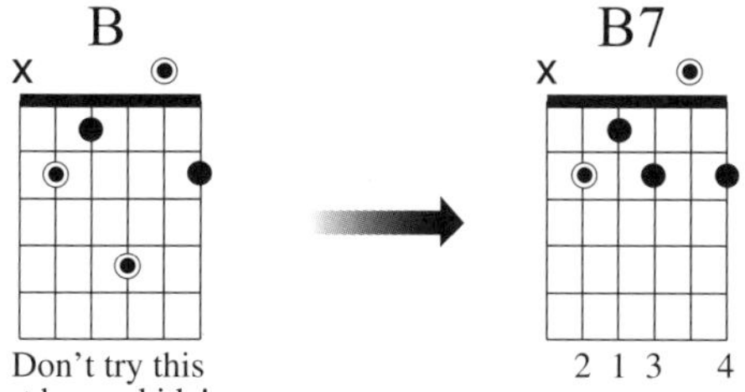

E → E7

2 3 1 → 2 1

A → A7

1 2 3 → 1 2

D → D7

1 3 2 → 2 1 3

C → C7

3 2 1 → 3 2 4 1

B → B7

Don't try this at home, kids! → 2 1 3 4

As you can see from examining the major-chord counterparts above, in the case of the G7 chord, the upper root (G) is omitted and replaced with the flat seventh (F); E is replaced with D for the E7 chord; A is replaced with G for the A7 chord; and D is replaced with C for the D7 chord. All of those replacement notes are two frets down from the roots. Get it? Good. Now, for the C chord, the higher root is left alone; instead, the flat seventh (B♭) is fretted on the third fret of the G string. The B major chord is virtually inhumane. Don't attempt playing it! It's only included as a visual aid for the origin of the B7 chord.

Dominant-seventh chords are constructed from the root, third, fifth, and flat-seventh scale tones of the major scale. For example, a C7 chord consists of the root, third, fifth, and flat-seventh (lowered-seventh) scale tones of the C major scale: C, E, G, and B♭.

THE SHUFFLE FEEL

The dominant-seventh progressions we're about to embark upon all involve new strumming patterns based on a *shuffle feel* ("feel" means the overall rhythm of a song). Sometimes called the *swing feel*, or *triplet feel*, the shuffle feel can be heard in many styles of music, but appears most frequently in blues ("Sweet Home Chicago," by Robert Johnson), rock ("Tush," by ZZ Top), and country ("Boot-Scootin' Boogie," by Brooks and Dunn).

The shuffle feel is based on triplet rhythms. Triplets are what you get when you divide a beat by three. For instance, we know that if you divide a beat by two you get eighth notes. When you divide a beat by three, you get triplets; specifically, eighth-note triplets. The figure below shows this breakdown process on the staff.

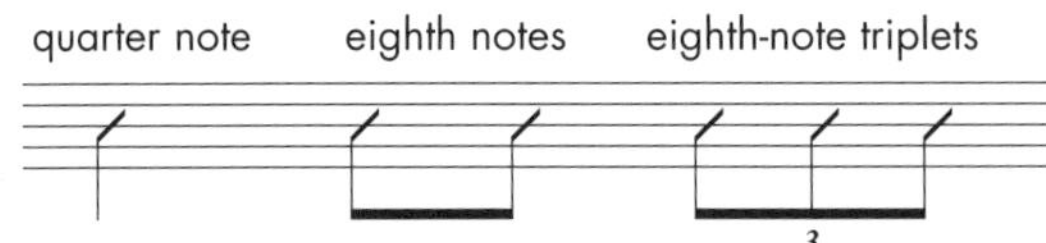

This next example pairs E7 and A7 chords with triplet rhythms. Keep track of the triplets by counting "one-trip-let, two-trip-let, three-trip-let, four-trip-let." The down-up-down/down-up-down strumming pattern may seem unusual at first, but just trust us for now. Also, remember to keep tapping your foot to the quarter-note pulse; don't let it tap along to the triplets. This may be difficult and very frustrating at first, but keep practicing; you'll get it.

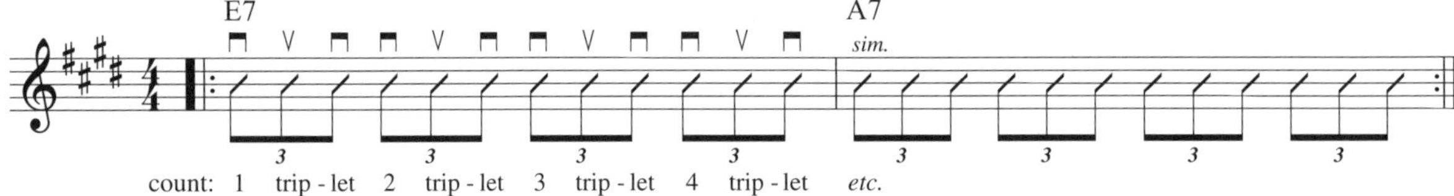

The Secret Strum

Now that you're working on advanced chords and rhythms, it's time to share some valuable information about a secret weapon. As a matter of fact, it's so secret that many pros aren't even aware that they themselves use it. It's called the *secret strum*.
The secret strum is actually a very simple procedure that takes little skill to perform. All you have to do is strum the open strings.

You may be asking, "What on earth is so secret about that?" The answer to that is: Used at the right time, the secret strum can save your life. Well, maybe not your life, but certainly your playing career.

Take a look back at the example we just played. There certainly are a lot of rhythms, but precious little time to switch between voicings. Secret strum to the rescue! On the very last eighth-note triplet of the first measure, lift your left-hand fingers off the strings and strum some of the open strings (the middle ones are likely targets). This allows time to get your left hand in place for the A7 chord. You can also insert the secret strum at the end of the second measure when changing back to the E7 chord.

You may be asking, "Won't that sound horrible?" Actually, in this case the secret strum happens so quickly that the ear barely picks it up. It also helps to keep the *groove* (overall rhythmic feel) going. (Note: The secret strum is used in this audio example. Listen to the performance to find out if you can hear it.)

We'll be mentioning the secret strum from time to time just to make sure you don't forget it. For now, just think of it as an ace you have up your sleeve. Keep it hidden; bring it out only in time of dire need.

The following figure shows a one-beat grouping of three eighth-note triplets. Notice that the first two are connected with a tie.

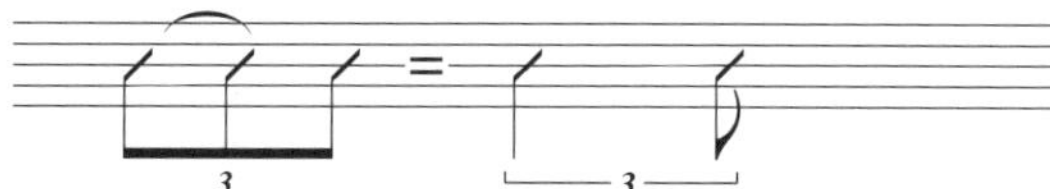

The tie lengthens the duration of the first eighth note, creating the rhythm notated to the right. Essentially, this notation tells you to play two notes in the space of one beat, with the first note lasting longer than the second. The example below combines this rhythm with the triplet rhythms you played earlier in this chapter. Play through the example using the strumming directions notated above the first measure. This keeps your right hand going in the same down-up-down motion used earlier, and should get you acclimated to the feel. Once you get used to the rhythm, you can graduate to the strumming pattern notated above measure 3.

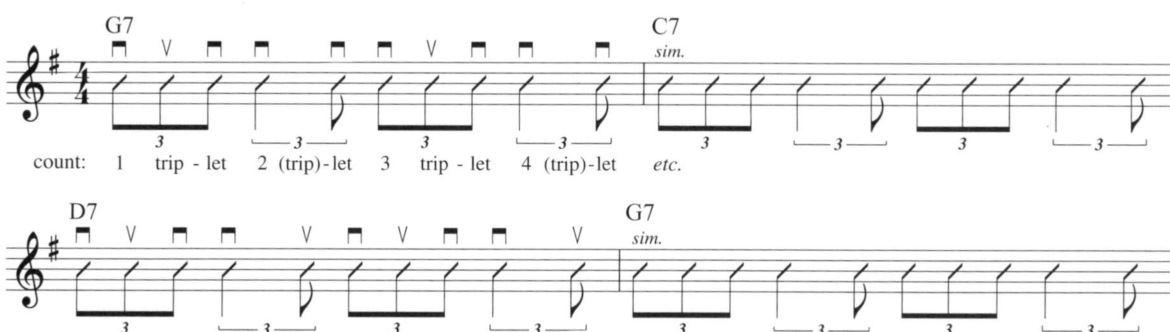

Look at the first measure in the following example. The quarter-note/eighth-note triplet rhythms on beats 2 and 4 are very common in songs with a shuffle feel. So common, in fact, that there is a short-cut method to notating them. If you look at the second measure, you'll see note values written above the staff. This information tells you that any one-beat grouping of two eighth notes should be played as quarter-note/eighth-note triplets. If you've ever heard a musician use the term "shuffled eighths," that's what he or she was referring to.

SHUFFLING DOMINANT-SEVENTH CHORDS

The next example gives you a chance to practice E7 and B7 chords along with a typical shuffle rhythm. (This is the underlying rhythm of the song "How Sweet It Is," by James Taylor.) Look above the time signature to see the shuffle-feel notation. Again, this means to shuffle the eighth notes, which appear on beats 1 and 3. There are two counting methods notated below the staff. You're familiar with the first. The second one keeps track of shuffled eighth notes with a drawn out "one" and a quick "and," as in "one… and, two… and, three… and, four… and." Using this method, triplets are counted as "1 & a, 2 & a, 3 & a, 4 & a."

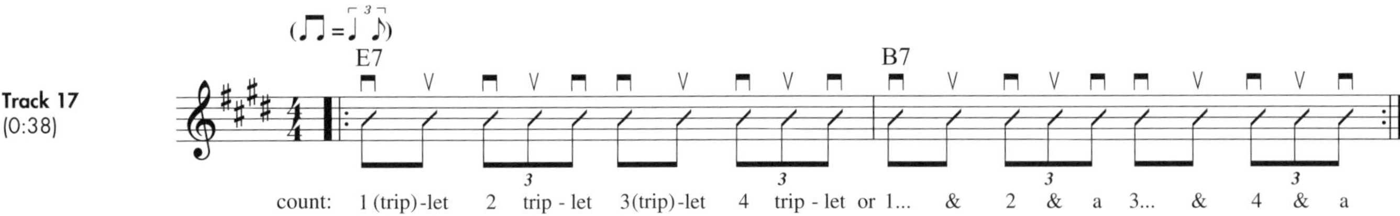

The following example features a popular shuffle rhythm you'll hear in country-rock songs such as "Drivin' My Life Away," by Eddie Rabbit. Be sure not to rush the second eighth notes on beats 2 and 3. Listen to the track to hear the groove.

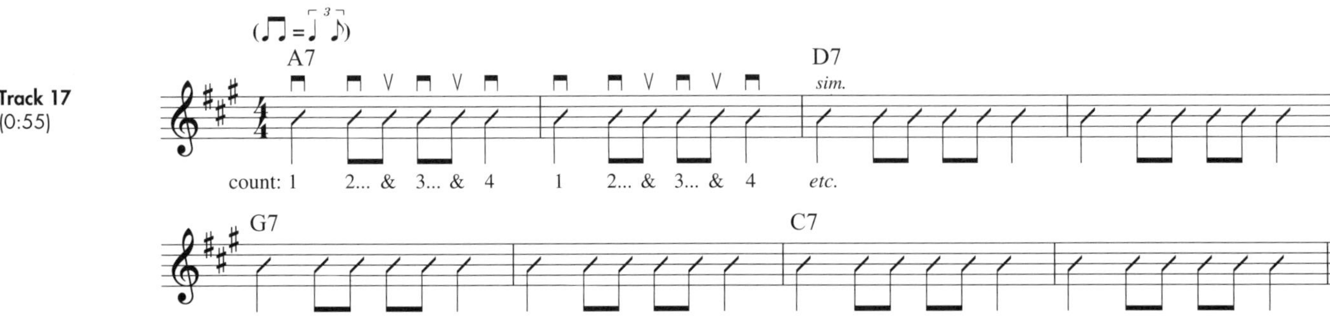

Always check above the time signature to see if there's a shuffle notation. You could end up in an embarrassing situation—grooving on straight eighths when the band is shuffling away!

MINOR-SEVENTH CHORDS

Minor-seventh chords are (you guessed it!) minor chords in disguise. Take a minor chord, plop down a flat seventh (two half steps below the upper root), and there you have it—a minor seventh chord. Minor sevenths carry a certain air of mystique. Sometimes they sound sad or bittersweet; other times they can be downright funky; and in certain situations they can be rather pretty. You'll hear minor seventh chords in songs such as "Oye Como Va," by Santana; "Long Train Running," by the Doobie Brothers; "Brick House," by the Commodores; "You Never Give Me Your Money," by the Beatles; "Miss You," by the Rolling Stones; "Any Colour You Like," by Pink Floyd; "Moondance," by Van Morrison; "Speed of Sound," by Coldplay; "So What," by Miles Davis; and "Rocket Man," by Elton John.

Em7, Am7, and Dm7 Chords

Next you'll see three minor-seventh chords (right frames) and how they relate to their minor-chord counterparts (left frames). (Note: Em7 stands for E minor seventh.) The Em7 and Am7 chords are a cinch to play with their corresponding minor chords; all you have to do is lift one finger off of the fretboard. The Dm7 chord is a little harder to play. It requires you to bar the top two strings (B and high E) at the first fret with your first finger.

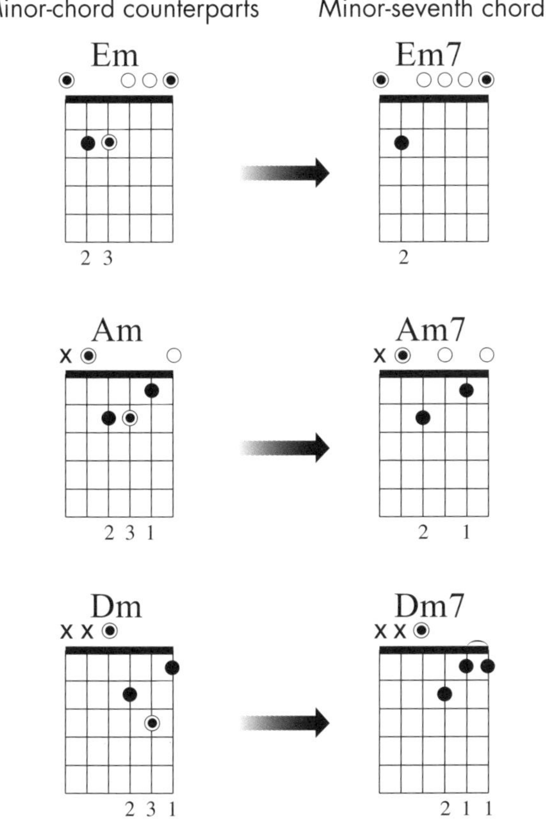

Minor-seventh chords are constructed from the root, flat-third (lowered-third), fifth, and flat-seventh (lowered-seventh) scale tones of the major scale. For example, a Cm7 chord consists of the root, flat-third, fifth, and flat-seventh scale tones of the C major scale: C, E♭, G, and B♭.

Alternate Em7 and Am7 Voicings

Below, you'll find alternate voicings (fingerings) for Em7 and Am7. This Em7 sounds jazzier than the Em7 shown above. You may recognize this Am7 chord as the first chord in "Rocky Raccoon," by the Beatles.

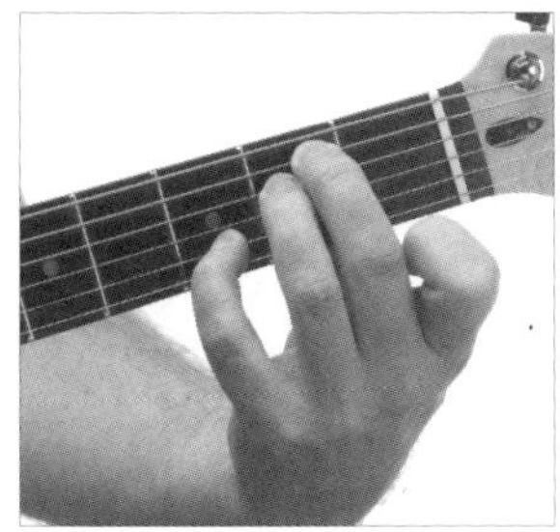

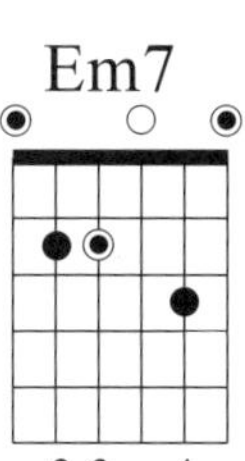

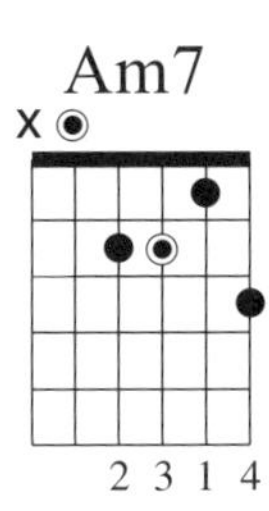

SIXTEENTH-NOTE RHYTHMS

With our new group of chords comes a new set of rhythms based on sixteenth notes. Sixteenth-note rhythms drive the beat of many rock ("Smells Like Teen Spirit," by Nirvana; "The Trooper," by Iron Maiden), and funk/dance songs ("Le Freak," by Chic; "Sex Machine," by James Brown). They are also the underlying rhythm of many rock and pop ballads, such as "Comfortably Numb," by Pink Floyd; "Space Oddity," by David Bowie; and "Your Body Is a Wonderland," by John Mayer.

Sixteenth notes are like eighth notes on steroids; you can play eight eighth notes in a measure, or you can be a he-man (or he-woman) and play 16 sixteenth notes instead. Seriously, though, when you divide a beat by two you get two eighth notes. When you divide a beat by four you get four sixteenth notes. Sixteenth-note rhythms often come in groups of four, but there are other combinations that involve eighth notes. Here are some of these combinations and how to count them:

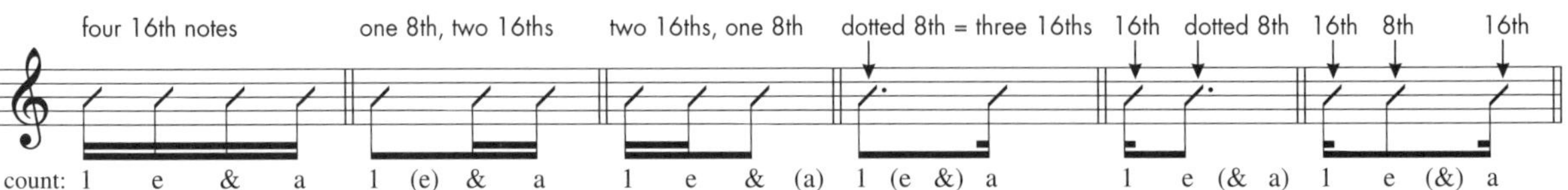

The first example above shows the basic count for keeping track of sixteenth-note rhythms: "1-e-&-a, 2-e-&-a," etc. The second figure pairs one eighth note with two sixteenth notes. This is known as the gallop rhythm because it sounds like a galloping horse. (If you're an Iron Maiden fan, this rhythm is ingrained in your music psyche.) The third figure is a reverse gallop, not because it sounds like a horse running backward (Is that possible?), but simply because it's the opposite of the gallop rhythm. The fourth figure wraps the first three sixteenth notes into a dotted eighth-note rhythm, followed by a single sixteenth note. This is the rhythm that Kurt Cobain uses to launch the beginning of "Smells Like Teen Spirit" (see Chapter 21). The next rhythm is its reverse counterpart. And the final rhythm is the engine that drives the groove of "Sing a Simple Song," by Sly & the Family Stone. A very syncopated (offset) rhythm, it tucks a single eighth note between two sixteenths.

GETTING FUNKY WITH MINOR-SEVENTH CHORDS

Now that you know how to count sixteenth-note rhythms, let's apply them to the minor-seventh chords you just learned.

The first progression involves Am7 and Em7 chords in sixteenth- and quarter-note rhythms. Strum down-up-down-up for the groups of sixteenth notes. Keep your right hand in a sixteenth-note motion (in midair) when sustaining the quarter-note rhythms. This will help keep you "in the groove" (in sync with the rhythms). (While all of this is going on, don't forget to keep tapping your foot in quarter notes.) The second progression sets the gallop rhythm in play in the first two measures. Strum down-down-up for the gallops. Measures 3–4 shift into the reverse-gallop rhythm. Strum down-up-down for the reverse gallops.

The third progression mixes the syncopated dotted-quarter/sixteenth rhythm, straight eighths, sixteenths, and a quarter note. (Listen to the track before you attempt this one.) Follow the strumming pattern carefully; it keeps your right hand swinging in a consistent down-up-down-up motion throughout. The final progression is the most difficult. Don't attempt it until you are comfortable with the others.

audio tracks 18

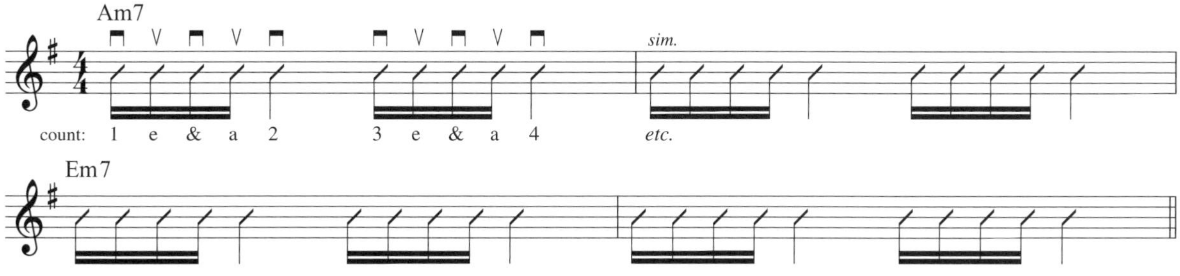

Am7

count: 1 e & a 2 3 e & a 4 *sim.* etc.

Em7

Track 18 (0:18)

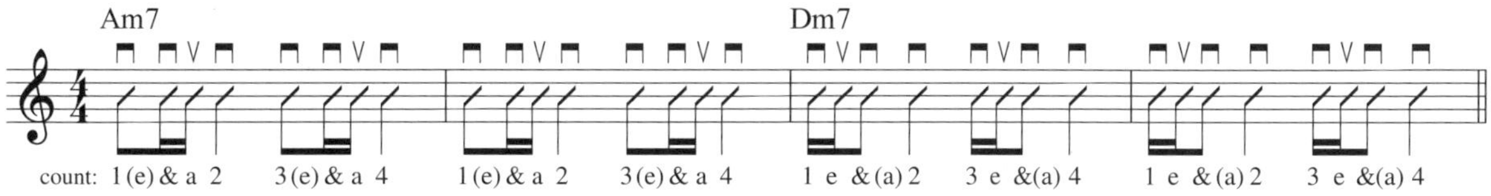

Am7 Dm7

count: 1(e) & a 2 3(e) & a 4 1(e) & a 2 3(e) & a 4 1 e &(a) 2 3 e &(a) 4 1 e &(a) 2 3 e &(a) 4

Track 18 (0:36)

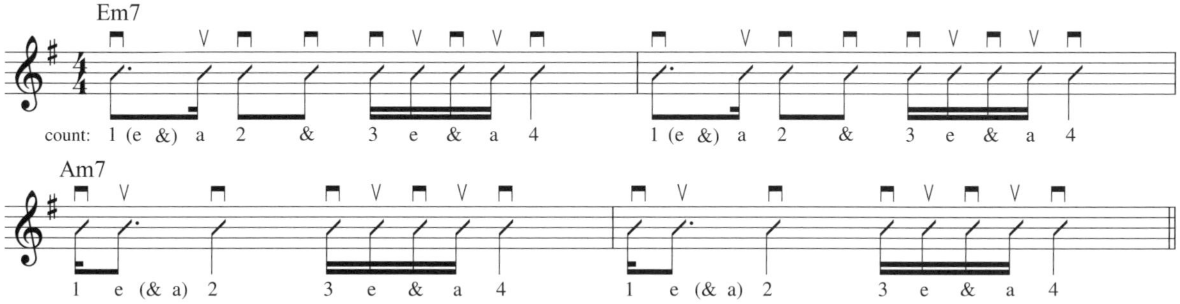

Em7

count: 1 (e &) a 2 & 3 e & a 4 1 (e &) a 2 & 3 e & a 4

Am7

1 e (& a) 2 3 e & a 4 1 e (& a) 2 3 e & a 4

Track 18 (0:54)

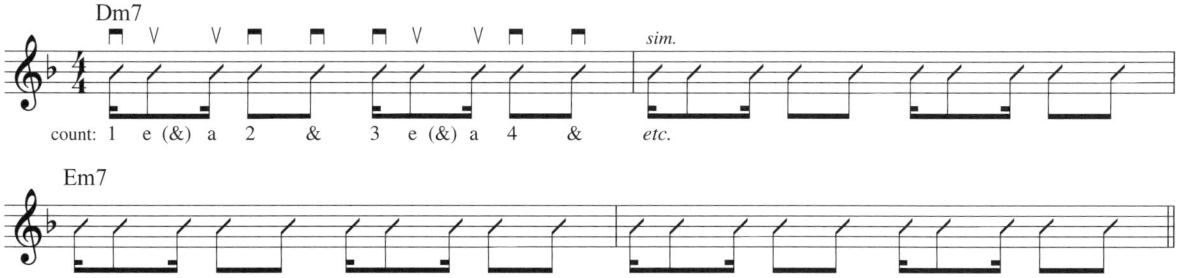

Dm7

count: 1 e (&) a 2 & 3 e (&) a 4 & *sim.* etc.

Em7

When playing rhythms involving sixteenth notes, it's important to keep your right hand loose and swinging, almost as if you were strumming every single sixteenth note. Don't exaggerate your movements, though; keep them subtle.

MIXING IT ALL TOGETHER

Following are some advanced progressions that mix in all of the chords you've learned so far: major chords, minor chords, and seventh chords.

The first one is a rock-style ballad. Use the "secret strum" on the last sixteenth note preceding each chord change. The second example is a popular progression used in many styles of music. Make sure you "shuffle" the eighth notes. The third progression uses a set of chords found in countless jazz tunes. Known as a ii–V–I progression (pronounced: "two–five–one"), it can also be heard in lighthearted pop tunes such as "Sunday Morning," by Maroon 5. The final example incorporates a haunting, folk-rock progression. Again, don't overlook the "shuffle feel" indication above the time signature.

audio tracks 19

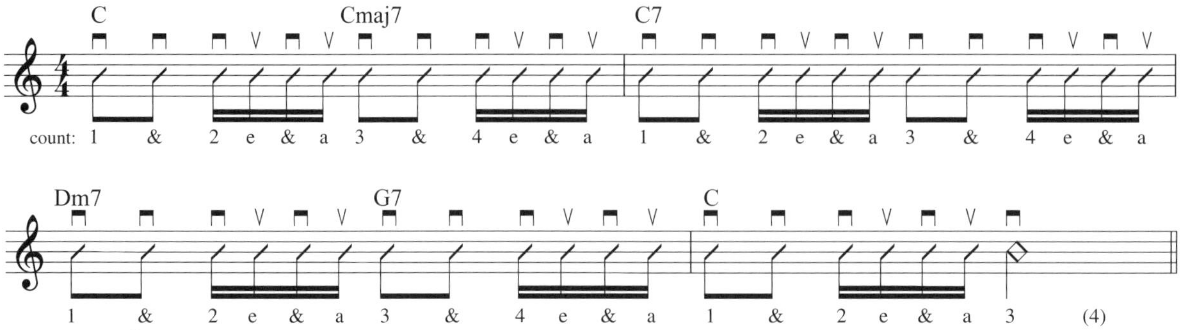

C Cmaj7 C7

count: 1 & 2 e & a 3 & 4 e & a 1 & 2 e & a 3 & 4 e & a

Dm7 G7 C

1 & 2 e & a 3 & 4 e & a 1 & 2 e & a 3 (4)

Track 19 (0:22)

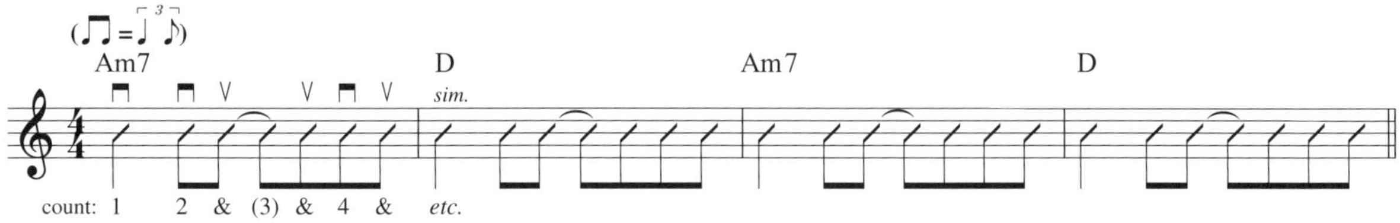

Am7 D Am7 D

sim.

count: 1 2 & (3) & 4 & etc.

Track 19 (0:37)

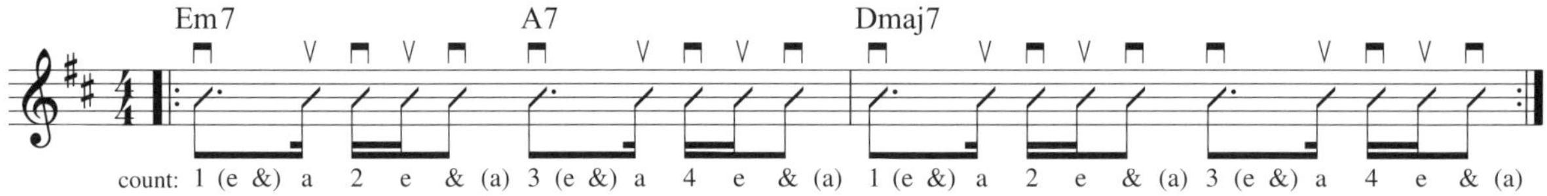

Em7 A7 Dmaj7

count: 1 (e &) a 2 e & (a) 3 (e &) a 4 e & (a) 1 (e &) a 2 e & (a) 3 (e &) a 4 e & (a)

Track 19 (0:57)

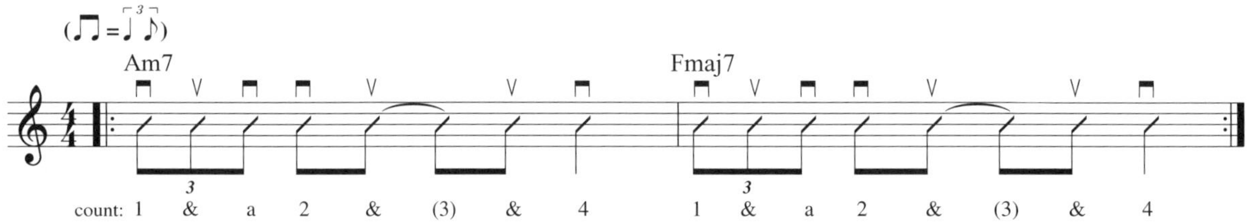

Am7 Fmaj7

count: 1 & a 2 & (3) & 4 1 & a 2 & (3) & 4

- Major-seventh chords are colorful substitutes for their major-chord counterparts.
- There are three types of seventh chords: major seventh (Cmaj7), dominant seventh (C7), and minor seventh (Cm7).
- The shuffle feel is based on eighth note–triplet rhythms.
- Keep your right hand swinging "in the groove" when playing sixteenth-note rhythms.
- The "secret strum" can be a musical lifesaver.

CHAPTER 10
BARRE CHORDS

What's Ahead:

- E-based barre chords
- A-based barre chords
- Barre-chord progressions
- Transposing
- Staccato technique

Fasten your seatbelts—we're about to travel out of the bounds of open position! In this chapter, you'll learn how to play chords all over the neck. But don't be scared; after you catch on to a few basics, it's a cinch. So get ready for a trip up the fretboard with movable chords!

BEYOND OPEN POSITION

So far, we've been playing chords that don't wander above the third fret. You could spend a lifetime of happiness jangling away on your favorite songs with these "grips" (chord voicings), but if you've got the wanderlust to venture out of open-position territory, you'll want to get a handle on *barre chords*.

Barre chords are movable chord voicings that use the first (index) finger to fret two or more strings, while the other fingers fret individual strings. The beauty of barre chords is that once you learn one shape, you can use it to create 12 different chords! Sounds like magic, huh? Actually, the principle is rather simple. Let's have a look.

THE E-BASED BARRE CHORD

Here's a simple, hands-on demonstration of how barre chords work: Take a look at the first chord frame below. You'll recognize this as the E major chord we learned back in Chapter 7. Next, play the same chord using the fingering notated in the second E chord frame. Notice that this leaves your first finger dangling in midair. Now, slide your other fingers up one fret each (third and fourth fingers move up to the third fret; second finger moves up to the second fret). Okay, now lay your first finger down on all six strings at the first fret. Be sure to press down hard while you apply pressure with your thumb behind the neck (keep your thumb aiming skyward), and strum across all six strings. Congratulations! You've just played your first barre chord. Hurts, doesn't it? Don't worry—with practice you'll strengthen those hand muscles in no time!

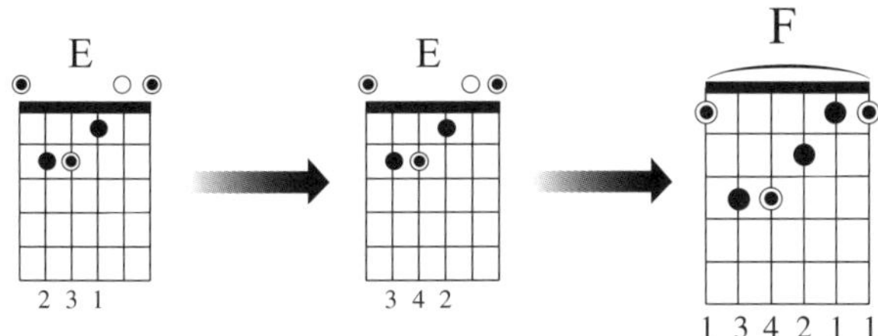

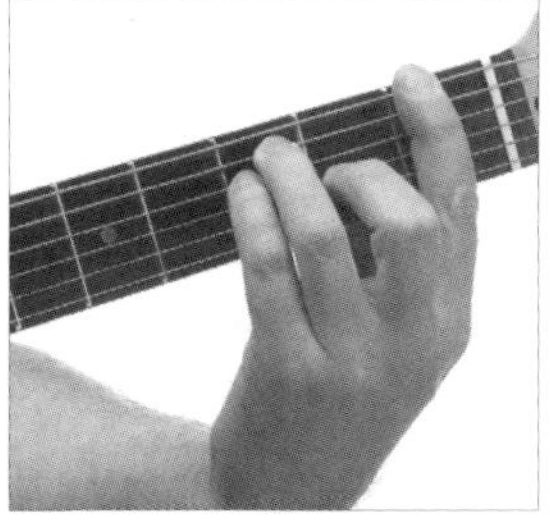

If you hear string buzz when you play a barre chord, your first finger is either out of position, or you're simply not pressing hard enough. Wiggle your first finger from side to side until you find the position where the strings ring loud and clear. For maximum leverage, position your thumb behind the fret that your first finger is barring.

Never practice beyond the pain. For instance, if your left hand starts to cramp up from practicing barre chords, take a break. When the pain subsides, resume practice.

It's easier to play barre chords on an electric guitar than it is on an acoustic because the strings of an acoustic are usually higher off the fretboard than on an electric.

By moving the open E chord up one fret and inserting a bar, you're raising the pitch of every note, creating a chord of the same quality (in this case, major) in a new key (F). You can also think of your first finger as a movable nut, or human capo. (A capo is a device that clamps to the neck of the guitar at a specified fret, raising the pitch of all the strings; see Chapter 16.) When you play an F barre chord, your first finger is the new nut, or temporary capo.

Now that you know how to play an E-based major barre chord, you can play every single major chord in existence! All you have to do is move the entire barre-chord shape to different frets. Whichever fret you stop at determines the name of the chord. For example, playing an E-based barre chord at the second fret creates an F♯ chord; at the third fret it's a G chord; and so on. Here's why: The note on the low E string is the root of the chord, thus the name of the chord. Get it? The more familiar you are with the names of the notes on the low E string, the faster you'll be able to determine where to place your barre-chord shape.

The neck diagram below shows all of the note names on the low E string. Memorize the location of the natural notes first (E, F, G, A, B, C, and D). That way, when you need to find a sharp or flat note, you can simply jump up or down one fret from its natural-note neighbor. For instance, B♭ is one fret below B; G♯ is one fret above G; and so on. (Note: B♭ can also be called A♯; G♯ can be called A♭; etc.) Once you reach the 12th fret, the note names repeat.

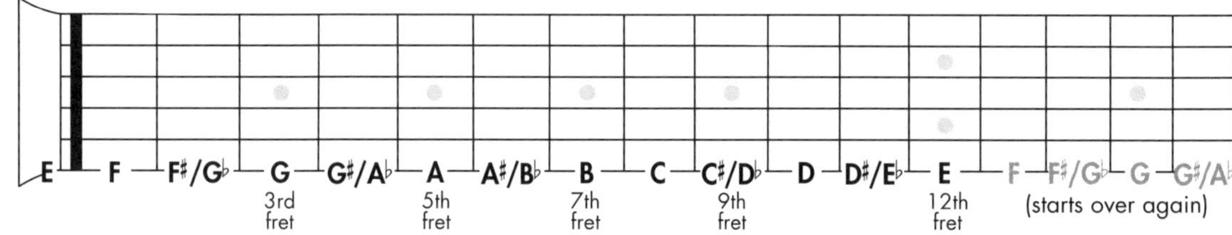

Notes of the same pitch but with different names (e.g., G♯ and A♭) are called *enharmonic equivalents*, or simply *enharmonic*.

The best way to practice barre chords is to put them together in a progression. The example below features a popular progression that you'll hear in many classic-rock songs. We've kept the strumming pattern simple so that you can concentrate on "targeting" the correct frets for each chord. To help you find your targets, fret numbers have been placed below the staff.

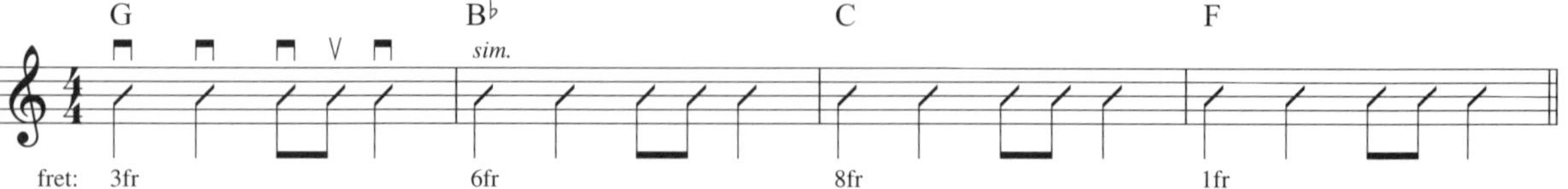

It takes stamina to play a barre-chord progression, but there's no need to keep gripping the neck like you're holding on for dear life. Give your left hand a break by releasing your grip when you slide from chord to chord. You'll still need to keep your fingers lightly touching the strings and your thumb on the back of the neck, but you can lighten your grasp between chords, albeit for a split second.

MINOR BARRE CHORDS

In Chapter 7, you learned that you could convert an open-position E major chord into an Em chord simply by lifting your first finger off of the G string. Well, guess what? This same procedure applies to barre chords. Here's how it works.

Take a look at the following figure. The chord frame to the left represents an F major barre chord. If you lift your second finger off of the G string, the first-finger bar automatically frets the same string at the first fret. This conversion process creates an Fm barre chord, pictured in the frame to the right. (Note: This type of barre chord is called an E-based minor barre chord.) Don't forget—this barre chord is movable to any fret. Therefore, you can play all 12 minor chords using this single barre-chord voicing.

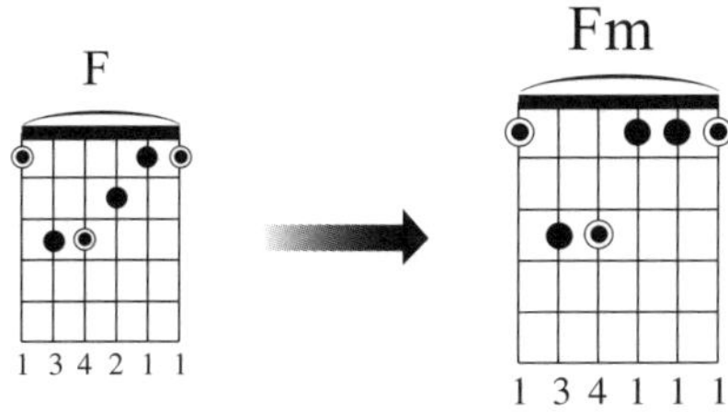

A minor chord is a major chord (1–3–5) with a lowered third (1–♭3–5). "1" = root.

Playing this minor barre chord requires a bit more leverage than its major counterpart. If some of the strings sound muffled, particularly the G string, check to make sure your first finger is pressed flat to the fretboard; don't let it arch upward. Now that your second finger is free from fretting, you might try pressing it down on top of your first finger to assist in the bar.

Below are a couple of progressions that mix the major and minor barre chords you've just learned. The first one is in the style of a '60s pop ballad. The second one is based on a progression that drives many classic-rock songs of the '70s. Again, the numbers below the staff indicate the fret at which to play your barre chords.

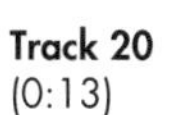

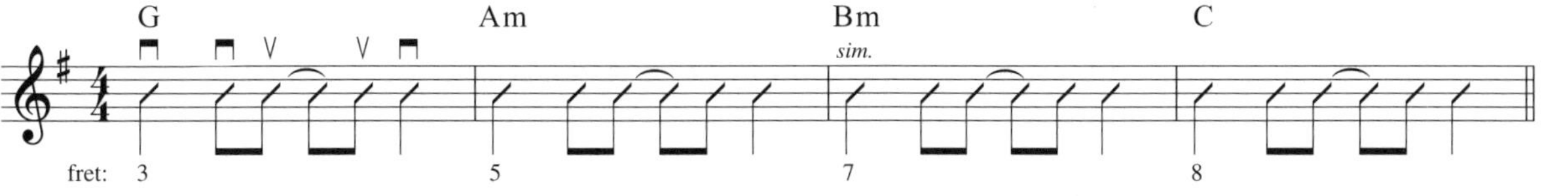

Track 20
(0:30)

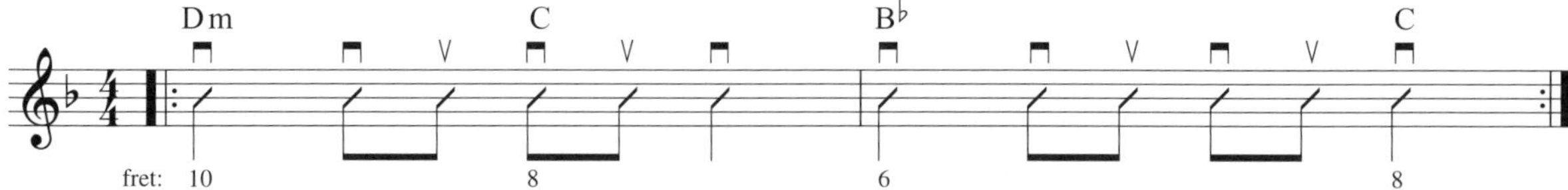

Once you're able to play the above progressions, try moving them to other keys. For example, the first progression is in the key of G. Move all of the chords up two frets (A–Bm–C♯m–D) and the progression is now in the key of A. Move the second progression (which is in the key of D minor) down five frets (Am–G–F–G) and it's now in the key of Am. Don't forget—you need to move every chord the same number of frets, in the same direction.

OTHER E-BASED BARRE CHORDS

In the following figure, you'll find two more barre-chord conversions. The first depicts the metamorphous of an F major barre chord to an F7 barre chord: The fourth finger is released to allow the D string to be fretted by the (already in place) first finger. In the same manner, the second example converts an Fm barre chord into an Fm7 chord by lifting the fourth finger from the D string. As with the major and minor barre chords, dominant-seventh and minor-seventh barre chords are movable to any key.

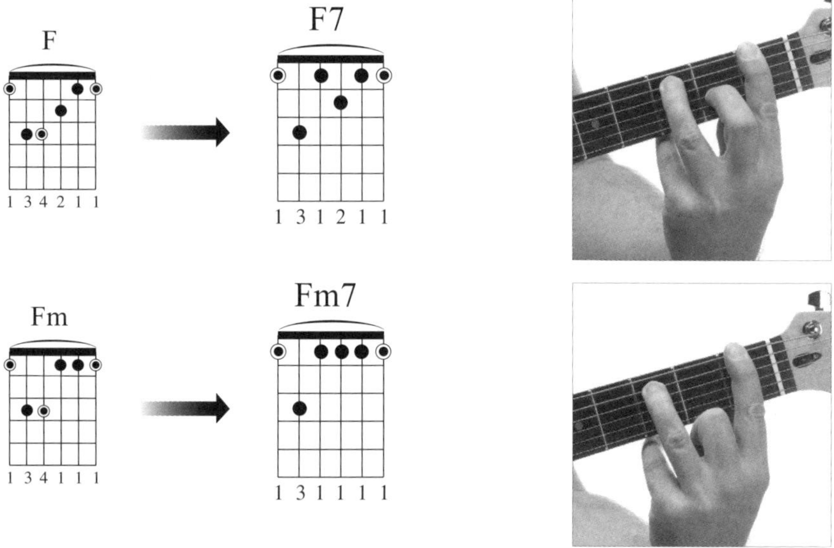

A dominant-seventh chord is a major chord (1–3–5) with an added lowered-seventh (1–3–5–♭7). A minor-seventh chord is a minor chord (1–♭3–5) with an added lowered-seventh (1–♭3–5–♭7).

Next, you'll see several progressions that mix all of the E-based barre chords you've learned. As before, the numbers below the staff represent the fret positions for the chords. Notice that in the first progression there is an eighth-note rest at the end of each measure. This gives you time to get to the next chord. (Remember to relax your left hand when changing chords.) The second progression is in a shuffle feel. Even though there are no eighth-note rhythms, you can imply the shuffle feel by adding a little pause (or rest) between each strum, on the "ands" of each beat. This is achieved by releasing pressure on your grip, as if you were going to change chords. Remember, this is a shuffle, so the "ands" arrive a little late. Listen to the track to hear where these rests occur. The last example is an "oldies" progression typical of the ballads from the '50s.

Track 20 (0:44)

Track 20 (0:58)

Track 20 (1:10)

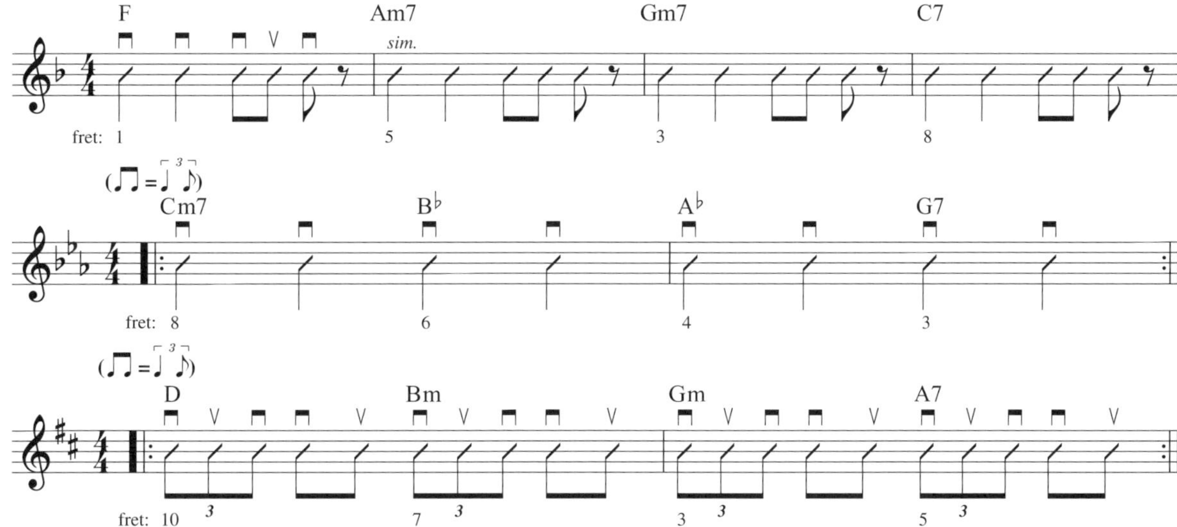

A-BASED BARRE CHORDS

Hands down, E-based barre chords are the most popular of all barre chords. Second in line, though, are those based on the open–A chord shape. Let's have a look at these chords.

Major, Minor, Dominant Seventh, Minor Seventh, and Major Seventh

Like E-based barre chords, A-based barre chords are directly related to their open–A chord counterparts. As you know, E-based barre chords have their roots on the low E string. A-based barre chords have their roots on the A string. The following figure gives a rundown of the most common A-based barre chords (in the key of C), along with their open-position counterparts.

Start with the open A chord first. Get your fingers in position to play the chord (the fingering notation leaves the first finger free to bar), and then slide all of the notes up three frets and bar the third fret with your first finger. There's no need to bar across the low E string, as it's not included in A-based barre chords. Many guitarists bar only the top five strings and lightly touch the low E with the tip of the barred first finger. This effectively mutes out the low E, keeping it from accidentally sounding.

Experiment with the "sliding up three frets" method with the other barre chords. As you did with the E-based barre chords, wiggle your first finger from side to side until you find the position where all of the strings ring loud and clear. And don't forget—positioning your thumb behind the fret where your first finger is barring will provide maximum leverage.

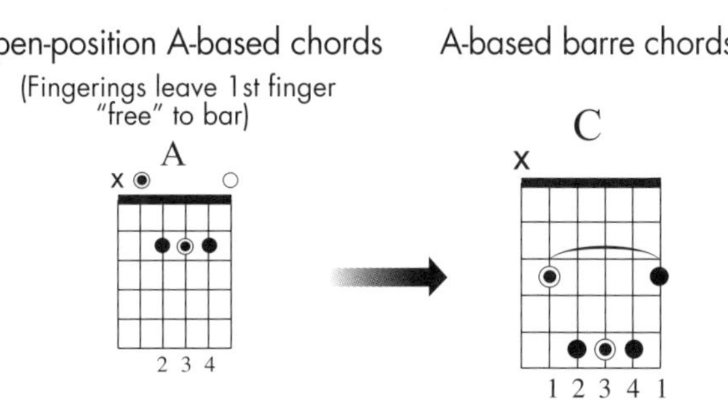

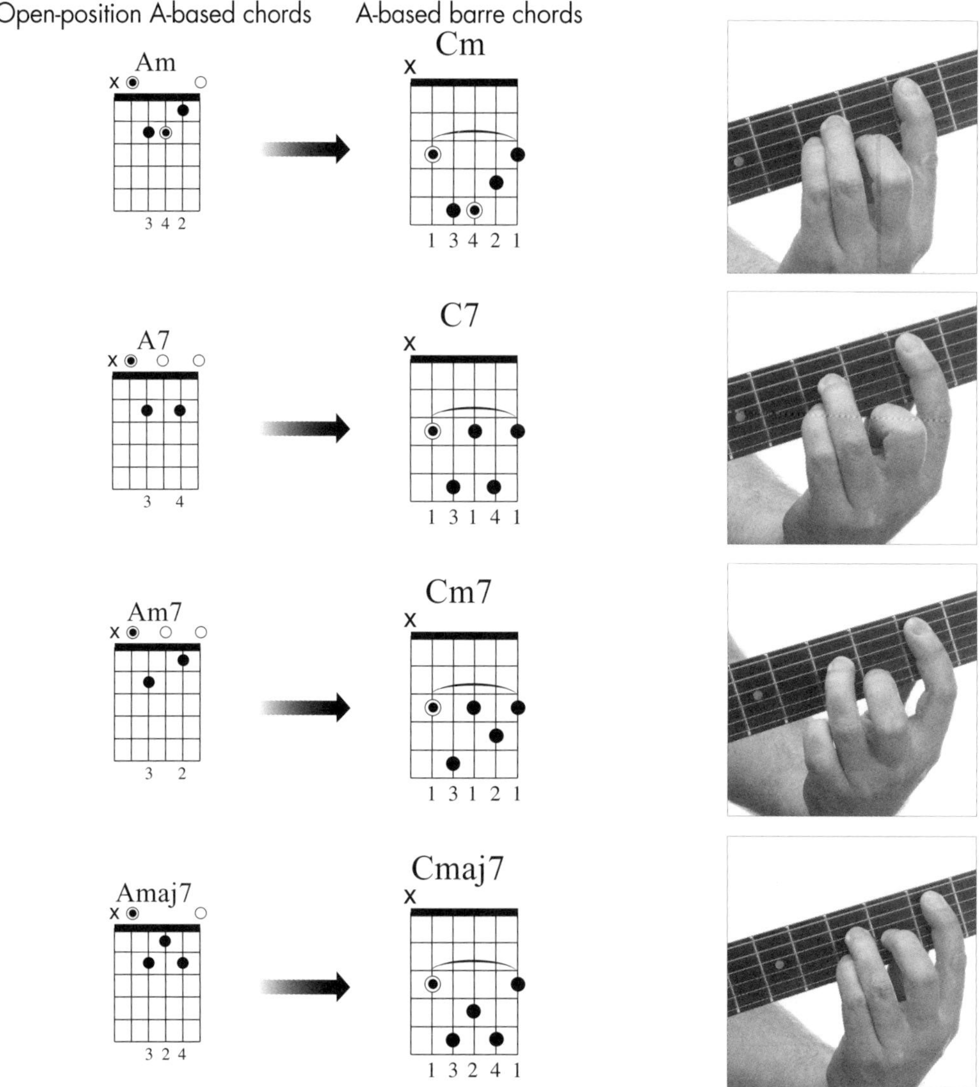

This next figure illustrates two alternate ways to finger an A-based, C major barre chord. The top voicing is like a double-barre chord: the first finger bars the top five strings at the third fret, while the third finger bars the D, G, and B strings at the fifth fret. This can be a difficult grip, as the top knuckle of the third finger has to collapse inward (see picture) to get out of the way of the high E string. Some people simply don't possess this double-jointed ability, thus the second voicing is a suitable (and much used) substitute. Instead of collapsing the knuckle, the third finger remains straight (see picture), gently laying across (and muting) the high E string.

Alternate fingerings for A-based major barre chord

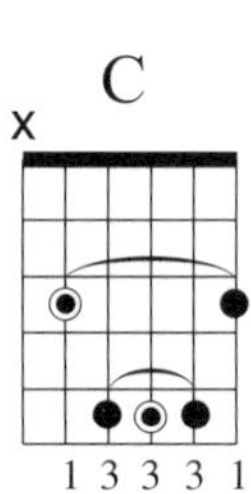

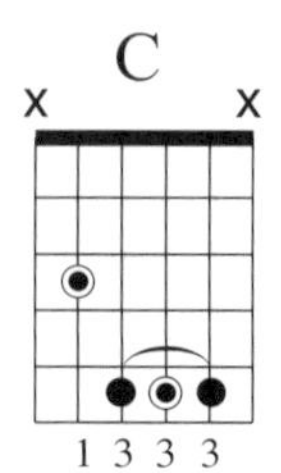

When using the second voicing of the A-based C major barre chord, be careful not to fret down on the high E string. Although this makes a pleasant-sounding chord (C6, if you're interested), it's no longer a C major chord.

Now that you know A-based barre-chord shapes, you can play them in any key. But, first, you need to learn the names of the notes along the fifth string (the roots of A-based barre chords are on the A string). You can use the neck diagram in the figure below for reference. As you did with the notes along the low E string, first memorize where the natural notes (A, B, C, D, E, F, and G) are located. Then locate the sharps and flats by relating them to their natural-note neighbors. (C♯ is one fret above C; E♭ is one fret below E; and so on.)

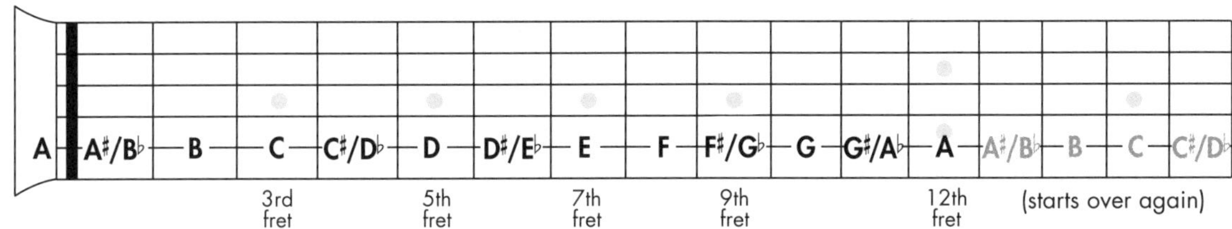

The notes and frets on a guitar are sort of like inches along a yardstick. Once you get to the 12th fret (or foot marking on a yardstick), they start over again.

PLAYING PROGRESSIONS WITH E-BASED AND A-BASED BARRE CHORDS

The following progressions include an assortment of both E-based and A-based barre chords. The numbers under the staff tell you which chord shape to use (E = E-based; A = A-based) and where to fret it (5 = fifth fret; 7 = seventh fret; etc.).

The first progression includes staccato notation (little dots above the hash marks). Staccato marks tell you to cut short the note duration. In this case, play the chord, and then immediately release your grip without letting go of the strings. This deadens the sound of all the strings. (Listen to the track for reference.)

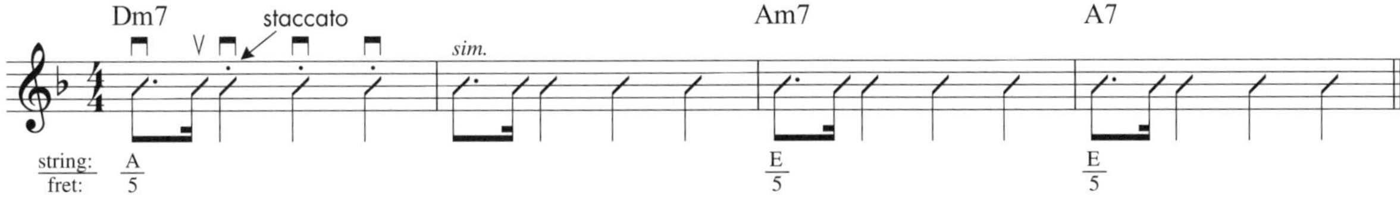

The second example features a progression favored by many a classic-rocker. Notice that the rests and the staccato markings allow you a chance to switch smoothly between voicings.

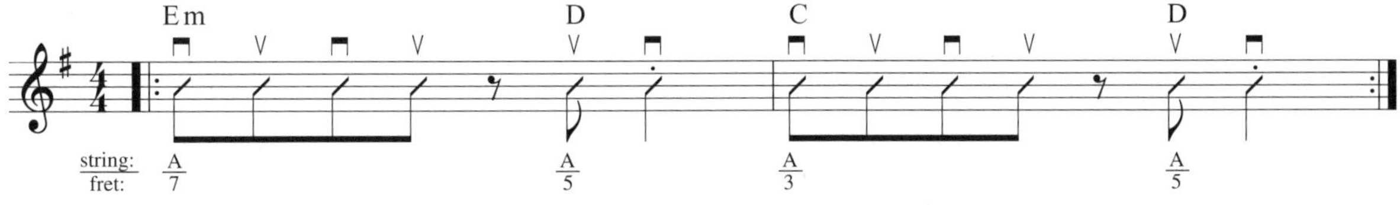

The third progression is described in jazz circles as a ii–V–I (pronounced: "two–five–one") in the key of C major. For now, just think of it as a musical way to practice three different types of seventh chords in one progression. Don't forget to shuffle (swing) the eighth notes.

Track 21
(0:30)

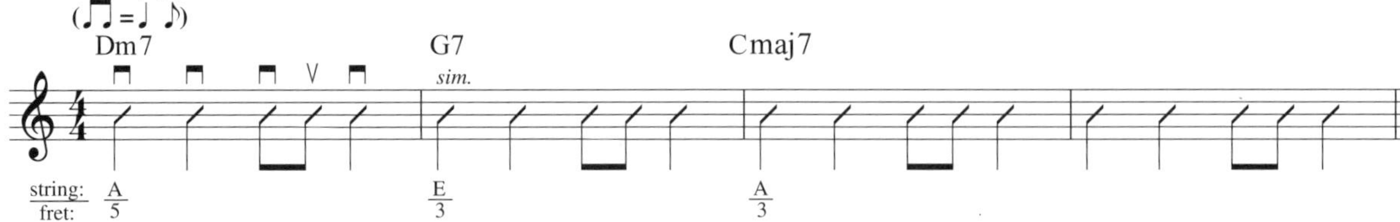

The final progression is in a Latin-rock vein. Notice that the C7 chord is placed on the "and" of beat 4 and held until the "and" of beat 1 of the next measure. This "early arrival" style of chord changing (in which the chord in the subsequent measure is rhythmically anticipated) is a common occurrence in many styles of music.

Track 21
(0:45)

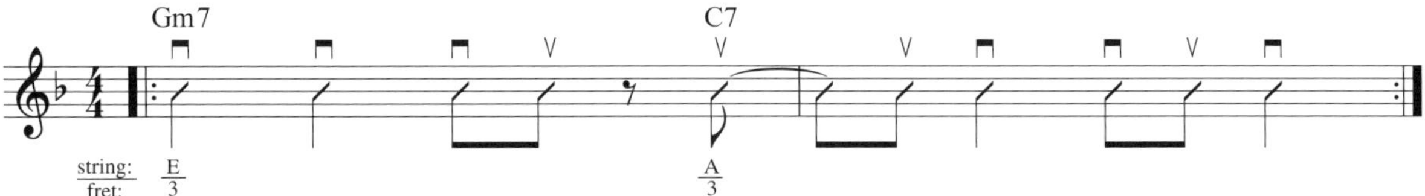

TRANSPOSING

You can play any of the chord progressions in this chapter in different keys. For example, the first chord in the first progression (on the previous page) is Dm7. This puts the progression in the key of D minor. (Don't worry about the theory for now—just take our word for it.) Notice that all of the chords are located at the fifth fret. If you play all of them at the seventh fret, you raise the key of the progression by a whole step (two half steps), to the key of E minor. (Now the chords read: Em7–Bm7–B7.) When you change the key of a progression, you are *transposing* it. It's easy to transpose this particular progression to any key. If you play the chords at the third fret (Cm7–Gm7–G7), you're in the key of C minor; at the tenth fret (Gm7–Dm7–D7) it's G minor; and so on.

- E-based barre chords are adapted from the open-position E chord. The roots of these chords are located on the low E string.
- A-based barre chords are adapted from the open-position A chord. The roots of these chords are located on the A string.
- Staccato rhythm markings indicate that a chord's duration is to be cut short.

CHAPTER 11
POWER CHORDS

What's Ahead:

- Power chords
- Muting techniques
- Power chord progressions
- Palm muting

Power chords are perhaps the easiest chords to play on the guitar. Then, you may ask, "Why didn't we start with those?" The reason is because they are specialty chords and best explained in relation to the barre chords you just learned. That said, let's power on!

WHAT IS A POWER CHORD?

A *power chord* is a two-note chord consisting of a root and a fifth. Since they contain only two notes, they're technically not chords (chords consist of three or more notes), but musicians refer to them as power chords anyway. Rock guitarists like to use power chords because they create a low, powerful sound. Listen to "Iron Man," by Black Sabbath, for the penultimate example of power chords.

Arguments rage on as to who invented the power chord, but many attribute it to Link Wray, the influential guitarist best known for his 1950s hits "Rumble" and "Rawhide."

E-BASED POWER CHORDS

Strip away all but the lowest two notes of an open E chord, and you're left with the root and fifth of the chord, the lowest power chord on the guitar (see adjacent). The suffix "5" is used to name a power chord. The E5 chord doesn't contain any other notes besides the root and fifth, therefore it can stand in for either an E major or E minor chord (and sometimes as a substitute for E7 or Em7).

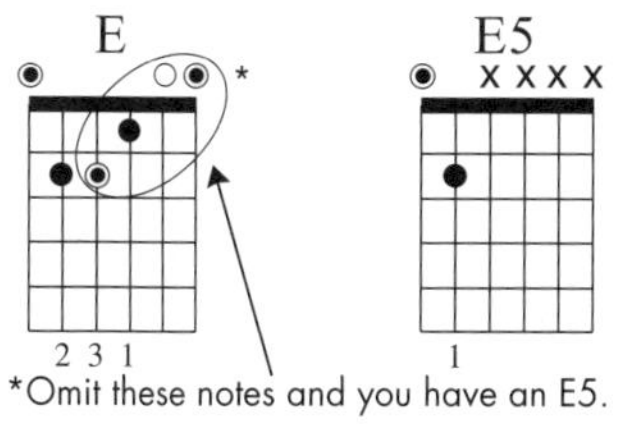

*Omit these notes and you have an E5.

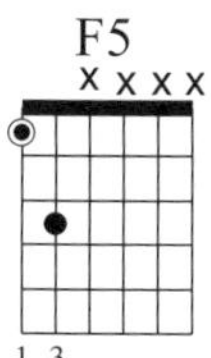

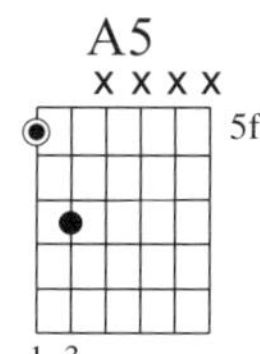

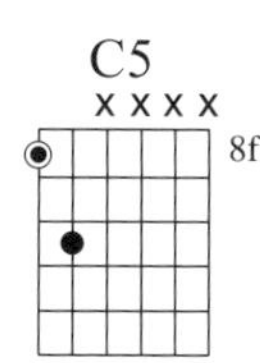

As you learned with E-based barre chords in Chapter 10, you can move an E-based power chord up and down the neck to different keys. Simply employ the two-finger voicings shown here. Again, the lowest note is the root, which gives the chord its name.

Here's a rock progression you can use to practice your new power-chord shapes. The numbers under the staff indicate the frets on which to place your first finger ("0" represents open position). Use all downstrokes for a more powerful sound.

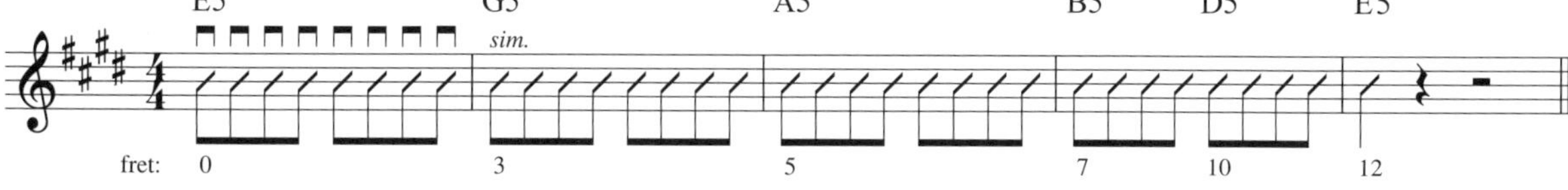

The previous progression is in the key of E minor. Move all of the chords up three frets to transpose it to the key of G minor.

Now that you know how to play E-based power chords, you can learn one of the most famous power-chord riffs in the annals of rock: "Iron Man," by Black Sabbath.

Iron Man

Words and Music by Frank Iommi, John Osbourne, William Ward and Terence Butler

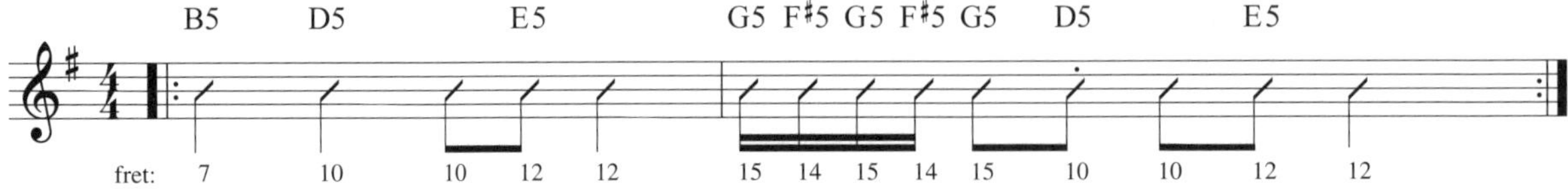

A-BASED POWER CHORDS

As illustrated below, if you omit all but the lowest two notes of an open A chord, you'll have an A power chord (A5). This shape (you guessed it!) can be converted to a movable, two-finger voicing. It's the same fingering as the E-based power chords, only the root is now on the A string.

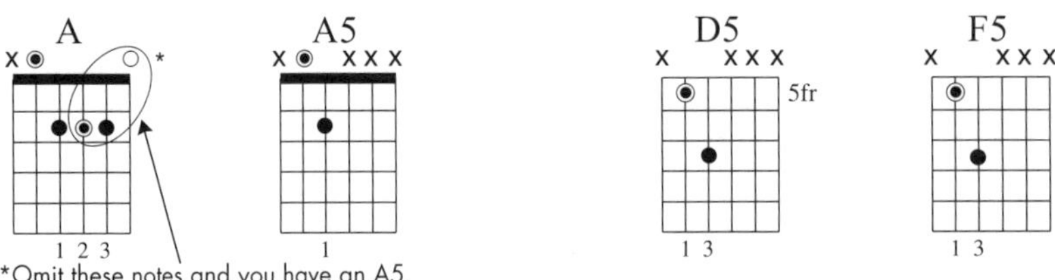

*Omit these notes and you have an A5.

Here's a progression that mixes A-based power chords with E-based power chords. The numbers below the staff indicate which chord shape to use (E = E-based; A = A-based) and where to fret it (5 = fifth fret; 3 = third fret; etc.). Use all downstrokes, and insert the "secret strum" (see Chapter 9) on the last eighth note before each new chord. Listen to the track to hear the sound.

Track 22
(0:15)

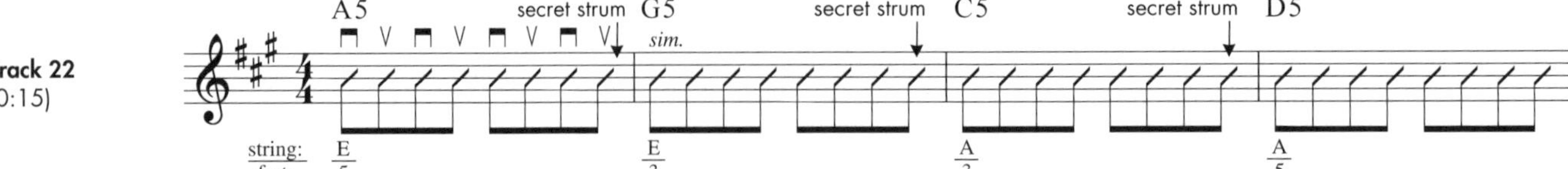

PALM-MUTING POWER CHORDS

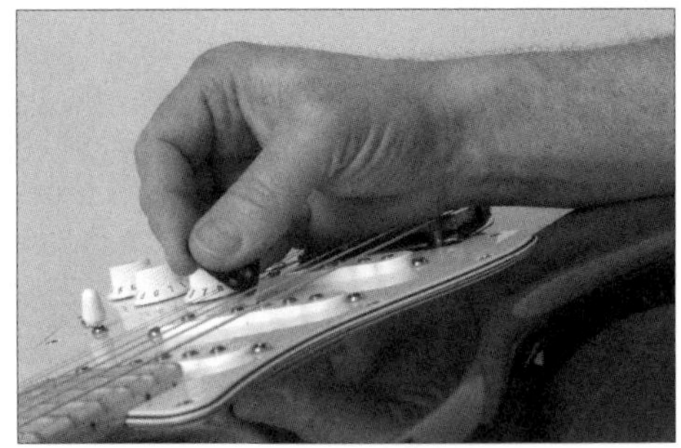

Palm muting is a technique in which the heel of the right hand lays lightly on the strings, just in front of the bridge (see picture). This deadens the sound of the strings and, when used in conjunction with power chords, creates a chunky, or thudding, sound favored by many rock guitarists. Listen to the introduction to "My Best Friend's Girl," by the Cars; "You've Got Another Thing Comin'," by Judas Priest; and "Basket Case," by Green Day to hear examples of muted power chords.

Play the open E5 chord shown earlier in the chapter, strumming it normally. Now, fan out the fingers of your right hand, laying the heel (fleshy side of the palm between the wrist and pinky finger) lightly against the lower strings, just in front of the bridge (the side toward the neck). Now strum the E5 again. If you can't hear the pitch of the chord (the actual notes), then you're pressing too hard with your muting hand, or you're too far away from the bridge. Reposition your right hand until your strumming produces a percussive, thudding sound.

Here's a collection of palm-muted power-chord progressions for you to practice. The first one is in a new-wave rock style, circa late '70s.

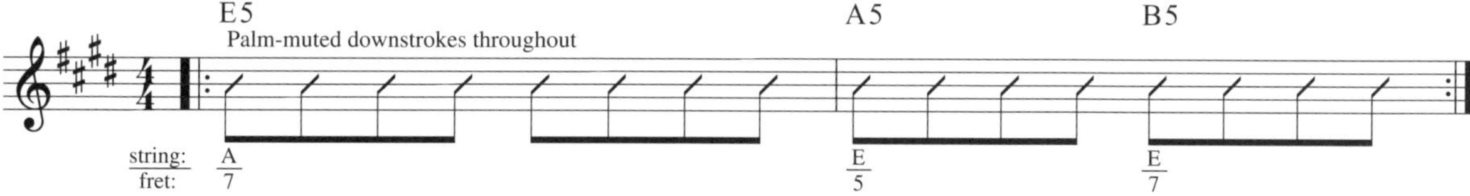

This next example is a typical classic-rock progression. After you learn it, transpose it to different keys. For example, move all of the chords up two frets to the key of E, or two frets down to the key of C.

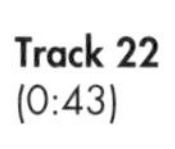

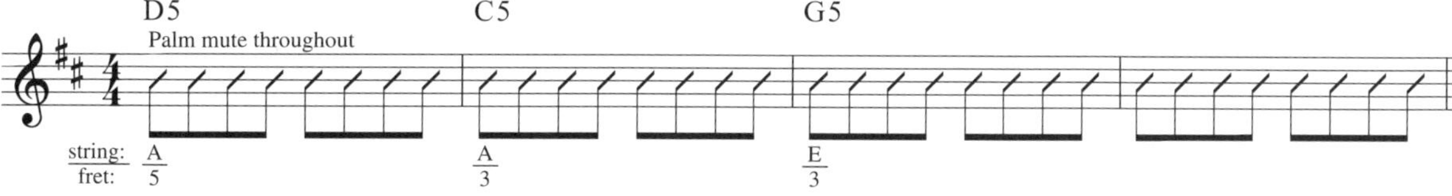

Here's a hard-rocking example played exclusively with A-based power chords. It features a series of *accents* (arrowheads pointed to the right) placed on the downbeat of beat 1 and the upbeat of beat 2 in each measure. These accents indicate to strum the corresponding beat with added emphasis. Listen to the example to hear the accents in action.

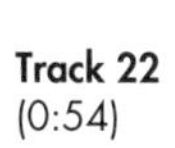

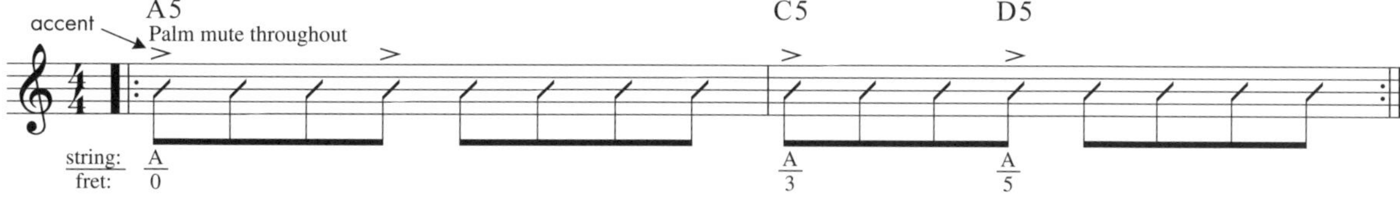

The following figure is a heavy-sounding progression in the style of classic metal bands such as Metallica and Megadeth, as well as modern metalists like Slipknot. If you're playing electric guitar through an amplifier, now's the time to crank the distortion! (See Chapter 23.)

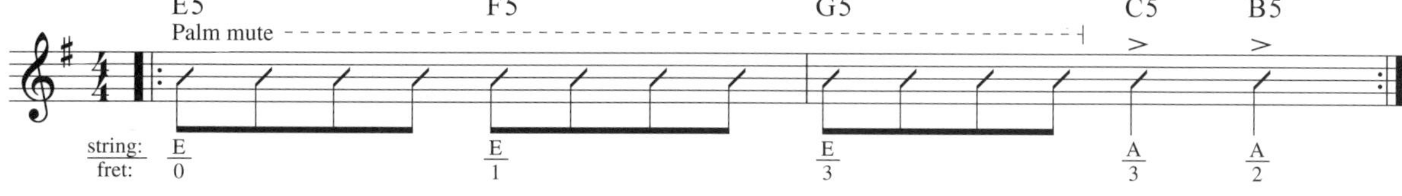

CHAPTER 12
THE PENTATONIC SCALE

What's Ahead:
- Movable minor-pentatonic scale patterns
- Minor-pentatonic licks
- Movable major-pentatonic scale patterns
- Major-pentatonic licks
- Jamming to your favorite tunes

Okay, now that you have all the basic tools you need to become a great rhythm guitarist, it's time to start talking lead guitar.

THE LEAD GUITARIST'S BEST FRIEND

Arguably, the pentatonic scale is *the* definitive scale in guitar-driven music. In the classic-rock vein, it forms the basis of just about every famous solo you've ever heard: "Crossroads," by Cream (Eric Clapton); "Stairway to Heaven," by Led Zeppelin (Jimmy Page); "Money," by Pink Floyd (David Gilmour); and "La Grange," by ZZ Top (Billy Gibbons). Blues guitarists also lean heavily on the pentatonic scale. Witness the three "kings" of the blues: "The Thrill Is Gone," by B.B. King; "Hideaway," by Freddie King; and "Crosscut Saw," by Albert King. Pentatonic scales also abound in country ("Chattahoochee," by Alan Jackson [Brent Mason]) and southern rock ("Ramblin' Man" and "Jessica," by the Allman Brothers [Dickey Betts]). You'll even hear pentatonic scales dispatched in jazz and jazz-rock (George Benson, John McLaughlin [Mahavishnu Orchestra], and Scott Henderson [Tribal Tech]).

WHAT IS THE PENTATONIC SCALE?

The word pentatonic literally means "five-note scale." Actually, there are a variety of pentatonic scales used around the world, but the one that we guitarists know and love best is the *minor-pentatonic scale*. The minor-pentatonic scale is essentially a stripped-down version of the natural-minor scale, which contains seven notes (see "The Relative A Minor Scale," Chapter 8). For example, the A natural-minor scale, or, simply, the A minor scale, contains the notes: A–B–C–D–E–F–G. Remove the B and F notes from the scale and you have the A minor-pentatonic scale: A–C–D–E–G. Okay, that's enough theory for now. Let's get to playing!

Omitting these notes (B and F) removes the "awkward" half-step intervals between the second and flatted third (B and C), and the fifth and flatted sixth (E and F) scale degrees. This makes for a streamlined, easy-to-apply, minor-scale alternative.

THE OPEN-POSITION E MINOR-PENTATONIC SCALE

The open-position E minor-pentatonic scale will be our starting point. You'll find out why in a moment. It's notated in tab and standard notation. Play through it using the fingering notated below the tab staff. (Note: The notes of the full E natural-minor scale are: E–F♯–G– A–B–C–D).

E minor-pentatonic scale

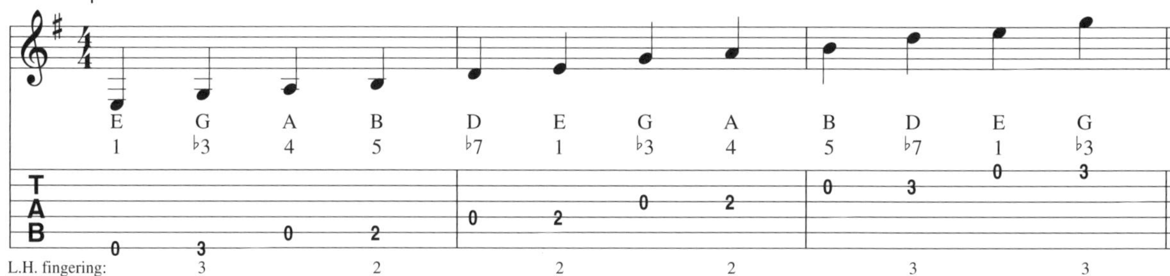

Strum an Em chord, and then play the E minor-pentatonic scale up to the top note (G on the high E string). Strum an Em chord again, and then play down the scale to the bottom note (open low E string). Strumming the chord before you play the scale helps you "tune in" to the sound of the scale.

E Minor-pentatonic Riffs and Licks

Now for some real fun: The following figures feature an assortment of licks and riffs using the E minor-pentatonic scale you've just learned.

A *lick* is a short, melodic phrase (either memorized or improvised), usually played once. Jimi Hendrix's opening guitar line in "All Along the Watchtower" is a lick. Lead guitarists combine various licks to form a solo.

A *riff* is a composed phrase or passage that is repeated, often throughout an entire song. The intro guitar figures in "Sunshine of Your Love," by Cream; "Pretty Woman," by Roy Orbison; and "I Feel Fine," by the Beatles are riffs.

The first example is a solid blues-rock lick. Picking directions (located between staves) and fingering suggestions (under the tab staff) are notated to help guide you through the lick. The "roll over" notation indicates to roll your second finger from the second fret of the D string to the second fret of the G string, instead of lifting it off of the fretboard. The roll-over technique is a great speed device, and one we'll visit often. The second lick is in a progressive-rock vein. Be careful here—you need to hold the G note in the first measure and the first A note in the second measure for 1-1/2 beats. Use the roll-over technique at the beginning of measure 2. The third lick is a heavy-metal example. It prominently features the low E string, and calls for an all-downstroke attack. When combined, the downstrokes form a powerful phrase. Last, we have an example of a classic-rock riff. Go slowly at first; this one is trickier than it looks.

Track 23
(0:12)

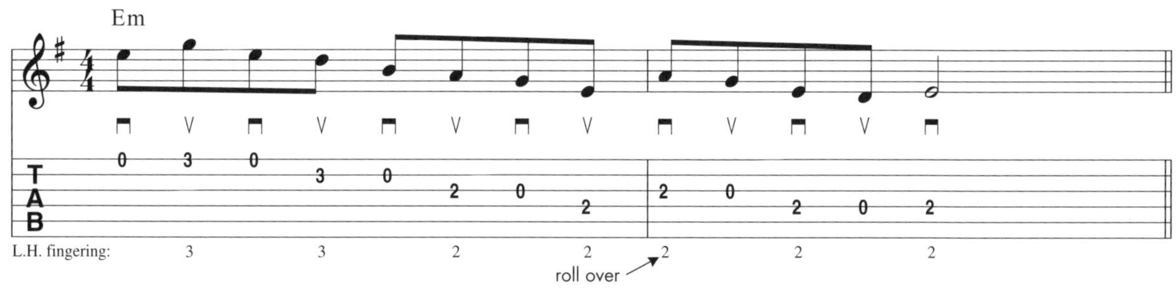

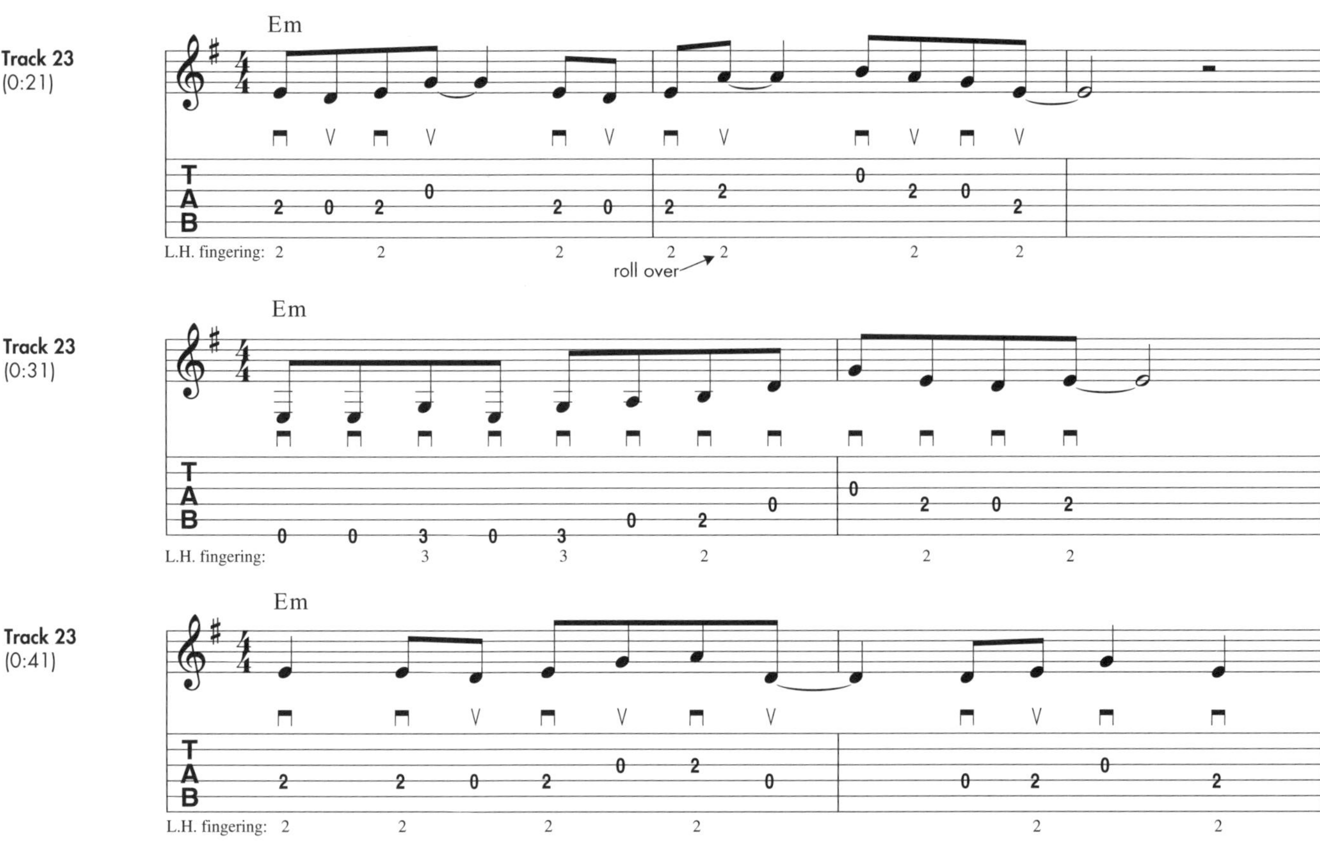

When the next note you're about to play is on the same fret and an adjacent string, you can roll your finger over to fret that note. If you're rolling to a higher string (e.g., D string to the G string), raise your left wrist as you roll. If you're rolling to a lower string (e.g., D string to the A string), drop your wrist as you roll.

SOLOING IN DIFFERENT KEYS

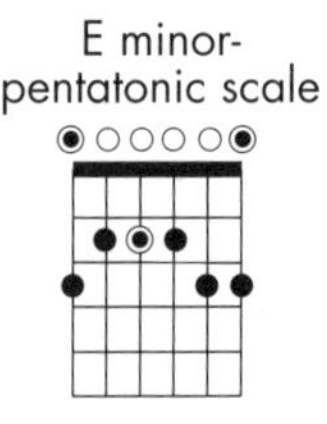

Take a look at the adjacent figure. This is the open E minor-pentatonic scale shown on a scale diagram called a *box pattern*, a visual snapshot of an isolated section of the fretboard. Like a chord frame, a box pattern is viewed as if the guitar's neck is out in front of you. If you haven't noticed yet, the lower "side" of the E minor-pentatonic scale pattern that you've been playing includes all of the open strings. The upper "side" is a pattern of notes played at the second and third frets. This is clearly evident when depicted in scale-box form.

Remember back in Chapter 10, in which we transformed an open E chord to an F chord with the help of a bar? Good, because we're going to do something very similar right now.

If we move every note in the open E minor-pentatonic scale up one fret, the result is the box pattern on the next page. We have just transposed the E minor-pentatonic scale up a half step to the F minor-pentatonic scale. See the similarities? They're exactly the same pattern, except now all the notes are fretted. We now have a pattern of the minor-pentatonic scale that, just like a barre chord, can be moved around the neck to every key! All you have to do is place the lowest note of the pattern (root) at the desired fret of the low E string. For example, if you place the box at the second fret, you have the F♯ minor-pentatonic scale; at the fifth fret, it's the A minor-pentatonic scale; and so on.

To cement this new-found knowledge, we're going to transpose the E minor-pentatonic licks from earlier in the chapter to different keys, using the box pattern you just learned (see below). The first lick is played in the G minor-pentatonic box at the third fret. The second is in the C minor-pentatonic box at the eighth fret. The third example is in the F♯ minor-pentatonic box at the second fret. And the last one is in the A minor-pentatonic box at the fifth fret. Try to memorize each lick, including its fingering and sound. Then move them to different keys.

audio tracks 24

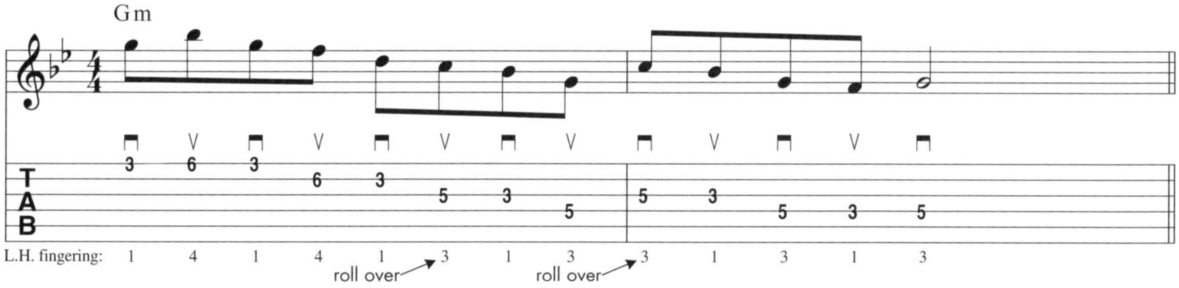

Gm

L.H. fingering: 1 4 1 4 1 roll over 3 1 3 roll over 3 1 3 1 3

Track 24 (0:09)

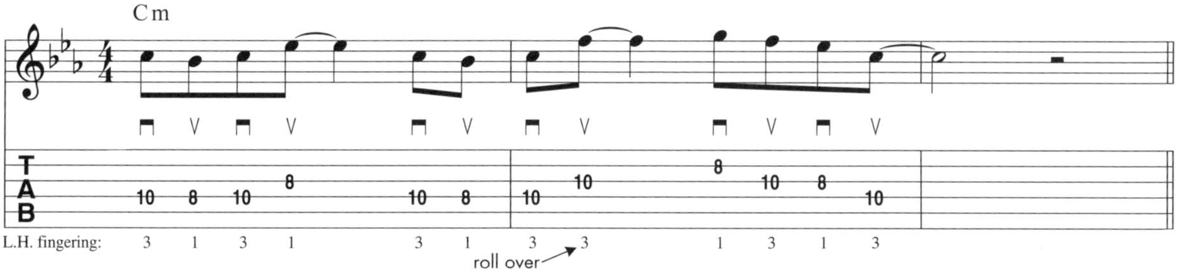

Cm

L.H. fingering: 3 1 3 1 3 1 3 roll over 3 1 3 1 3

Track 24 (0:20)

F♯m

L.H. fingering: 1 1 4 1 4 1 3 1 roll over 1 3 1 3

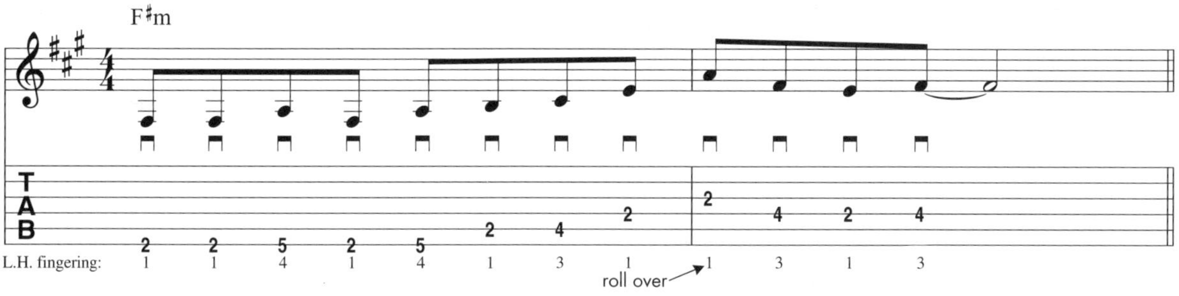

Track 24 (0:30)

Am

L.H. fingering: 3 3 1 3 1 3 1 1 3 1 3

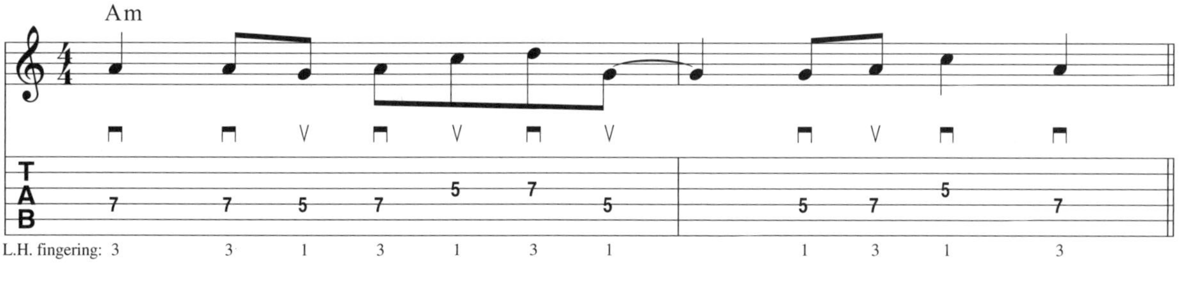

JAMMING WITH THE MINOR-PENTATONIC SCALE

The minor-pentatonic scale is sort of a "one size fits all" jamming device. (Jamming is the art of making music spontaneously, or improvising.) That is, once you're in the right key, most of the notes are "safe" choices at any given time. For example, many rock and blues songs use very few chords, staying in the same key throughout the tune. If you know the key of the song (many times you can go fishing for the key by playing notes up and down the low E string until you find the one that sounds like the tonic, or central tone of the music), you can go hog-wild by playing notes from the minor-pentatonic scale pattern in the same key. Here are some songs with which to start:

- "All Along the Watchtower," by Jimi Hendrix; use the C minor-pentatonic box at the eighth fret
- "Are You Gonna Be My Girl," by Jet; use the A minor-pentatonic box at the fifth fret
- "I Shot the Sheriff," by Eric Clapton; use the G minor-pentatonic box at the third fret
- "Miss You," by the Rolling Stones; use the A minor-pentatonic box at the fifth fret
- "Smells Like Teen Spirit," by Nirvana; use the F minor-pentatonic box at the first fret
- "Somebody Told Me," by the Killers; use the B♭ minor-pentatonic box at the sixth fret
- "The Thrill Is Gone," by B.B. King; use the B minor-pentatonic box at the seventh fret
- "Vertigo," by U2; use the E minor-pentatonic box at the 12th fret or open position

THE MAJOR-PENTATONIC SCALE

Yes, there is another pentatonic scale—the major-pentatonic scale. This scale is used in major keys and is quite prevalent in styles such as country, southern rock, rockabilly, and blues. Essentially, the major-pentatonic scale is a stripped-down version of the complete major scale. Omitting the fourth and seventh scale degrees of the major scale creates the major pentatonic. For example, the C major scale contains the notes: C–D–E–F–G–A–B (1–2–3–4–5–6–7). If you remove the F (fourth) and the B (seventh), you have the C major-pentatonic scale: C–D–E–G–A (1–2–3–5–6).

Omitting the fourth and seventh scale degrees removes the "awkward" half-step intervals between the third and fourth, and seventh and octave. This creates a streamlined, major alternative to the full-on major scale.

THE OPEN-POSITION G MAJOR-PENTATONIC SCALE

We're going to start with the G major-pentatonic scale for a very good reason. You'll find out why momentarily.

The following figure illustrates the open-position G major-pentatonic scale (G–A–B–D–E) both ascending (going up in pitch) and descending (going down in pitch). (Note: The notes of the entire G major scale are: G–A–B–C–D–E–F♯.) Do you sense anything familiar as you play through the scale? Of course you do! It's the same batch of notes, played on the same strings and frets, as the E minor-pentatonic scale.

G major-pentatonic scale

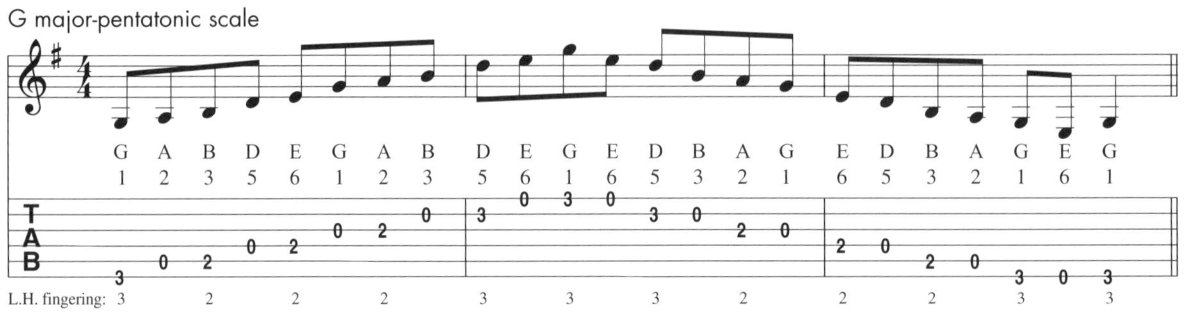

Remember back in Chapter 8 when you discovered that the C major scale has the same notes as the A minor scale? We told you that the two scales are relative because they share the same notes. Well, the same goes for G major pentatonic and E minor pentatonic. They share the same notes; therefore, they're related, or relative. You may be asking, "If they have the same notes, why do they have different names?" Good question. The answer lies in which note is designated as the root, or central tone. For example, if you play the E minor-pentatonic scale from E to E, it has a sad, minor sound. If you play the E minor-pentatonic scale from G to G, it sounds happy, like the major scale. Again, let's put the theory aside for now and see what we can do with the major-pentatonic scale.

THE MOVABLE MAJOR-PENTATONIC PATTERN

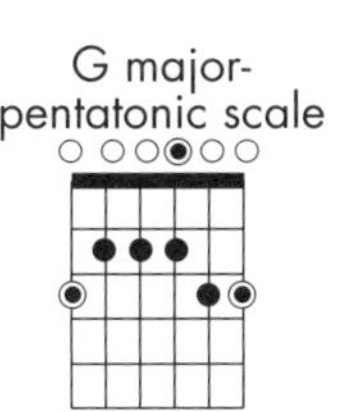

Since the E minor-pentatonic scale and the G major-pentatonic scale are relative, or share the same notes, it stands to reason that you can use the same box patterns for each one, right? Right! The adjacent box shows the G major-pentatonic scale pattern in open position, which is same scale as the open-position E minor pentatonic, except the root is now on the third fret.

If you move all of the notes up two frets, you have the A major-pentatonic scale. (Remember, the scale gets its name from the root, which is at the fifth fret of the low E string.) Now you have a box pattern of the major-pentatonic scale that you can move around the neck to different keys.

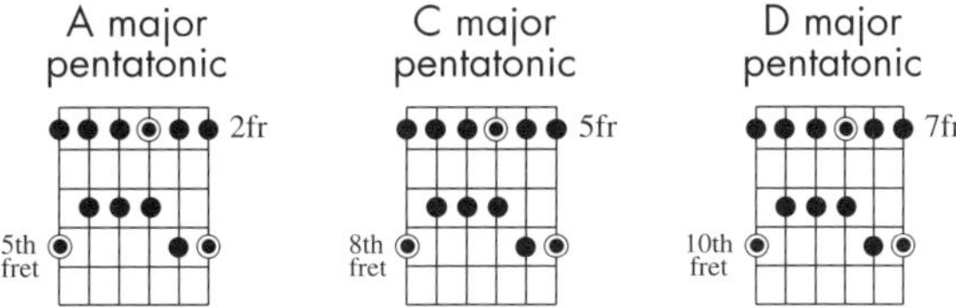

MAJOR-PENTATONIC LICKS

Now let's use our major-pentatonic box to play some licks (see below). The first example is a '60s soul-rock melody that simply climbs the A major-pentatonic scale. The second one is a southern-rock lick. The third example is pure country. And the fourth lick is in a classic-rock vein. Go through these examples slowly, working out the picking directions and the roll-over techniques, all notated for your convenience.

Track 25 (0:32)

C

L.H. fingering: 4 1 3 1 3 3 1 1

roll over roll over

Track 25 (0:39)

D

L.H. fingering: 4 4 1 1 4 3 1 1 3 3 1 3 1

roll over roll over roll over roll over

MAJOR-PENTATONIC JAMS

The major-pentatonic scale is a great jamming device for songs in major keys. Here's a list of suggested songs with which to experiment:

- "Anyway You Want It," by Journey; use the G major-pentatonic box at the 15th fret (root at the 15th fret)
- "Chattahoochee," by Alan Jackson; use the C major-pentatonic box at the eighth fret
- "Dammit," by Blink-182; use the C major-pentatonic box at the eighth fret
- "Ramblin' Man," by the Allman Brothers; use the G major-pentatonic box at the 15th fret
- "She Will Be Loved," by Maroon 5; use the E♭ major-pentatonic box at the eleventh fret
- "Slide," by the Goo Goo Dolls; use the G♯ major-pentatonic box at the fourth fret
- "Start Me Up," by the Rolling Stones; use the F major-pentatonic box at the 13th fret
- "Sweet Home Alabama," by Lynyrd Skynyrd; use the D major-pentatonic box at the tenth fret

- The minor-pentatonic scale is a five-note scale derived from the natural-minor scale.
- The open-position E minor-pentatonic scale forms the basis of movable, minor-pentatonic patterns.
- The major-pentatonic scale is a five-note scale derived from the major scale.
- The G major-pentatonic scale at the third fret (open position) forms the basis of movable major-pentatonic patterns.
- When moving to the same fret of an adjacent string, you can "roll over" your finger to fret the note.

CHAPTER 13
MAKING YOUR GUITAR SING

What's Ahead:

- Playing hammer-ons and pull-offs
- Playing slides
- String bending
- Vibrato techniques

The guitar is a wonderfully expressive instrument. With the right touch you can make it cry or sing. In fact, in the hands of a fine player it can almost be made to talk! With the proper technique, just a few notes from the guitar can speak volumes of emotion. It's all in the articulation, or the way those notes are played. In this chapter we'll teach you the techniques you need to make your guitar sing.

LEGATO

Listen carefully to a good singer, and you'll notice that he or she doesn't hit every single note "dead-on," pitch-wise or volume-wise. The human voice has a tendency to slur, or slide into pitches from above or below, resulting in a smooth, connected sound musicians refer to as *legato.* Many instrumentalists strive to emulate the human singing voice when they play, and guitarists are no exception. To emulate this vocal-like sound, guitarists use a number of legato techniques including hammer-ons, pull-offs, slides, bends, and vibrato.

Hammer-ons

The hammer-on is one of the most popular of all the legato techniques used by guitarists. A *hammer-on* is executed by first picking a note, then slamming (hammering) a left-hand finger down onto a higher fret of the same string. In other words, the second note is played without picking it with your right hand.

Open-string hammer-ons are often the easiest to learn how to play. Take a look at the next example. The first measure is a hammer-on from the open D string. First, pick the open D string, then, with your second finger, hammer-on to the second fret while the string is still ringing. (The curved line in the tab staff is called a *legato slur.*) You need to use a lot of force to get the hammered note to sound as loud as the picked one. Try to picture your finger as a little hammer that is slamming down on the fretboard. Keep at it, and you'll develop the strength and mind control required to perform the hammer-on. When you're ready, move on to the second measure. This is a hammer-on to the third fret of the B string, which you can practice to help get your third finger in hammer-on condition.

The next example features a musical exercise for the open-string hammer-on technique. Yes, it's our old friend, the open-position E minor-pentatonic scale. But instead of picking every note, we're going to just pick the open strings, and hammer-on to all of the fretted notes. Work through the exercise slowly and carefully, striving to make all the notes equal in volume. Use all downstrokes and be careful not to rush the hammer-ons. Keep all of the eighth notes nice and even.

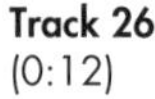

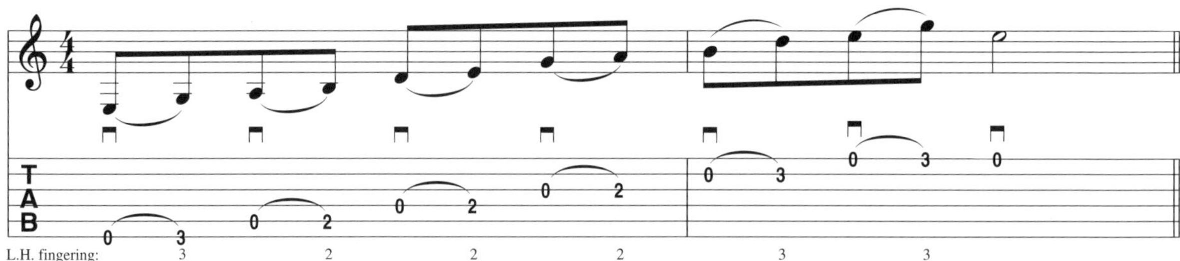

Next is a heavy-metal riff. It starts with an open E5 power chord (see Chapter 11), then moves to open A- and open D-string hammer-ons. Crank the distortion (if you have it) and dig in.

Track 26
(0:23)

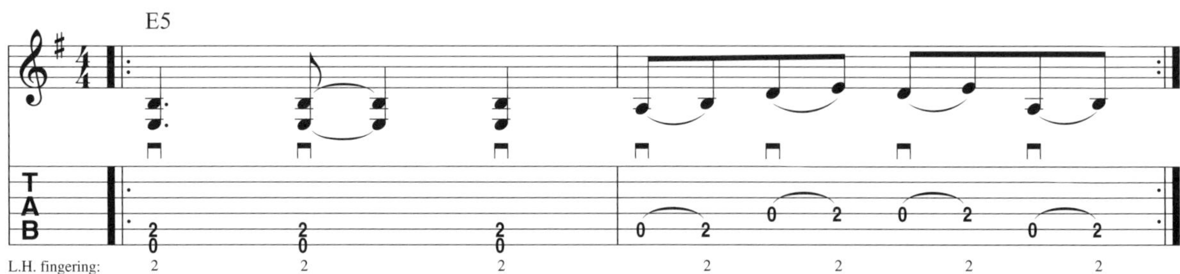

When performing hammer-ons, think of your fretting fingers as little hammers slamming down on the fretboard.

Pull-offs

Like the hammer-on, the pull-off technique plays a major role in legato phrasing. Musically speaking, a *pull-off* is the opposite of a hammer-on: Where a hammer-on allows you to slur into a note higher in pitch, a pull-off provides a slur to a lower note. Technique-wise, the pull-off is a bit more complex than the hammer-on. Here's a step-by-step explanation of how to perform a pull-off to an open string. The procedure is notated in tab in the first measure of the following example.

- Place your second finger on the second fret of the D string and pick the note as you normally would.
- While your finger is still pressing the second fret, drag it toward the G string until your finger is completely off the string. If you're pressing down hard enough, the motion should cause the D string to ring.

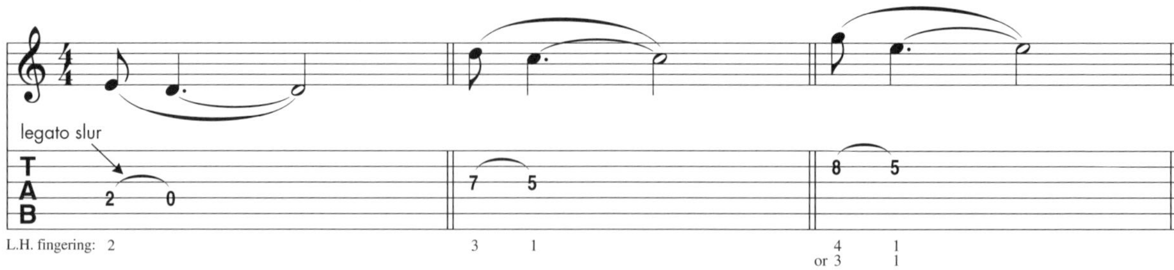

Tab notation is the same for both hammer-ons and pull-offs: an upward curving line above the fret numbers. If the second note is on a higher fret, it means it's a hammer-on. If the second note is on a lower fret, it's a pull-off.

Don't be confused by the term "pull-off." If you take it by its literal meaning, you may be inclined to simply lift your finger off the string. This motion won't allow the second note to be loud enough. A pull-off is more like a tiny finger pluck performed by your fretting hand.

The second measure in the previous example depicts a pull-off to a fretted note. This technique is a little trickier as it calls for you to fret both notes ahead of time. In this case, you need to press the fifth fret of the G string with your first finger and the seventh fret of the same string with your third finger, both at the same time. Then strike the string with your pick, and, while the seventh-fret note is still ringing, pull-off your third finger to sound the note on the fifth fret. Remember, don't lift your third finger straight up off the fretboard; pull it off in a sideways motion toward the B string.

The third measure in features a pull-off with the fourth finger. Give it a try, but if it proves too difficult, you can use your third (stronger) finger.

The next figure shows a couple of pull-off licks in the fifth-position A minor-pentatonic scale box. These are typical blues-rock licks used by guitarists such as Jimmy Page (Led Zeppelin), Slash (Guns N' Roses), and Ace Frehley (KISS). The first lick advises you to use all downstroke picking for extra power. The second lick suggests an up/down/up/down pattern. This makes it easier to get the lick up to speed. Use a first-finger barre to fret the high E and B strings at the fifth fret. This will allow the notes to ring together. Listen to the track to hear the sound of these licks.

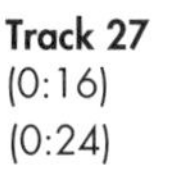

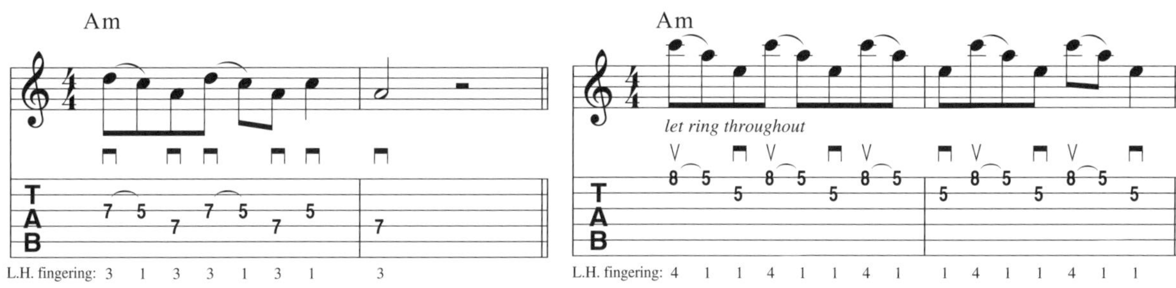

Combining Hammer-ons and Pull-offs

Many guitarists combine hammer-ons with pull-offs. The most common combinations are the *hammer/pull-off* and the *pull/hammer-on*. Following is an example of a country lick (in the seventh-position D major-pentatonic box) that uses a hammer/pull-off. The lick begins with two standard hammer-ons (from the seventh to the ninth fret) on the A and D strings. Another similar hammer-on is played on the G string, but when the third finger hammers, it immediately pulls-off again to the first finger at the seventh fret. It's like getting three notes for the price of one pick!

Next is another D major-pentatonic country lick, but this one employs pull/hammer-ons. The first one is on the G string, where the third finger pulls-off the ninth fret to the seventh fret (fretted by the first finger), then hammers back to the ninth fret again. Again, three notes for the price of one pick attack. Another pull/hammer-on occurs on the same frets of the D string.

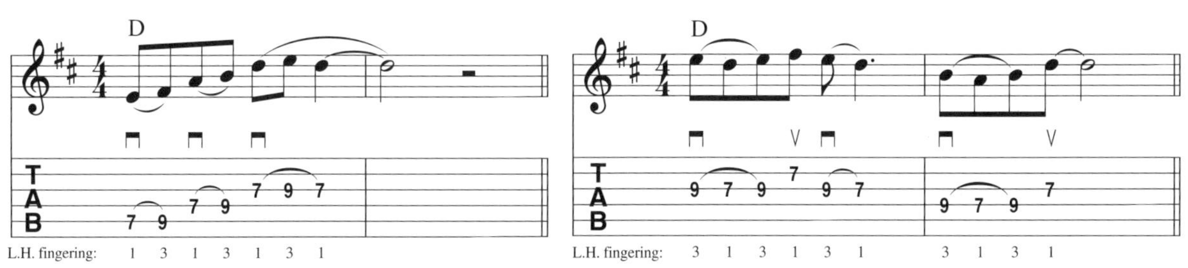

There are a great many different types of hammer-ons, pull-offs, and various combinations in the guitar vernacular (see Sections 4 and 5), but they are all based on the fundamental techniques we just learned.

Slides

The *slide* is probably the easiest of all legato techniques. All you have to do is slide your finger up or down a string, from one note to another. This allows you to connect two notes smoothly and quickly.

The following figure shows various types of slides and how they are notated on the tab staff. The first two are *legato slides*. To play a legato slide you strike the first note and slide the same fretting finger up or down the string to the second note. With a legato slide, the second note is not picked. Legato slides are notated on the tab staff with an upward or downward slanting line (telling you to slide up or down), and a slur over the line. To play it, strike and hold the first note until the count of "2," then quickly slide up to the second note. Do not pick the second note. To play the second slide, strike and hold the first note until the count of "2," then quickly slide down to the second note. Again, do not pick the second note.

The third slide is an example of a *shift slide*. A shift slide is executed exactly the same way as a legato slide, except that you *do* pick the second note. A shift slide is notated on the tab staff in the same manner as a legato slide, except there is no slur above the slanted line. To play it, strike and hold the first note until the count of "2," then quickly slide up to, and pick, the second note.

The fourth slide is called an *indeterminate slide*. You can think of this as a quick slide from nowhere. With indeterminate slides you can start one, two, three or more frets below the target note; the choice is up to you. Start your slide with minimal finger pressure, gradually increasing it until you arrive at your destination. Once you reach the target note, exert full pressure, but do not strike the string again. Tab notation for an indeterminate slide is simply a slanted line pointing toward the target fret. There is no "departure" fret notated on the left side of the line.

Next we have an example of a *fall-off slide*. To play a fall-off slide you pick the note, then slide down the string (how far you slide is your choice), gradually releasing finger pressure as you go. A fall-off slide is notated in tab with a downward slanting line. (There is no destination fret notated.)

Last is an example of a *grace-note slide*. A grace-note slide is played in exactly the same manner as a legato slide, but the slide is immediate. Tab notation is also similar except that the departure fret number is smaller in size than the destination fret number. The small note on the upper staff is a grace note. A *grace note* takes up no time value and is played quickly before the beat.

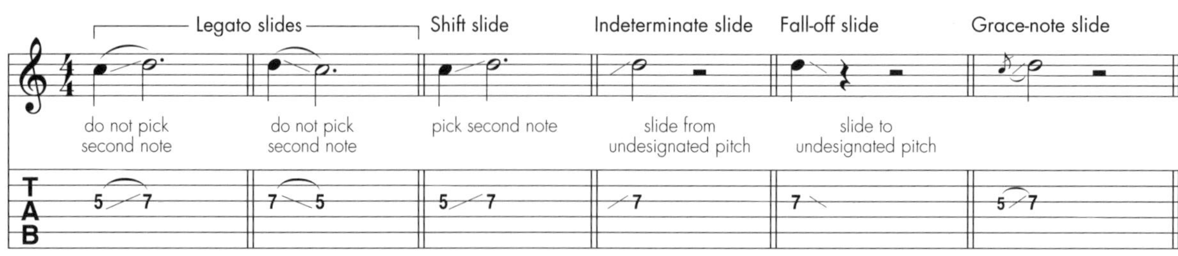

Besides being used for legato effects, slides can also facilitate position shifts from one area of the fretboard to another. Next we have a bluesy example, which travels up the fretboard from the third fret to tenth position.

Track 28 (0:30)

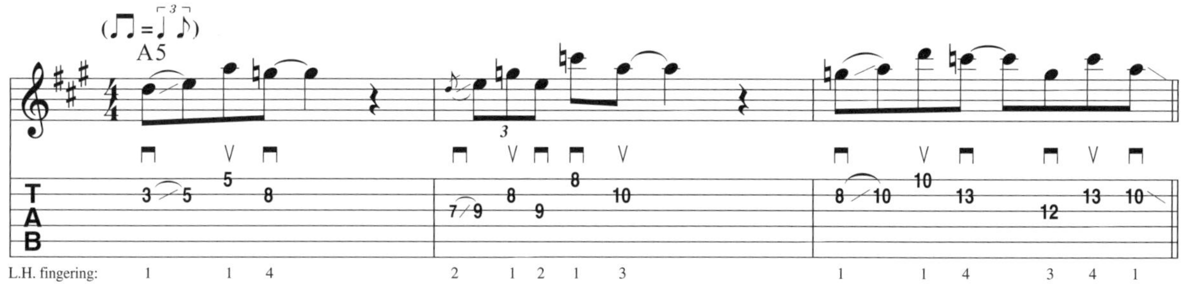

BENDS

Of all the legato techniques, the *string bend* is the most emotive. Guitarists use string bends to produce the moaning, crying, and singing sound of the human voice. The technique takes practice, but the principle is simple: The finger frets a note, then pushes the string up or down (across the fret) to raise the pitch. In other words, a string bend allows you to change the pitch of a fretted note without having to change positions.

Do not attempt the following examples on an acoustic guitar. You may break a string, or worse, injure your left hand. Beginners should learn string-bending techniques on an electric guitar equipped with light-gauge strings (see "Strings" Chapter 24), ideally a .009–.042 or .010–.046 set.

Although it's possible to bend any of the six strings on the guitar, the G string is the easiest to start with. We're going to begin with a whole-step bend (a whole-step is the distance of two frets) from F at the tenth fret, to the target pitch, G.

First, you want to get the sound of the bend in your head. Do this by playing F (tenth fret) and G (twelfth fret) slowly, back and forth. Try to memorize the difference in pitch. Now, place your third finger at the tenth fret of the G string, and position your second and first fingers behind it. (The first and second fingers don't produce any sound, but will add support to the actual bend.) Pick the string and, using all three fingers, push the string up, toward the ceiling, until you reach the pitch that is a whole step higher. It's important to push your fingers into the neck as you bend. Also, you should wrap your thumb over the neck for extra leverage. The adjacent example shows the tab notation for the above procedure. The first two notes are the example pitches (F and G) played at the tenth and twelfth frets. The bend is notated on the tab staff with an upward curving arrow which points to the number "1." This tells you to bend the tenth fret of the G string up a whole step (1 = 1 step).

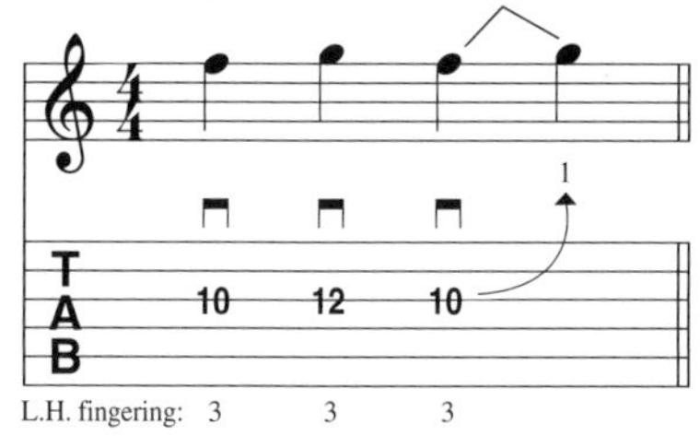

Following are various bending techniques and how they are notated. First is the *grace-note bend*. To play this grace-note bend, place your third finger at the tenth fret of the G string and immediately bend it up a whole step. Tab notation for the grace-note bend is similar to a regular bend, except that the fret number is written a little smaller in size than usual. Compare it to the size of the normally fretted note next to it.

The second bend is called a *bend/release*. To play this bend/release, place your third finger at the tenth fret of the G string, hold it until the count of "2," then quickly bend up a half step (distance of one fret) and hold it until the count of "3," then release the bend (without picking) to its normal position. The release is notated with a downward curving arrow pointing to the fret number in parentheses.

Last is the *pre-bend*. To play a pre-bend you need to bend the string to pitch before striking it. To play this pre-bend, place your third finger at the tenth fret of the G string and bend it up the distance of a whole step before striking it with your pick. The pre-bend is the most difficult of the bunch because you can't rely on your ear to help you bend the correct distance. It's more of a "feel" thing—like working the clutch while driving with a stick shift. Keep working on normal bends and eventually you'll develop the skills needed to accurately execute pre-bends.

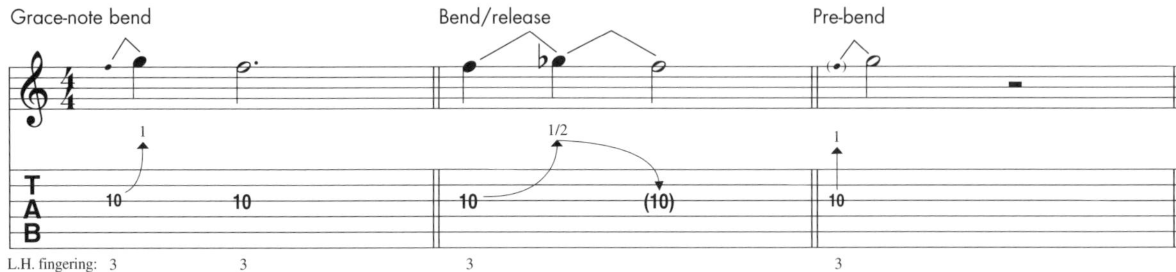

String-bending Practice

Next you'll find some examples you can use to practice your bending techniques. The first is designed to help you find the pitch for a whole-step bend on the G string. Listen carefully as you play the fretted notes in the first measure, and then try to match the pitches as you perform the bend in measure 2. When you play the two measures back to back, the melody should sound the same. If it doesn't, you're either bending the string too far (making the note sound sharp), or you're not bending it enough (which will make the note sound flat).

The rest of the examples follow the same procedure: The first measure contains the fretted version of the target pitch, while the second is the string-bending version of the same pitches. The next example is designed to whip your pinky into bending shape. (Place your second and third fingers on the B string, behind your pinky, to help assist in pushing the string up to pitch.) If it's not up to the task, use your third finger, which is usually stronger. The third example features a half-step pre-bend. (A half step is the distance of one fret.) Remember, bend the B string to pitch before striking it with your pick. Be careful not to overbend, as half-step bends require less pushing power. The last example is a half-step bend/release move. Again, you don't have to push the string very far to achieve a half-step bend.

Track 29
(0:27)

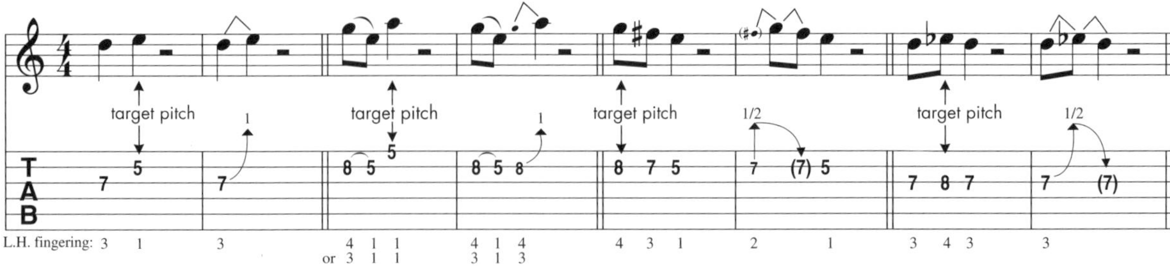

Bendy Licks

The following licks employ the practice bends from the previous example. First is a classic blues-rock lick that uses the bending maneuvers from the first two practice bends. The trickiest part of this lick is when you move from the G-string bend to the fifth fret of the B string. Make sure you reduce finger pressure before releasing the bend; otherwise the note will go flat. (Reducing finger pressure before releasing the bend effectively mutes the string, which is what you want.) The second lick is a variation on the first lick. Here, we have a grace-note bend on the G string. Again, make sure you reduce your finger pressure before releasing the bends. The last lick is a quirky, psychedelic-rock lick fashioned from the half-step bends in the previous practice example. Be careful; it's easy to go sharp (bend too far) on those half-step bends.

Track 29
(1:04)

Most string bending is delegated to the top three strings (G, B, and high E), but it's also common to bend the lower three (D, A, and low E). When bending the low E and A strings, you should bend down, toward the floor. Otherwise they'll slip right off the fretboard! The D string can be bent up or down, depending on the situation.

Vibrato

Vibrato is most often defined as a slight, steady fluctuation in pitch. It's a pretty sterile definition for a technique that can actually breathe life into any fretted note you play. A guitarist's vibrato technique can be as personal as a fingerprint. Indeed, some players can be recognized in a single note, just by the speed and intensity of their vibrato. Are you familiar with the opening moments of "Foxey Lady," by Jimi Hendrix? Enough said!

There are three ways to produce vibrato on the guitar: 1) the bend-and-release technique, in which a note is bent slightly then released in a repeated fashion; 2) the side-to-side finger motion technique (also called the classical technique), where the fretting finger rocks back and forth in a steady motion; and 3) the whammy-bar technique, which involves a special, "string-tension altering" mechanism found on certain electric guitars.

Bend-and-release Vibrato

Bend-and-release is by far the most common vibrato technique in the guitar world (except for classical guitar). You can think of this technique as a gentle form of string bending. Here's a step-by-step procedure:

- Place your third finger on the seventh fret of the G string.
- Position your hand as if you were going to perform a regular bend.
- Bend the string a tiny amount (less than a half step) and release it, in a steady motion, over and over.

The figure below shows the tab notation for normal vibrato (less than a half step) which involves the fret number on the designated string, with a wavy line written above the staff. This doesn't tell you the speed of the vibrato; that's up to the player to decide. In the second measure, the wavy line is exaggerated. This is the notation for wide vibrato. The technique for wide vibrato is the same as normal vibrato, except you need to bend the note about a half step or more. Try these vibrato techniques with each finger, on different frets, and on all strings. Which direction (up or down) you bend is up to you, but you need to bend up for notes on the high E and B strings, and down for notes on the low E and A strings (otherwise the strings slip off the fretboard).

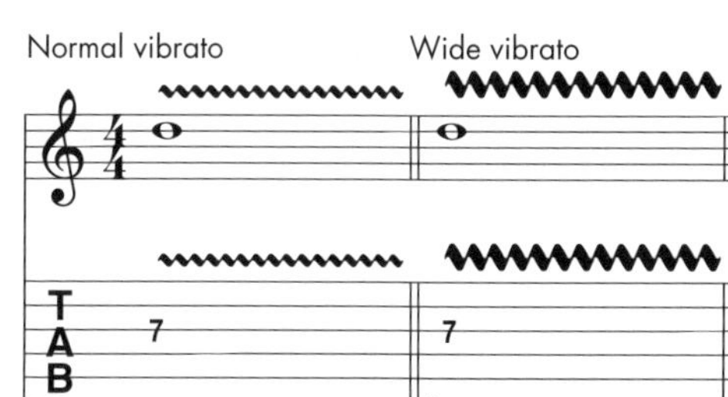

The speed, depth, and intensity of vibrato varies from guitarist to guitarist: Angus Young of AC/DC favors a fast, quivery vibrato; David Gilmour (Pink Floyd) often uses a wide, even vibrato; B.B. King is famous for his aggressive "butterfly" vibrato; and Carlos Santana is known for his delayed-vibrato technique, in which he sustains a long note without vibrato, then adds vibrato just before the note dies out.

Classical Vibrato

Classical vibrato (side-to-side motion) is much more subtle than the bend-and-release technique. Classical vibrato is achieved by pressing down firmly and rapidly rocking your finger back and forth along the length of a string, within the distance of one fret area. This motion increases and decreases the string tension, causing the note to go sharp and flat. This technique is used mostly on classical guitars with nylon strings.

Whammy-bar Vibrato

Track 30
(0:14)

A whammy bar is a special mechanism located at the bridge of some electric guitars. The unit has a bar attached to it, which can be moved up and down with the right hand, to raise and lower the pitch of all the strings. The whammy bar allows you to add vibrato to open strings and chords, as depicted in this example. (Tab notation for whammy-bar vibrato includes the instructions "w/ bar" written above the wavy line.)

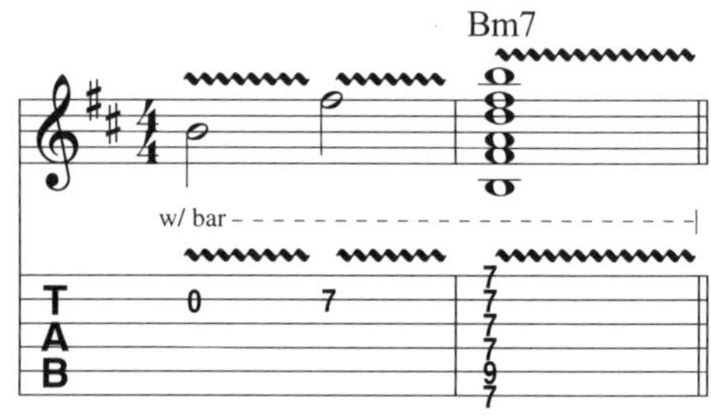

We're going to close this chapter with a quick lesson on the power of legato techniques. Following is a blues melody played without embellishments—every note is simply picked and held. The second example is the same melody but now it's fortified with all of the legato techniques covered in this chapter. Listen to the track to hear the example with no embellishments. Sounds rather dull, doesn't it? Now, listen to the example with the legato embellishments (hammer-ons, pull-offs, slides, bends, and vibrato). Hear the difference? The first example is simply a melody with rhythms. The second is an emotion-packed musical statement.

Track 30
(0:25)
(0:37)

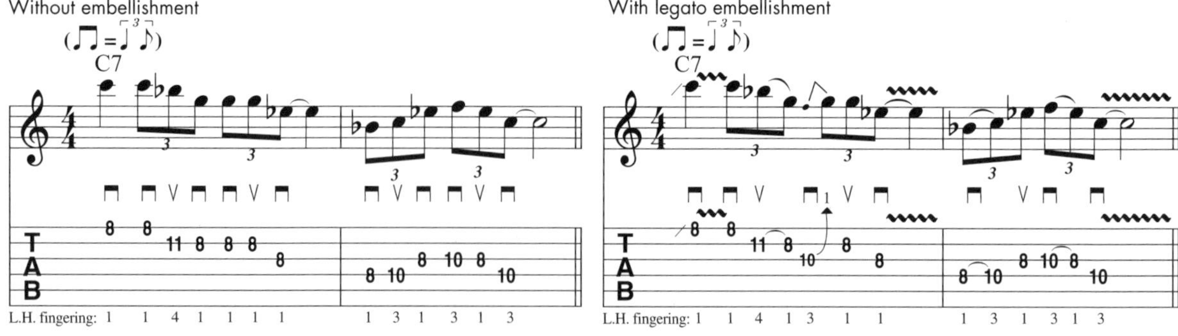

- When you play a hammer-on, your finger is like a tiny hammer slamming onto the fretboard.
- A pull-off is like a tiny finger pluck performed by the fretting hand.
- When bending with the third finger, allow your first and second fingers to help push the string.
- Bend-and-release is the most popular vibrato used by blues, rock, and country guitarists. Vibrato breathes life into sustained notes.

SECTION 4

Stylistic Playing

CHAPTER 14
ROCK

What's Ahead:

- Rock rhythm playing
- Chordal riffs
- Lead-guitar riffs
- Rock soloing

Congratulations! You've just earned your diploma from the College of Guitar Fundamentals. Now it's time to get your master's degree.

In this section, we'll explore the techniques unique to rock, blues, country, and folk. So whether your guitar hero is Jimmy Page, B.B. King, Chet Atkins, or Melissa Etheridge, in this versatile section you'll find the rhythm, soloing, and guitar tricks that they, and others like them, use and rely on.

Chuck Berry ("Johnny B. Goode") started it; Dick Dale ("Miserlou") splashed on some water; Eric Clapton ("Sunshine of Your Love") beefed up the tone; Jimi Hendrix ("Purple Haze") psyched it out; Eddie Van Halen ("Eruption") reinvented it; Kurt Cobain ("Smells Like Teen Spirit") stripped it back to a primal level; and now, in the new millennium, players such as Joe Satriani, Steve Vai, Eric Johnson, John Petrucci, and Derek Trucks, among many others, are sending it soaring to new heights. Of course, we're talking about rock-guitar playing.

ROCK RHYTHM GUITAR

Believe it or not, the major portion of rock-guitar playing involves rhythm techniques (chords and rhythms). While rock rhythm guitar employs its fair share of standard open-position chords (see Chapter 7), seventh chords (see Chapter 9), barre chords (see Chapter 10), and power chords (see Chapter 11), there's usually some kind of twist or special technique thrown into every rhythm part. Let's start our rock rhythm guitar journey with the man who started it all, Mr. Chuck Berry.

Chuck's Boogie

Elvis Presley may be the "King of Rock 'n' Roll," but Chuck Berry is the "King of Rock 'n' Roll Guitar." He was the genre's first bona-fide guitar hero, and many modern rock-guitar techniques point back to his early creations. Moreover, Berry established a template for rock rhythm (and rock lead) that is still applied to this day.

Inspired by the boogie-woogie piano patterns of blues music, Berry ("You Never Can Tell," "Roll Over Beethoven," and "Johnny B. Goode") developed a style of rhythm playing that remains the cornerstone of rock rhythm guitar. In its basic form, it consists of two *dyad voicings* (two-note chords), which are played in driving eighth-note patterns and palm-muted. The fundamental dyad is called a root-fifth chord, which is pictured in the first chord frame on the next page. This chord is called A5. The second dyad, which is generally used as a passing (or temporary) chord, is called a root-sixth chord, and is pictured to the right of the A5 chord. This chord, called A6, is difficult to play because it requires a wide stretch with the pinky. Practice changing back-and-forth between these two voicings. (When you play the A6, don't lift your third finger; instead, keep it planted on the seventh fret of the A string.) Move on to the other chords (D5, D6, E5, and E6) once you get A5 and A6 under your fingers. Then we'll put them all together in a classic rock 'n' roll progression.

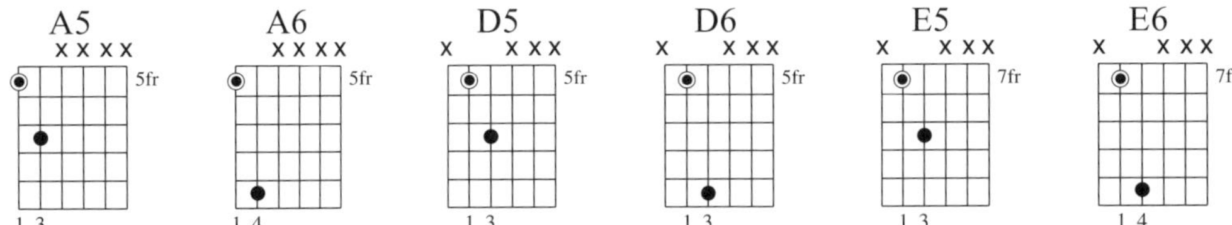

This next example is a typical early rock 'n' roll rhythm part that features all of the dyad voicings from the previous chord frames. Dig in with your pick, use all downstrokes, and don't forget to use palm muting.

audio tracks 31

A5 A6 A5 A6 A5 A6 A5 A6 A5 A6 A5 A6 A5

P.M. throughout

A6 A5 A6 A5 D5 D6 D5 D6 D5 D6 D5 D6 D5

A5 A6 A5 A6 A5 A6 A5 A6 A5 E5 E6 E5 E6 E5

D5 D6 D5 D6 D5 A5 A6 A5 A6 A5 A6 A5

The root-fifth/root-sixth pattern has been used in one form or another to power a thousand rock songs: "Rocky Mountain Way," by Joe Walsh; "Fun, Fun, Fun," by the Beach Boys (see Chapter 17); "Keep Your Hands to Yourself," by the Georgia Satellites; "Bang a Gong," by T. Rex; and "Come Together," by the Beatles; just to name a few. There are many variations (see "Blues," Chapter 15), but few are as memorable as Randy Bachman's opening riff in "Takin' Care of Business" (Bachman-Turner Overdrive).

Takin' Care of Business

Words and Music by
Randy Bachman

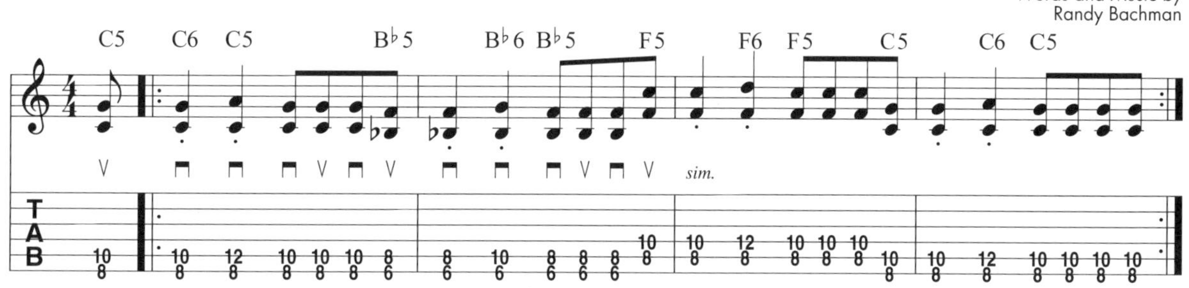

Two-note Rock

As with the "Chuck Berry" boogie pattern, much of rock rhythm guitar is based on the interplay of power chords with other dyads. This form of "two-note rock" makes for many memorable rhythm parts and riffs.

Inverted Power Chords

An *inverted power chord* is one in which the fifth is the bottom note and the root is on top; sort of like turning the chord upside down. Below are several examples of inverted power chords, along with suggested fingerings.

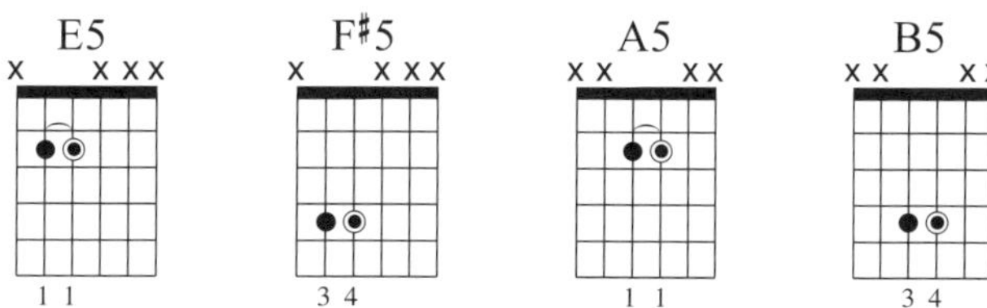

You'll hear the sound of inverted power chords in songs such as "Smoke on the Water," by Deep Purple (see Chapter 19); "Frankenstein," by the Edgar Winter Group; "Cat Scratch Fever," by Ted Nugent; "Sharp-Dressed Man," by ZZ Top; "Rock and Roll Hoochie Koo," by Rick Derringer; "You've Got Another Thing Comin'," by Judas Priest; "Shout at the Devil," by Mötley Crüe; "The Number of the Beast," by Iron Maiden; and "Shot in the Dark," by Ozzy Osbourne. Below is a hard-rocking rhythm pattern that uses the inverted power chords shown above. Listen to the track to hear how it sounds.

Track 31
(0:26)

Slash-chord Dyads

No, we're not talking chords that Slash (of Guns N' Roses fame) uses. *Slash-chord dyads* are two-note chords that most often come in the form of major-triad inversions in which the third of the chord is the lowest note, followed by the root (the fifth is omitted). The following figure shows several slash-chord dyads. Notice how they're notated: a letter name, followed by a forward slash, and another letter name; thus the term "slash chord." The letter on the left refers to the top note, while the number on the right indicates the bottom note. For example, E/G♯ indicates to play a G♯ in the bass (bottom of voicing) with an E note on top. Incidentally, this is the equivalent of an E major triad with the fifth (B) omitted.

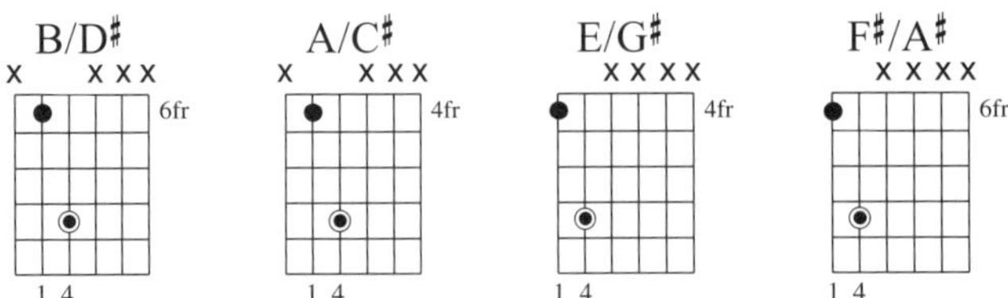

Slash-chord dyads usually appear in progressions that feature power chords. You'll hear these types of progressions in songs such as "Hold On Loosely," by .38 Special; "Anyway You Want It," by Journey; and "Cold Gin," by Kiss. The next example features power chords mixed with slash-chord dyads. Be sure to use right-hand palm muting throughout.

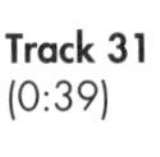

If you fret the power chords in the above example with the same first finger/fourth finger grip as the inverted dyads, it's much easier to make the changes.

Octave Octane

Octaves are unique types of dyads consisting of matching pitches (e.g., F and F) voiced an octave apart. Octaves have a big sound and are often used as alternatives to power chords. You'll hear octave riffs in songs such as "Third Stone From the Sun," by Jimi Hendrix; "Mountain Song," by Jane's Addiction; "My Own Worst Enemy," by Lit; "Somebody Told Me," by the Killers; and "25 or 6 to 4," by Chicago.

Octaves are most often voiced on the low E and D strings or the A and G strings, as depicted in the adjacent chord frames. Notice that, in both cases, there is a string that lies between the two fretted strings (the A string in the first voicing; D string in the second). In both voicings, this "inner" string should be muted with the fleshy underside of the first finger (the finger fretting the lowest string). Avoid striking any of the other strings with your pick.

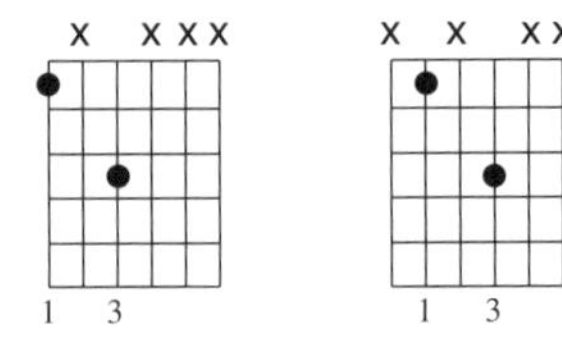

The following example features the main riff from "1979," by Smashing Pumpkins. Billy Corgan plays octave shapes over an open low E drone (a *drone* is a note that continues at the same pitch for an extended time), followed by single-note movement over a low A drone. Use all downstrokes, except on the sixteenth notes, and be sure to mute the D string with the underside of your first finger. You may find that the higher strings will ring out, even if you aren't striking them with your pick. This is called *sympathetic vibration*, and usually occurs at high volume levels. You can stop this from occurring by gently laying the lower section of your fretting-hand's first finger across the B and high E strings.

1979

Sixths Intervals

Sixth-interval dyads are two notes that are either eight or nine half steps apart, and are similar to octaves in that they're generally played on non-adjacent strings. Unlike octaves, though, sixths are usually voiced on the higher strings. The following figure includes some common grips, along with their suggested fingerings. In all cases, the "inner string" should be muted with the fleshy underside of your second finger. Sixth dyads are used in many forms of rock, from folk rock to hard rock. You'll hear them featured prominently in songs such as "Soul Man," by Sam and Dave; "Peace Train," by Cat Stevens; and "Wanted Dead or Alive," by Bon Jovi.

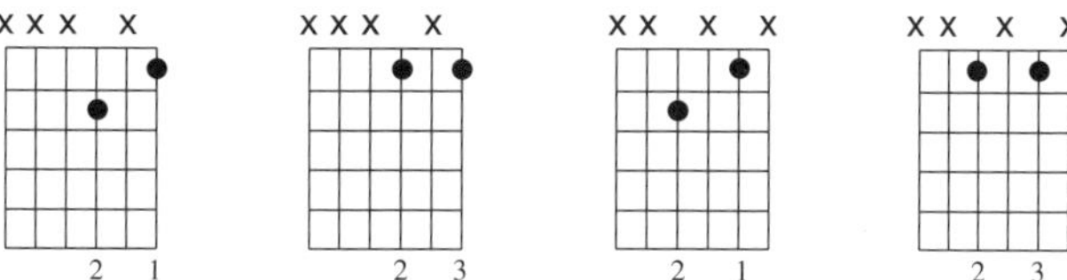

This next example, a funky alternative to simply playing G and C chords, is an example of sixths intervals in action. Remember to mute the B string with the underside of your second finger, which is fretting the G-string notes.

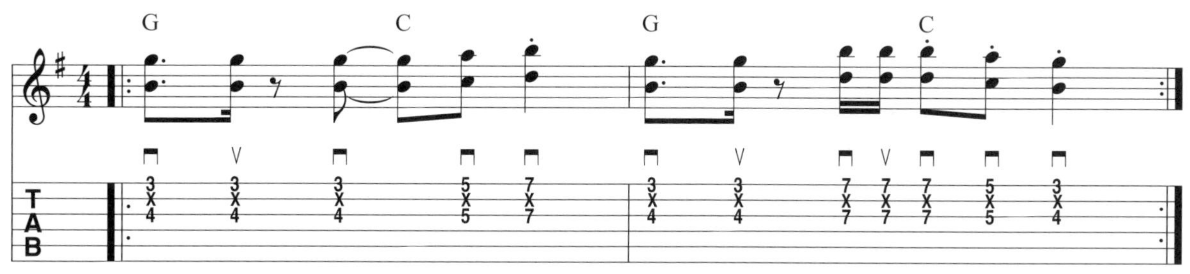

The Power of Thirds and Fourths

Another popular dyad approach to rock rhythm guitar involves the use of *thirds* (notes that are either three or four half steps apart) and *fourths* (notes that are five half steps apart). Most often voiced on the top strings, these dyads sparked such memorable riffs as "Brown Eyed Girl," by Van Morrison; "The Wind Cries Mary," by Jimi Hendrix; "Heaven," by Los Lonely Boys; "Pride (In the Name of Love)," by U2; and "Rhiannon," by Fleetwood Mac.

Here are the most common voicings of minor-third, major-third, and fourth-interval dyads, along with fingering suggestions.

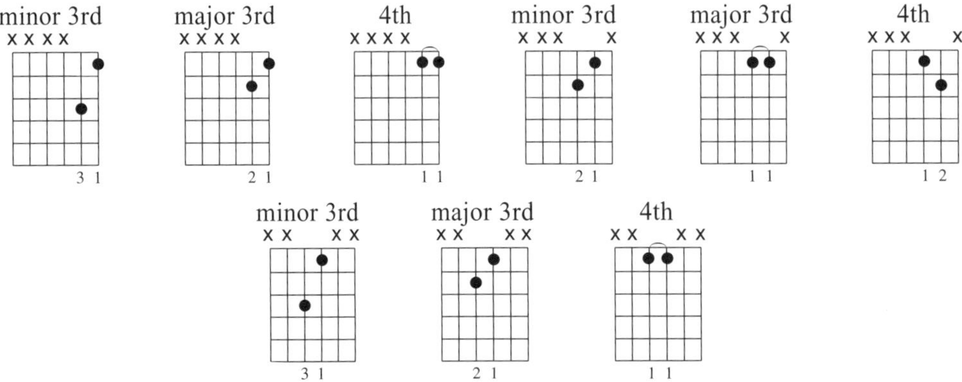

The first example below is a soul-rock example that combines major-third and minor-third intervals on the G and B strings. (Left-hand fingering suggestions are written under the tab staff.) The second figure is an R&B (rhythm & blues) lick that mixes major and minor thirds, as well as fourths. Curtis Mayfield, Cornell Dupree, and Jimi Hendrix are the reigning kings of this style of playing.

In the following example, you'll find the main riff from the song "Rhiannon," by Fleetwood Mac. Like the R&B example above, it combines thirds and fourths. Again, you'll find the left-hand fingering suggestions notated underneath the tab staff. This song was originally played fingerstyle. Try playing it with your fingers as well as a pick.

Rhiannon

Words and Music by
Stevie Nicks

Big, Fat Open Chords

Back in Chapter 11 you learned how to play two-note (root-fifth) power chords. Although two-note power chords rule in rock, it's also common to double-up on the root, and sometimes the fifth, to create fatter-sounding voicings. The figure below features a variety of open-position power chords and slash chords. These are the type of chords that Angus and Malcolm Young (AC/DC) use in songs such as "Back in Black" and "Highway to Hell." Since they involve open strings, they're very loud and powerful, and have a tendency to ring longer than their fretted companions. The D5/A is simply a D5 chord with the root doubled an octave up and an open A string on the bottom. The D/F♯ is the same chord, but with an F♯ (third of the chord) fretted on the low E string with the thumb. (Many rock and blues guitarists use their thumbs to fret notes on the low E string.) The G5 chord requires that you mute the A string with the fleshy underside of your second finger, which is fretting the low E string.

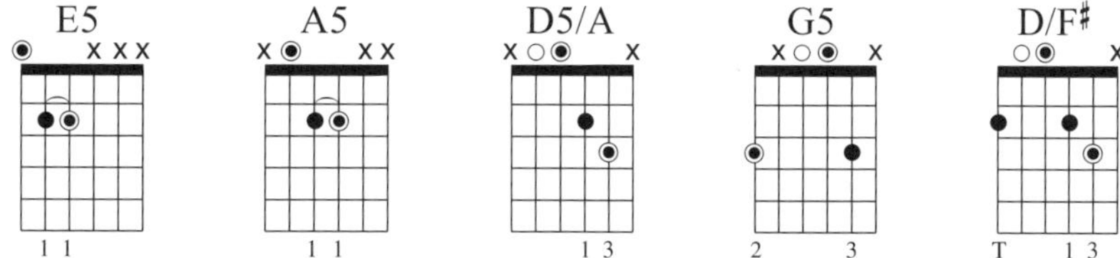

Here's a hard-rocking example of the above chords in action. The rhythms in this example require that you quickly mute the strings with the heel of your picking hand immediately after you strike the E5, A5, and D5/A chords.

Track 32
(0:28)

Barring the E5 and A5 voicings with your first finger is handy for changing chords rapidly, but it can be dangerous. If you press down too hard on the higher strings with your barring finger, you'll produce some unwanted tones. Simply use the upper joint of your first finger to bar the strings, gently overlapping the higher strings with the lower part of your finger.

Sus Chords and Add Chords

A *sus chord*, short for "suspended chord," is a major or minor triad whose third has been replaced with a suspended second or suspended fourth. What the heck does that mean? Well, a major chord is formed from the first, third, and fifth steps of its corresponding major scale. For example, to build an A major chord, you use the first, third, and fifth notes (A–C♯–E) of the A major scale (A–B–C♯–D–E–F♯–G♯). Get it? Good. Now, take the third (C♯) out of the chord, replace it with the second note of the scale (B), and you have an Asus2 chord (A–B–E), which is shown in the first frame below. Sus2 chords sound ambiguous and rather mysterious, and because they lack a third degree (the tone that distinguishes the basic quality of a chord), they can stand in for either major or minor chords. You'll hear sus2 chords in songs like "Message in a Bottle," by the Police; "Behind Blue Eyes," by the Who; "What Would You Say," by the Dave Matthews Band; "What I Am," by Edie Brickell and the New Bohemians; and "If," by Bread.

If you replace the third of an A chord (C♯) with the fourth note of the A major scale (D), you have an Asus4 chord (A–D–E), which is pictured in the third frame below. Sus4 chords usually resolve to their corresponding major or minor counterparts. For instance, in the main riff of "Pinball Wizard," by the Who, the Bsus4 chord resolves to a B chord. Below, you'll find a variety of sus2 and sus4 chords. The first row consists of open-position sus chords. The second row reflects their barre-chord counterparts.

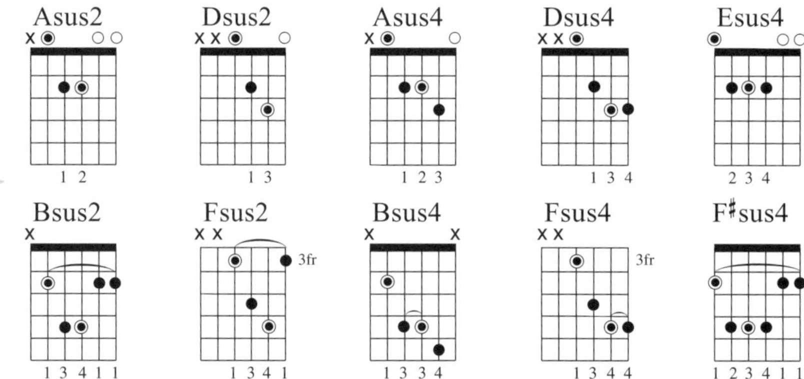

Here are two progressions designed to help you practice sus chords. The first example is a country-rock progression that uses open-position sus chords. The second example is a classic-rock rhythm that uses barre-chord versions of sus chords.

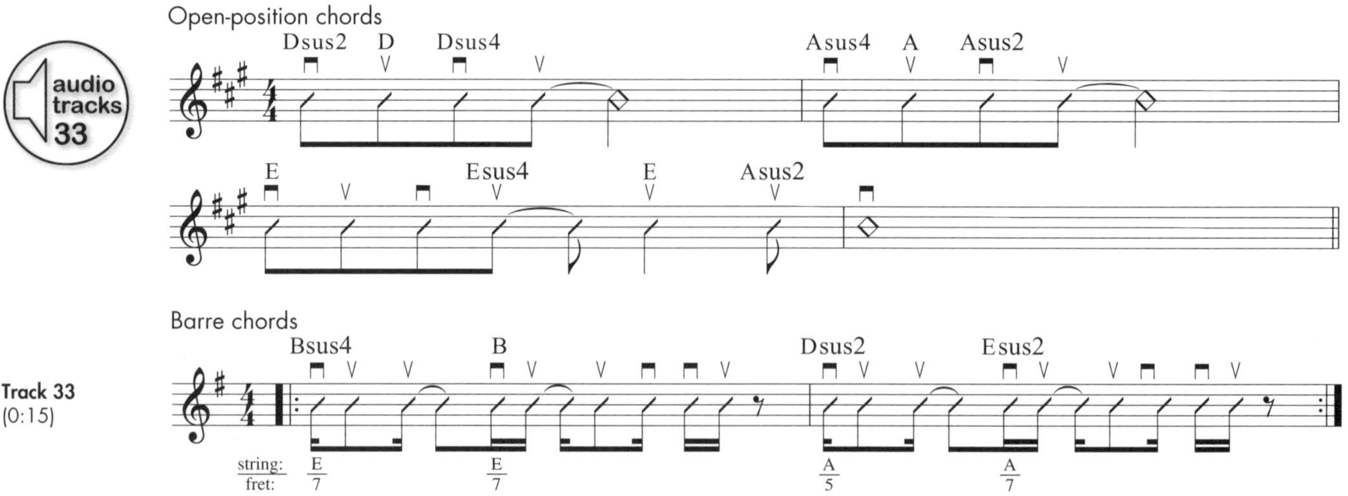

Add chords are chords with added tones. The most common add chords are major and minor chords with added seconds or ninths (an octave above a second), as in Em(add2), which is an Em chord with an added F♯ note; Cadd2, which is a C major chord with an added D note; Cadd9, which is a C chord with an added D note in the upper register; and Am(add9), which is an Am chord with an added B note in the upper register (all chords shown below). Other add chords include add4, as in Cadd4, which is a C chord with an added F note (see below), and, believe it or not, Dadd$^{2}_{4}$, which is a D chord with added E and G notes (see below). Another extremely common add chord is the E7♯9 chord, which is an E7 chord with an added G note (see below). Sometimes called the "Hendrix chord" (it's the central chord in "Purple Haze"), it's often used as an ending chord in hard-rock songs in the key of E minor.

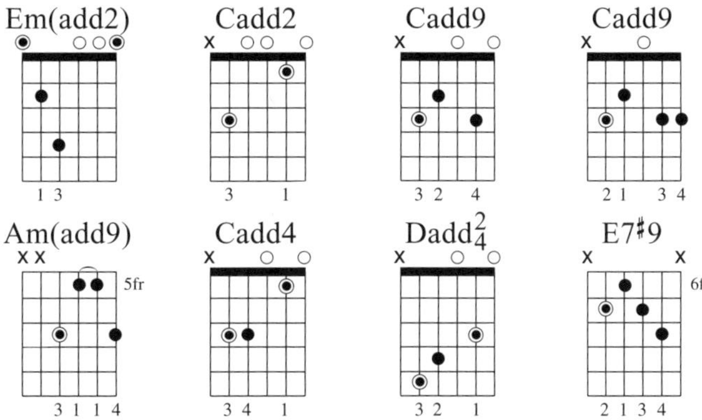

Here's a hard-rock ballad example using selected add chords. The chords are played arpeggio-style (one note at a time). Pick downward on all of strings until you get to the high E. Once there, pick upward on all of the strings until you get to the next chord change, and then repeat the process.

Track 33
(0:30)

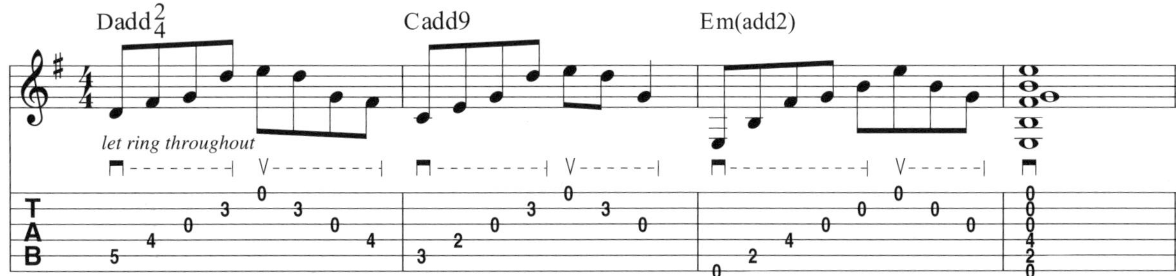

Sus2 chords don't contain a third degree. Add2 chords contain a minor or major third.

Triads and Pedal-tones

Triads are three-note chords and form the basis for many of rock's classic riffs. Usually voiced on either the top three strings or the D/G/B string set (see the following figure), these three-note chords are often mated with low E-, A-, or D-string pedal tones (repeatedly sounded note). You'll hear pedal-tone/triad riffs in songs such as "Crazy Train," by Ozzy Osbourne; "Substitute," by the Who; "Run Like Hell," by Pink Floyd; "The Song Remains the Same," by Led Zeppelin; "Running On Empty," by Jackson Browne; "All Right Now," by Free; "Running With the Devil," by Van Halen; "Brown Sugar," by the Rolling Stones; and "Rock and Roll All Nite," by Kiss; just to name a few.

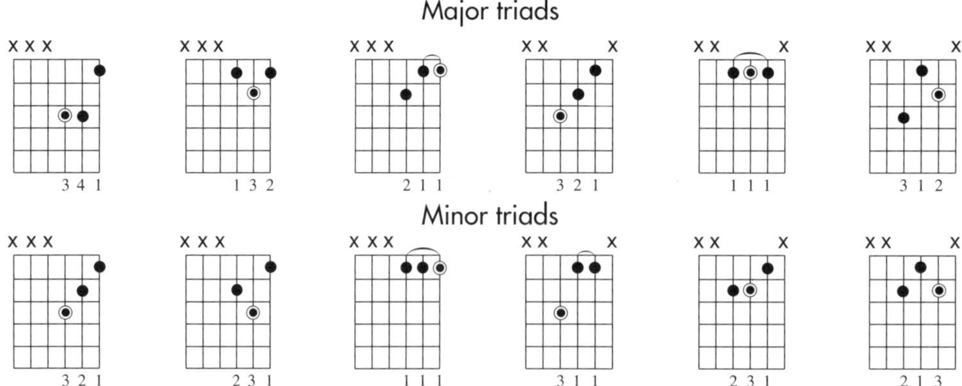

Here are a couple of riffs that incorporate some of the above triads. The first example places whole-note B♭, C, and Dm triads on the top three strings, and fortifies them with an open D–string pedal tone. Be sure to let the triads ring as you pedal the D string. The second example features A, E, and D triads on the D/G/B string set, all sandwiched between an open A–string pedal pattern.

The rhythms in this example are pretty tricky. You may want to listen to the audio example before attempting it.

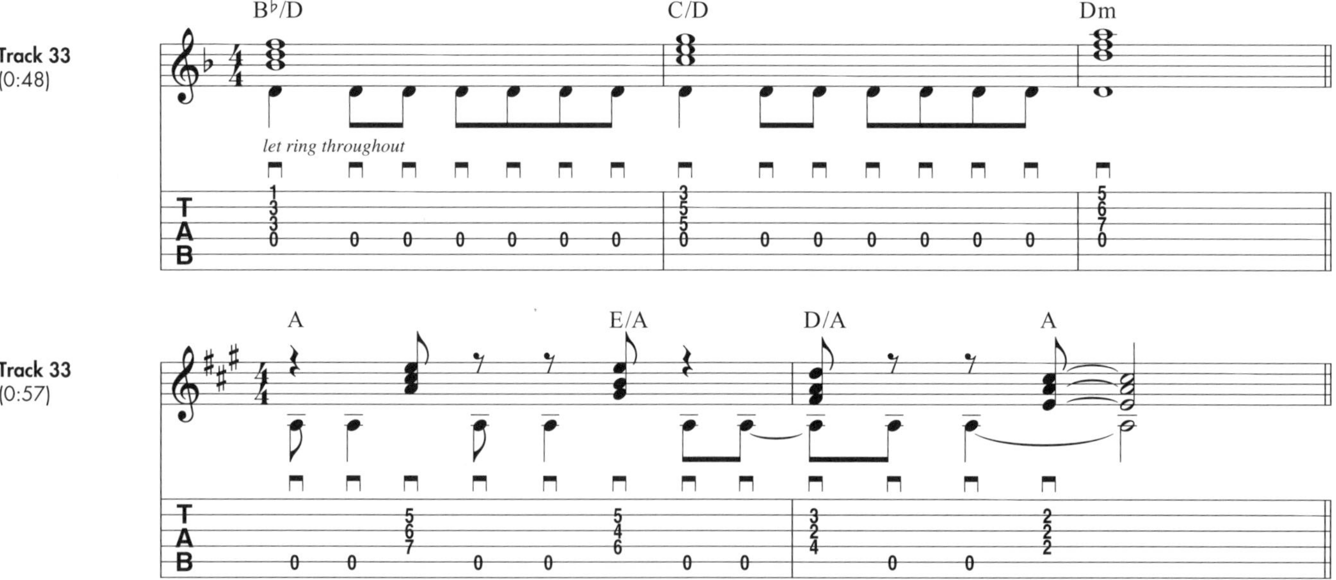

The next example features the main riff from "Substitute," by the Who. Performed by rock–rhythm guitar god Pete Townshend, it mixes D, A, and G triads with a Dsus2 chord, all played against an open D–string pedal tone.

Substitute

Words and Music by
Peter Townshend

D A/D G/D Dsus2 D

Who guitarist Pete Townshend is considered by many to be one of rock's most influential rhythm guitarists. Townshend's playing style in the mid-'60s laid the groundwork for many genres to come, such as hard rock, heavy metal, and punk.

Rock Guitar: A Brief Timeline

1955 • "Rock Around the Clock," arguably the first rock 'n' roll recording, hits the airwaves. Following a 12-bar blues format (see "Blues," Chapter 15), and featuring a hot guitar solo played by Danny Cedrone, it sets the template for rock 'n' roll records to follow.

• Chuck Berry makes his mark with "Maybelline."

1956 • Elvis Presley makes his television debut, singing and strumming an acoustic guitar (Scotty Moore backs him up on electric lead guitar). The music world is never the same.

1957 • Buddy Holly, one of a precious few guitar heroes to sport spectacles, debuts with "That'll Be the Day," the first of a long string of hits.

1958 • Rockabilly, a mixture of rock 'n' roll and country, is at its peak, spurned on by Eddie Cochran's smash hit "Summertime Blues."

1959 • The '50s end on a tragic note. A plane crash claims the lives of rock 'n' roll idols Buddy Holly and Ritchie Valens ("La Bamba").

1960 • "Walk Don't Run," an instrumental hit by the Ventures, serves as a precursor to surf music.

1961 • Roy Orbison rides the top of the charts with "Crying" and "Running Scared."

1962 • The Beach Boys debut with "Surfin' Safari," and the surf craze hits the ground running.

1963 • The Pacific Northwest becomes a hotbed (not for the final time) for a new phenomenon in rock—the garage band. Among them, the Kingsmen, the Wailers, Paul Revere and the Raiders, and the Sonics.

1964 • The Beatles appear three weekends in a row on the Ed Sullivan show. Beatlemania explodes worldwide, ushering in a new era in rock. Subsequently, guitar sales hit the stratosphere.

1965 • The British Invasion is in full swing with guitar bands such as the Rolling Stones, the Who, the Kinks, and the Yardbirds, the latter of which boasts three famous alumni: Eric Clapton, Jeff Beck, and Jimmy Page.

• The Byrds, featuring Roger McGuinn on 12-string guitar, invent folk rock with their hits "Mr. Tambourine Man" and "Turn! Turn! Turn!"

1966 • The Beatles retire from live performances to concentrate full time on studio recording.

• "The Monkees" television show ushers in teenybopper "bubblegum" rock.

1967 • Already a star in England, Jimi Hendrix makes his show-stopping debut at the Monterey Pop Festival, burning his guitar during the curtain-closer.

- Psychedelia is in full swing, spurred on by San Francisco bands Jefferson Airplane, the Grateful Dead, and Quicksilver Messenger Service.
- The Beatles release *Sgt. Pepper's Lonely Hearts Club Band,* the yardstick by which all future rock albums will be judged.

1968
- Blues rock is all the rage in Britain, fueled by guitar-gods Eric Clapton (Cream), Peter Green (Fleetwood Mac), and Jeff Beck.
- Stateside, heavy bands such as Steppenwolf, Blue Cheer, and the Amboy Dukes (featuring Ted Nugent) take up the gauntlet.

1969
- Led Zeppelin (featuring Jimmy Page) and Black Sabbath (featuring Tony Iommi) release their debut albums, signaling the birth of heavy metal.
- All looks hopeful with the huge success of Woodstock, but the '60s close on a hostile note with the infamous Rolling Stones concert at Altamont Raceway.

1970
- The decade opens on a sensitive note with James Taylor's moody ballad "Fire and Rain." His crafty acoustic lines influence a legion of acoustic-rockers to follow.
- The Beatles break up.

1971
- A new music coined "progressive rock" is quickly gaining momentum in England. Top bands include Yes, King Crimson, Jethro Tull, and ELP (Emerson, Lake and Palmer).

1972
- The Eagles release "Take It Easy," the first in a long line of country-rock hits.

1973
- Southern rock begins to take hold of the country with the release of Lynyrd Skynyrd's immortal classic "Free Bird."

1974
- The theatrical, glam-rock band KISS releases its self-titled debut album.

1975
- Queen releases its signature song, "Bohemian Rhapsody."

1976
- Rearing its "ugly little head," punk rock takes hold of the music scene. Among the most prominent bands are the Sex Pistols, the Ramones, and the Clash.

1977
- Disco sweeps across the globe. Doomsayers erroneously predict the death of rock music.

1978
- Eddie Van Halen stuns the guitar world with jaw-dropping performances on his band's debut release, *Van Halen.*

1979
- The decade closes with yet another rock offshoot—"new wave." Bands such as the Cars, the Police, and the Knack dominate the rock airwaves.

1980
- Wielding a Fender Telecaster and fronting her band, the Pretenders, Chrissie Hynde inspires a generation of young girls to compete in the male-dominated rock scene.

1981
- Randy Rhoads joins Ozzy Osbourne's band and heavy metal quickly resurges.

1982
- Heavy rotation on MTV, a fledgling music station, helps the Go-Go's become the first mega-successful all-girl rock group.
- Brian Setzer and his Stray Cats spark a rockabilly revival.

1983
- Stevie Ray Vaughan debuts with *Texas Flood* and single-handedly brings the blues back to rock.

1984 *Rising*
- Neo-classical rocker Yngwie Malmsteen forever raises the bar on rock-guitar gymnastics with his stunning debut, *Force.*

1985
- Bruce Springsteen takes on the world with his *Born in the U.S.A* tour.

1986
- Sammy Hagar replaces David Lee Roth in Van Halen, and the group releases *5150.*

1987
- Sunset Strip band Guns N' Roses, featuring top-hatted lead guitarist Slash, hit the ground running with the release of *Appetite for Destruction.*

1988
- Hair-metal bands like Bon Jovi, Def Leppard, Warrant, and Poison enjoy a very good year.

1989
- The decade closes on a syncopated note, with bands like the Red Hot Chili Peppers, Primus, Jane's Addiction, and Faith No More experimenting with funk-rock grooves.

1990
- Bonnie Raitt wins multiple Grammy Awards for her multi-platinum album *Nick of Time.*

1991
- Seattle band Nirvana officially kicks off the grunge era with its debut album, *Nevermind,* featuring the hit single "Smells Like Teen Spirit."

1992
- While grunge grinds on, Eric Clapton sits down for an "unplugged" version of "Layla" on MTV.

1993 • Melissa Etheridge scores big for women in rock with the release of *Yes I Am*, which has sold more than six million copies in the U.S. alone.

1994 • The death of Kurt Cobain signifies the end of the grunge era. Many point to nü metal as the next big thing.

• The Beatles reunite… well, almost. Paul, George, and Ringo add finishing touches to a posthumous John Lennon demo recording and title it "Free as a Bird."

1995 • Led Zeppelin is inducted into the Rock and Roll Hall of Fame.

1996 • The first G3 tour launches, featuring Steve Vai, Joe Satriani, and Eric Johnson.

1997 • Dave Matthews' popularity sparks renewed interest in steel-string acoustic guitars.

1998 • The seven-string guitar makes rock heavier and darker than ever. Bands such as Korn, Deftones, Limp Bizkit, Soulfly, Coal Chamber, and Sevendust flourish.

1999 • Against all odds, ex-Red Hot Chili Peppers guitarist John Frusciante kicks his addictions and returns to the band. The foursome's first effort, *Californication*, goes multi-platinum.

2000 • Carlos Santana collects an unprecedented eight Grammy Awards in recognition of his *Supernatural* album and its singles.

2001 • U2 enjoy a well-earned comeback with the chart-topping hit "Beautiful Day."

• *Billboard*'s top album of the year is the Beatles' *One*. It comes 31 years after the group split up.

2002 • Ex–Van Halen vocalists David Lee Roth and Sammy Hagar hit the road for a joint summer tour.

2003 • McFarlane toys mass produces a Jimi Hendrix action figure fashioned after his famous Woodstock performance.

2004 • Retro bands such as the Darkness and Jet spark renewed interest in classic rock.

2005 • Eric Clapton reunites with Cream for a string of concerts at the Royal Albert Hall in London.

2006 • Veteran rockers the Rolling Stones headline the Super Bowl halftime concert. Classic rock is alive and well.

ROCK LEAD GUITAR

No doubt about it—second only to the lead singer, the lead guitarist gets the lion's share of the glory in a rock band. The lead guitarist gets to play all of the main riffs and step up front to perform the blazing solos. If you've ever dreamed of being the lead guitarist in a rock 'n' roll band, then this is the section for you.

Single-string Riffs

One of the most fun things about lead guitar is that you get to play all the cool, single-string riffs. Single-string riffs differ from chordal riffs in that they are generally played one note at a time, and often run through major sections of a song. The opening guitar melody from "Down on the Corner," by Creedence Clearwater Revival (see below), is an example of a single-string riff that's very easy and fun to play. As you can see, all of the notes are on the lowest two strings (low E and A). Pick down on all of the notes for a uniform attack, and use the suggested fingerings written below the tab staff. If you look at the music notation (upper staff), you'll see that some of the noteheads have little dots under them. These are called *staccato dots* and tell you to play the notes short.

Down on the Corner

Words and Music by
John Fogerty

"Come As You Are," by Nirvana, is a cool-sounding riff that's also quite easy to play (see below). Like "Down on the Corner," it's also played on the lowest two strings. This riff sounds best when you let all of the notes ring together. Suggestions for picking directions are notated above the tab staff.

Come As You Are

Words and Music by
Kurt Cobain

"La Bamba," by Ritchie Valens, is a classic rock 'n' roll riff that's a bit more involved (see below). This riff is akin to arpeggiating (playing a chord one note at a time) C, F, and G chords.

La Bamba

By Ritchie Valens

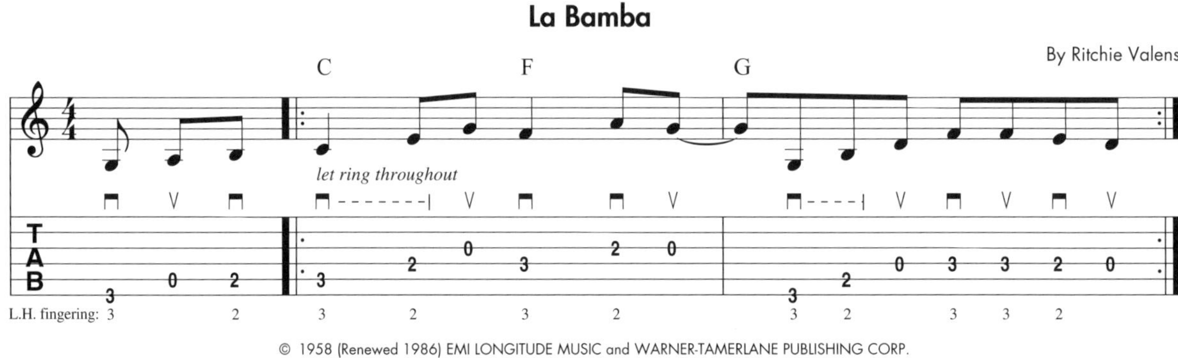

Here's a rock anthem if there ever was one. It's the opening riff of "Sweet Child O' Mine," by Guns N' Roses. Two different fingering suggestions are notated below the tab staff. One involves the fourth finger; the other does not. Use alternate picking (down-up-down-up) for this riff, which sounds best on the neck-pickup setting with a distorted tone.

Distortion is the fuzzy sound you get when you overload an amplifier's circuitry. Rock guitarists love this sound. Many modern amplifiers include distortion controls, sometimes called "overdrive" or "crunch." If your amplifier doesn't have an overdrive section, there's a wide-variety of foot-pedal distortion devices that, when activated, produce the fuzz effect.

Sweet Child O' Mine

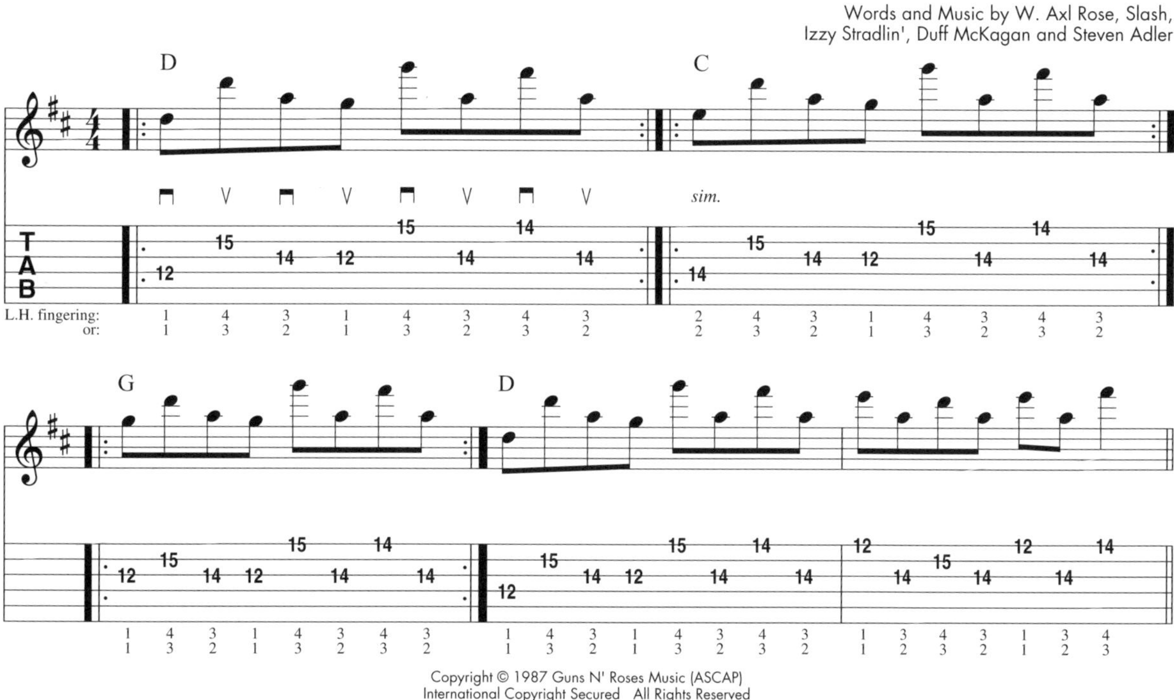

Rumor has it that it took an entire afternoon to successfully record the intro to "Sweet Child O' Mine," proving that even the best of us have a bad day.

The riff below is courtesy of one of the greatest "riff-meisters" in rock: Eddie Van Halen. It's the opening line of "Ain't Talkin' 'Bout Love," from Van Halen's debut album. Like "La Bamba," this riff is based on the arpeggiating of chords (Am, F, and G5). The hardest part about this riff is that the picking has to be very precise. Practice it slowly, using the picking directions notated above the tab staff, and then gradually get it up to speed. Dial in some distortion and don't forget to use right-hand palm muting, except for the last two notes.

Ain't Talkin' 'Bout Love

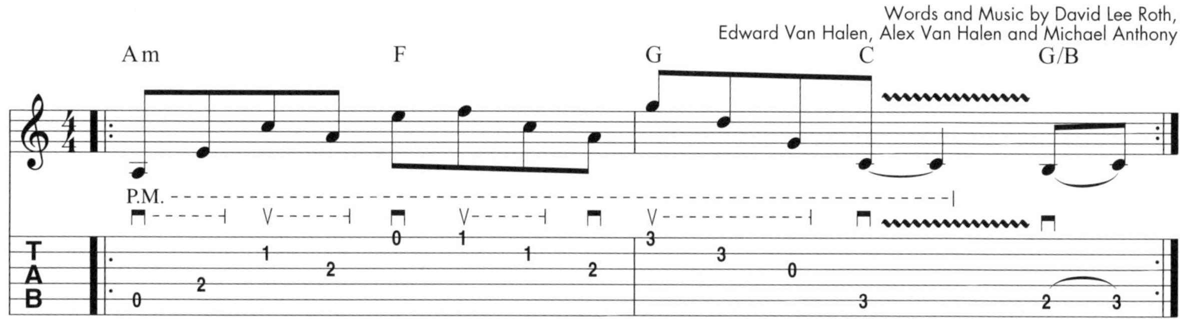

Rock Soloing

The chief job of the lead guitarist is to play the solos. A solo is when you play licks and melodies, either memorized or improvised, over the chord progression or riff that the band is playing. Licks are short melodies, which you string together to make solos—much like putting sentences together to form a paragraph. The sentences are the licks; the solo is the paragraph. This is the fun part: when you step up to the lip of the stage, hold your head high, and wow the audience with your amazing guitarmanship.

Pentatonic Soloing

A great many rock guitarists use minor- (1–♭3–4–5–♭7) and major- (1–2–3–5–6) pentatonic scales to build their solos. (If you feel you need a refresher course on pentatonics, visit Chapter 12.) It's the way each player puts the notes together that distinguishes them from other guitarists. For instance, guitarists like Chuck Berry and Keith Richards (of the Rolling Stones) often combine major- and minor-pentatonic melodies with two-string voicings called *double stops*, or *dyads*. For example, the two scale boxes shown here represent the upper portions of the C major-pentatonic and C minor-pentatonic scale patterns. Chuck and Keith use these combinations of notes to come up with licks like the one below. Use a partial bar (bar two strings with the same finger) to fret all of the dyads. The arrows pointing to the 1/4 fraction in the last bar indicate to bend both strings a quarter step.

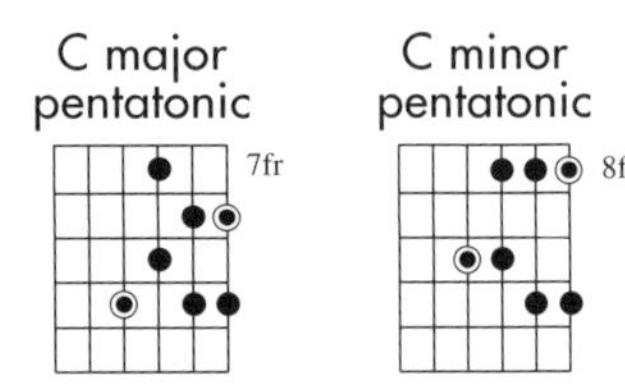

Blues-rock guitarists like Eric Clapton, David Gilmour (Pink Floyd), and Slash (Guns N' Roses) lean toward the minor-pentatonic scale boxes shown here. All of these players use a liberal amount of legato techniques (hammer-ons, pull-offs, and slides). They also use moderate-to-heavy distortion to help give body and sustain to their lines. The lick below is a four-bar example of blues-rock phrasing using the E minor-pentatonic (E–G–A–B–D) boxes, as well as an assortment of bends, pull-offs, hammer-ons, and vibrato. The symbol "8va" above the notation means "an octave higher," and tells you to play the notated music an octave higher than written. It doesn't affect the tab, it's just a way to make the notation easier to read by eliminating too many ledger lines.

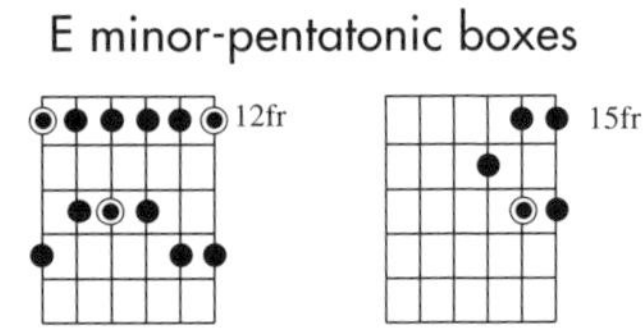

Track 34
(0:08)

Here's an excerpt from Eric Clapton's solo in "Crossroads," by Cream. Captured live at San Francisco's Fillmore West in 1968, it still stands as one of the best blues-rock solos ever recorded. In this section, Clapton is using the minor-pentatonic boxes shown in the previous figures, but in the key of A (A–C–D–E–G), in fifth and eighth positions. (He also throws in a passing major third [C♯] over the A7 chord. "Passing" means it's a temporary note that is not in the scale.)

Southern-rock and country-rock guitarists such as Gary Rossington (Lynyrd Skynyrd), Dickey Betts (Allman Brothers), and Bernie Leadon (Flying Burrito Brothers and the Eagles) favor the major-pentatonic scale (see below), often flavoring it with *fixed-string bends*. A fixed-string bend is an adjacent-string technique in which the higher string is fretted and held stationary, while the lower string is bent to a certain pitch. The lick below provides an example, using the D major-pentatonic (D–E–F♯–A–B) box. The example opens with a fixed-string bend involving the G and B strings. Bend the G-string note as you normally would, but at the same time hold your fourth finger down on the tenth fret of the B string. Try not to let it move as you perform the G-string bend.

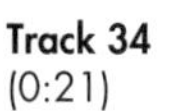

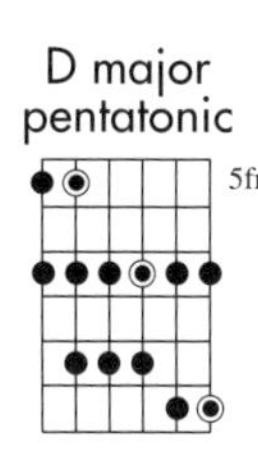

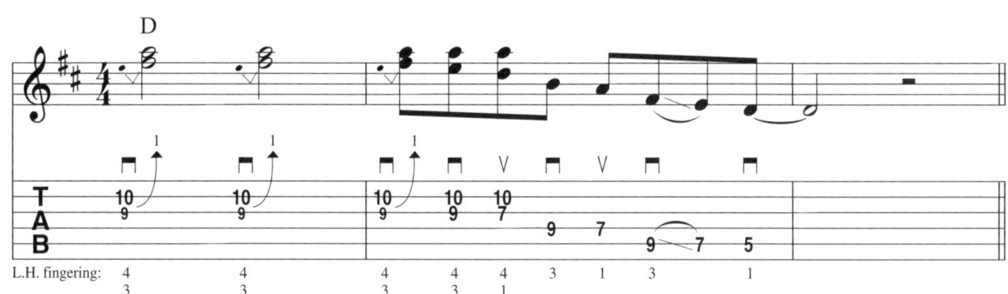

Hard-rock and heavy-metal guitarists like Jimmy Page (Led Zeppelin), Tony Iommi (Black Sabbath), and Jimi Hendrix often employ a different type of fixed-string bend called a *unison bend*, or *oblique bend*. A unison bend involves fretting the higher string normally, and bending the lower string to the same pitch. The example below contains four unison bends on the G/B string set. In each case, fret the B-string note with your first finger, and bend the G string up a whole step to match the pitch of the B-string note. Measure 3 involves an A minor-pentatonic *scale sequence*. A scale sequence is a specific pattern of notes (usually two to four) that is repeated at various starting points within the same scale. This sequence is called a "groups of 3" sequence, because it comes down the scale three notes at a time. Scale sequences are very common in hard rock and heavy metal.

Track 34
(0:30)

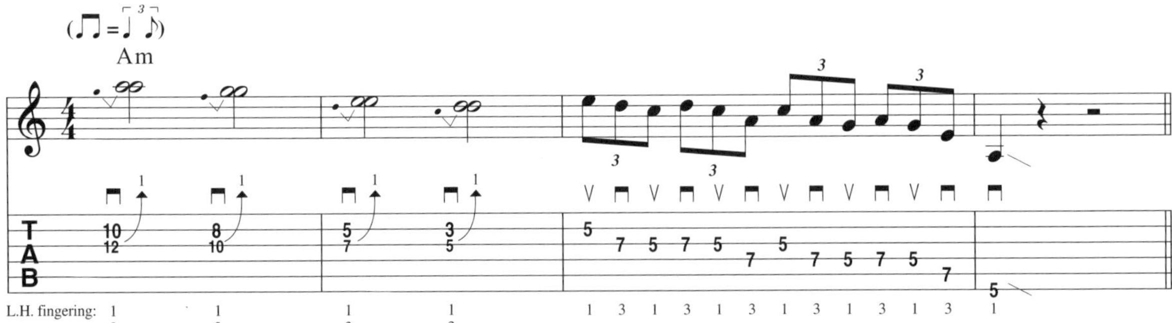

The next example is the top of Billy Gibbons' first solo in "La Grange," by ZZ Top. Drawn from the extended C minor-pentatonic box, it contains a scale sequence (measure 2), slides, pull-offs, and a bent note with vibrato. The latter is a difficult maneuver that requires you to bend the note a whole step, release it about a quarter step, and then bend it back to pitch again in a rapid, continuing motion.

La Grange

Minor Scale Rock

Many rock solos go beyond minor-pentatonic licks and into the realm of minor scales (1–2–♭3–4–5–♭6–♭7). Here's an early-rock example from the Ventures' "Walk Don't Run," which uses the open-position A minor scale (see "The Relative A Minor Scale," Chapter 8). Notice that the example includes single-note lines, as well as thirds and fourths dyads, similar to those from Fleetwood Mac's "Rhiannon" (see previous excerpt). The D♯ note in measure 5 is a passing tone, which means it's a note outside of the scale that is used briefly.

Walk Don't Run

By Johnny Smith

Mark Knopfler (Dire Straits) uses the D minor scale (D–E–F–G–A–B♭–C) for his solo and fills in "Sultans of Swing" (see below). Chock-full of legato techniques such as bends, slides, hammer-ons, and pull-offs, it's a veritable *tour de force* of rock-guitar nuances. The succession of downpicked notes that crosses the bar line between measures 3 and 4 is called an A major triad arpeggio. In soloing, an arpeggio is made up of three or more notes of a chord played individually. In this case, the notes are A, C♯, and E. Another arpeggio appears in measure 5. This is a D minor triad arpeggio, or the notes of a D minor chord (D, F, and A) played individually. Take your time putting it together, note by note. Your hard work will reward you in the long run. (The G♯ note at the end of measure 6 is a passing note.)

Sultans of Swing

Words and Music by Mark Knopfler

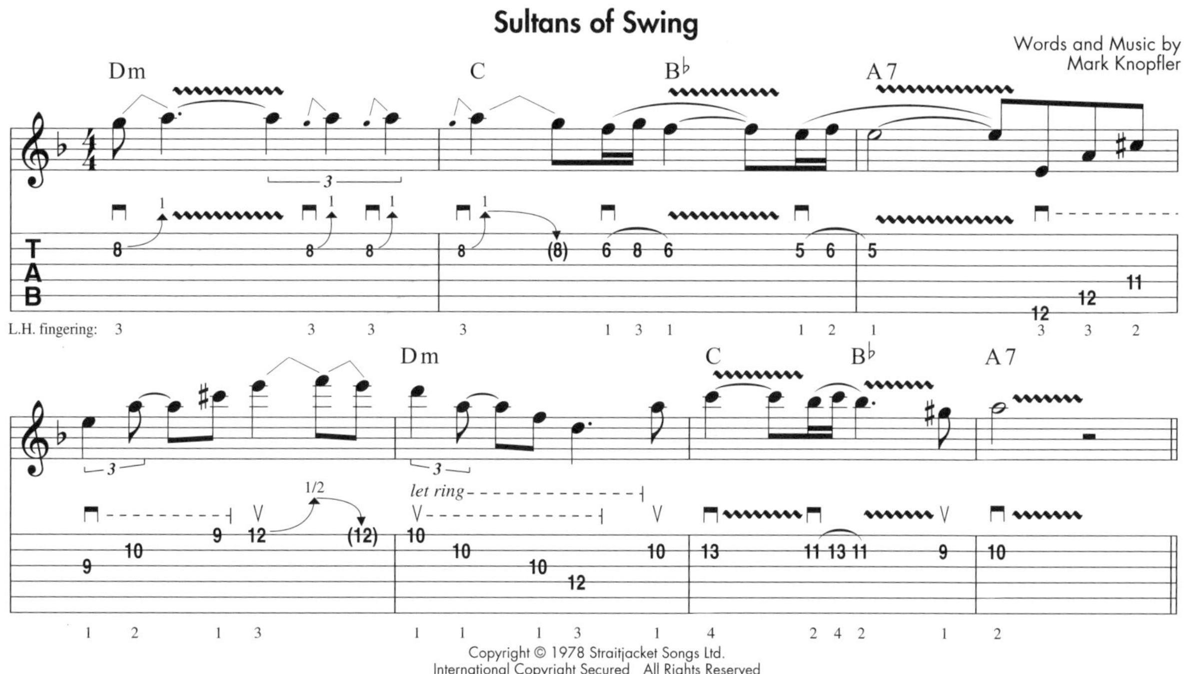

The next example is from Knopfler's arpeggiated outro solo in "Sultans of Swing." A shining moment in classic-rock history, it consists of three triad arpeggios: D minor (D–F–A), B♭ major (B♭–D–F), and C major (C–E–G). At first sight, the licks look pretty scary, but, in fact, they're comprised of consistent picking and pull-off patterns. Work it out very slowly and you'll be fine.

Sultans of Swing
(Outro Solo)

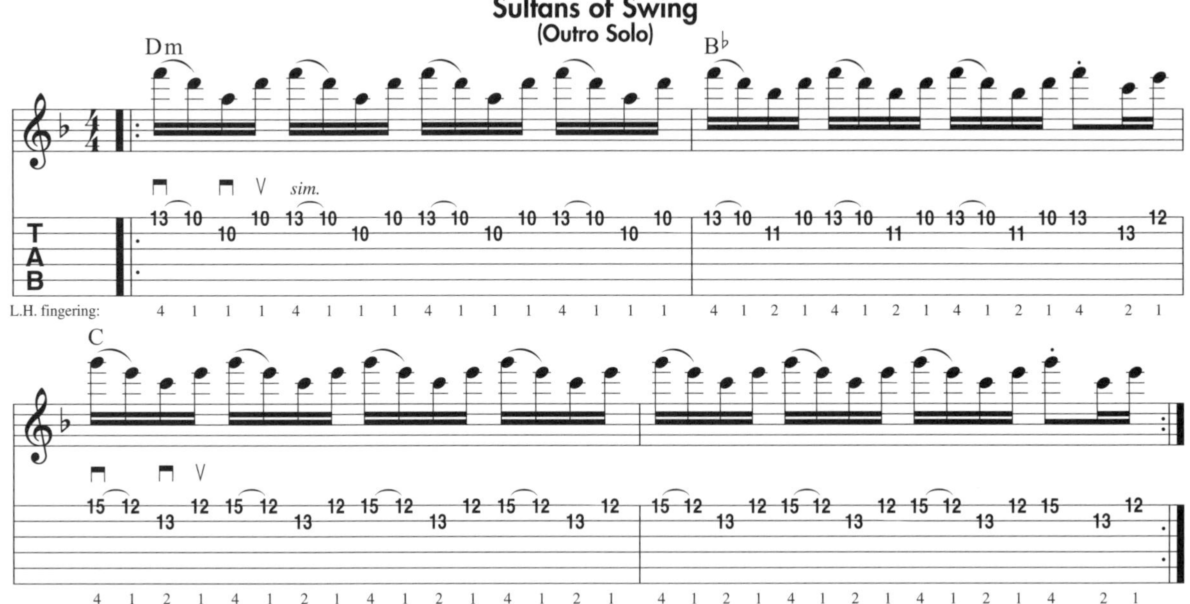

Rock Soloing in a Major Way

The major scale (1–2–3–4–5–6–7) is another scale source used by many rock guitarists. Such players include David Gilmour of Pink Floyd ("Time" and "Comfortably Numb"); Neal Schon of Journey ("Anyway You Want It"); Tom Scholz of Boston ("More Than a Feeling"); Joe Satriani ("Always With Me, Always With You"); and Eric Johnson ("Cliffs of Dover"). David Gilmour uses the A major scale (A–B–C♯–D–E–F♯–G♯) toward the end of his solo in "Time," by Pink Floyd. Instead of staying in box patterns, though, he slides up and down the G and B strings.

Time

Words and Music by Roger Waters,
Nicholas Mason, David Gilmour and Rick Wright

Building a Rock Solo

Most rock lead guitarists know how to improvise a solo. (To improvise means to create music instantly, without preparation.) To a beginner, this may seem like some magical ability, but, in reality, it's something that can be learned.

Many guitarists learn to improvise by first memorizing a lot of licks, and then practicing them in different keys. That way, when it comes time to improvise, they can put these licks together in different combinations, with variations in melody and rhythm. Eventually, with practice and experience, soloing becomes second nature; something they don't think about, they just do it. As an introduction to the creation process, let's build a solo using some of the licks from this chapter.

The solo below features a common Am–G–F rock progression. A minor pentatonic and the A minor scale work well for these chords. Let's start off by popping in a lick similar to the one in "La Grange"; except we have to transpose it from C to A. Also, the rhythms have been changed from eighth-note triplets to sixteenth notes. Measure 3 begins with a phrase from "Crossroads," but with slightly different note combinations. That group of sixteenths at the end of measure 4 is influenced by "Sultans of Swing," but transposed down five frets from D minor to A minor. Measure 5 carries on with more ideas from the same example, and the solo goes out with a fixed-string bend lick, similar to the one from earlier in the chapter. This last lick is transposed down two frets from the key of D major to the key of C major. C major is relative to A minor; therefore, it works in this situation.

- A major portion of rock guitar playing involves rhythm guitar techniques.
- Chuck Berry's rhythm and lead work is the foundation of rock 'n' roll guitar.
- A chordal riff involves two or more strings; a single-string riff is generally played one note at a time.
- Blues-rock and hard-rock guitarists favor the minor-pentatonic and natural-minor scales.
- Southern-rock and country-rock guitarists favor the major-pentatonic scale and fixed-string bends.
- Many rock lead guitarists use distortion to add body and sustain to their solos.

CHAPTER 15
BLUES

What's Ahead:

- 12-bar blues form
- Blues comping
- Blues soloing
- Intros and turnaround licks
- Other blues forms

The blues just may be the most universally understood style of music. Its simple structure provides common ground for players of any language or culture to get together and instantly make music. Besides all of that, it's relatively easy to play, and with a few basics, you'll be sounding like a blues cat in no time.

THE 12-BAR BLUES FORM

The vast majority of blues music is based on a system called the 12-bar blues. The *12-bar blues* is a 12-measure system consisting of a set of chords that keep repeating through the course of a tune. The most basic 12-bar blues form uses the I, IV, and V chords (Roman-numeral notation for one, four, and five) of the major scale, or the chords based on the first, fourth, and fifth steps of the major scale. In other words, a 12-bar blues in the key of C uses C, F, and G chords; in the key of A: A, D, and E chords; and so on. Most often, these chords are dominant seventh in quality. So a 12-bar blues in the key of A would use A7, D7, and E7 chords. Now you know about the 12-bar form and the chords that are used. Next you need to know where those chords go.

The following example illustrates a basic 12-bar blues in the key of A. Notice that the progression is divided into three sections of four bars each. In these three sections, the I, IV, and V chords have their designated slots. The first section introduces the I chord, which establishes the key; the middle section moves to the IV chord and then returns to the I chord; and the third, and most active section, begins with all three chords in descending succession (V–IV–I), and then ends on the V chord, which turns the progression back around to the beginning.

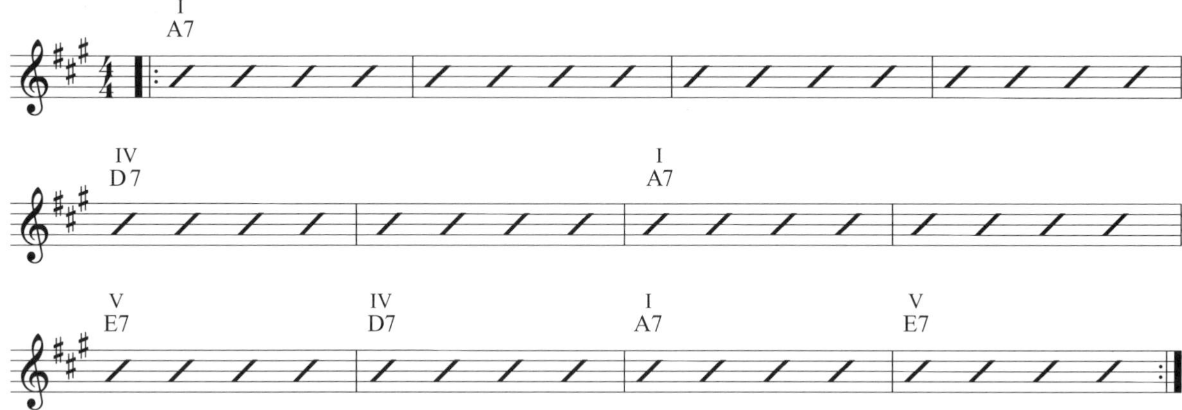

The next example is a common variation on the basic 12-bar form. If you look closely, there are only two differences, which occur in the second and last measures. In this example, the IV chord (D7) arrives "early" in the second measure, and then measure 3 goes back to the I chord. This situation is called a *quick change*, and is a very common occurrence in the blues. (When the first four bars stay on the I chord, it's called a *slow change*.)

The second variation occurs in the final bar, in which the V chord (E7) is delayed until the "and" of beat 2, and an F7 chord is placed on the downbeat of beat 2. This is called a *♭VI–V turnaround*, another common occurrence in the blues.

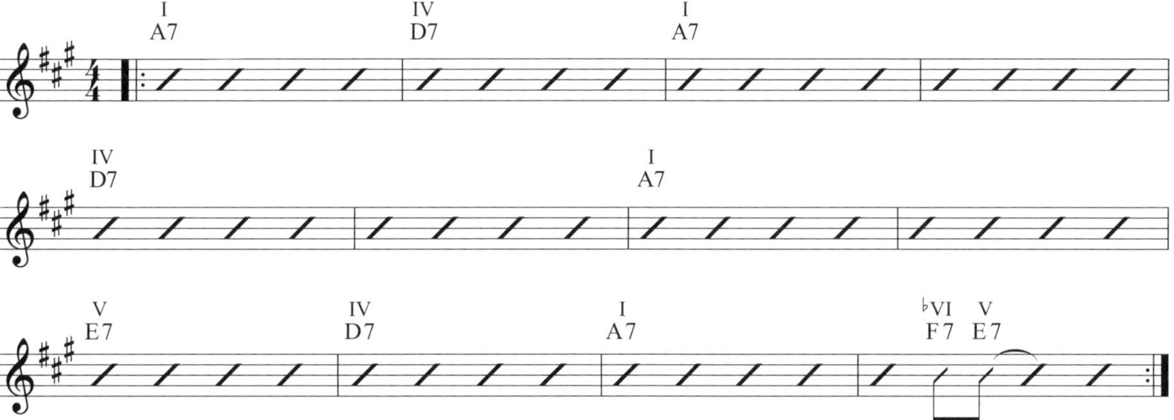

BLUES COMPING

Now that you know where the chords are placed in a 12-bar blues, let's move on to a few typical voicings and comping patterns. Incidentally, *comping* is music jargon for "accompany," or, in our case, playing rhythm guitar.

Boogie Patterns

Boogie patterns are the most widely used rhythm patterns in the blues. From basic to complex, they're all based on two-note power chords with roots on the low E or A strings (see "Power Chords," Chapter 11). The next example features a basic boogie pattern that hearkens all the way back to Robert Johnson ("Sweet Home Chicago"), the famous bluesman from the '30s. Played over the 12-bar, quick-change blues in A, it's based on A5, D5, and E5 voicings. You can use alternate strumming (down-up-down-up) or all downstrokes—whatever feels comfortable—but just remember to shuffle the eighth notes (see "The Shuffle Feel," Chapter 9). The final measure (second ending) features a typical ending in blues: ♭II–I (B♭7–A7). Above measure 12 is a line with the number "1" under it. This is called a *first ending*, and signifies to go back to the repeat sign, a double bar line with two dots at the beginning of the piece. From there, you play through to measure 11, and then skip to the *second ending*, which is the last bar. In a real-life situation, you would play the first 12 bars repeatedly, not just twice.

audio tracks 36

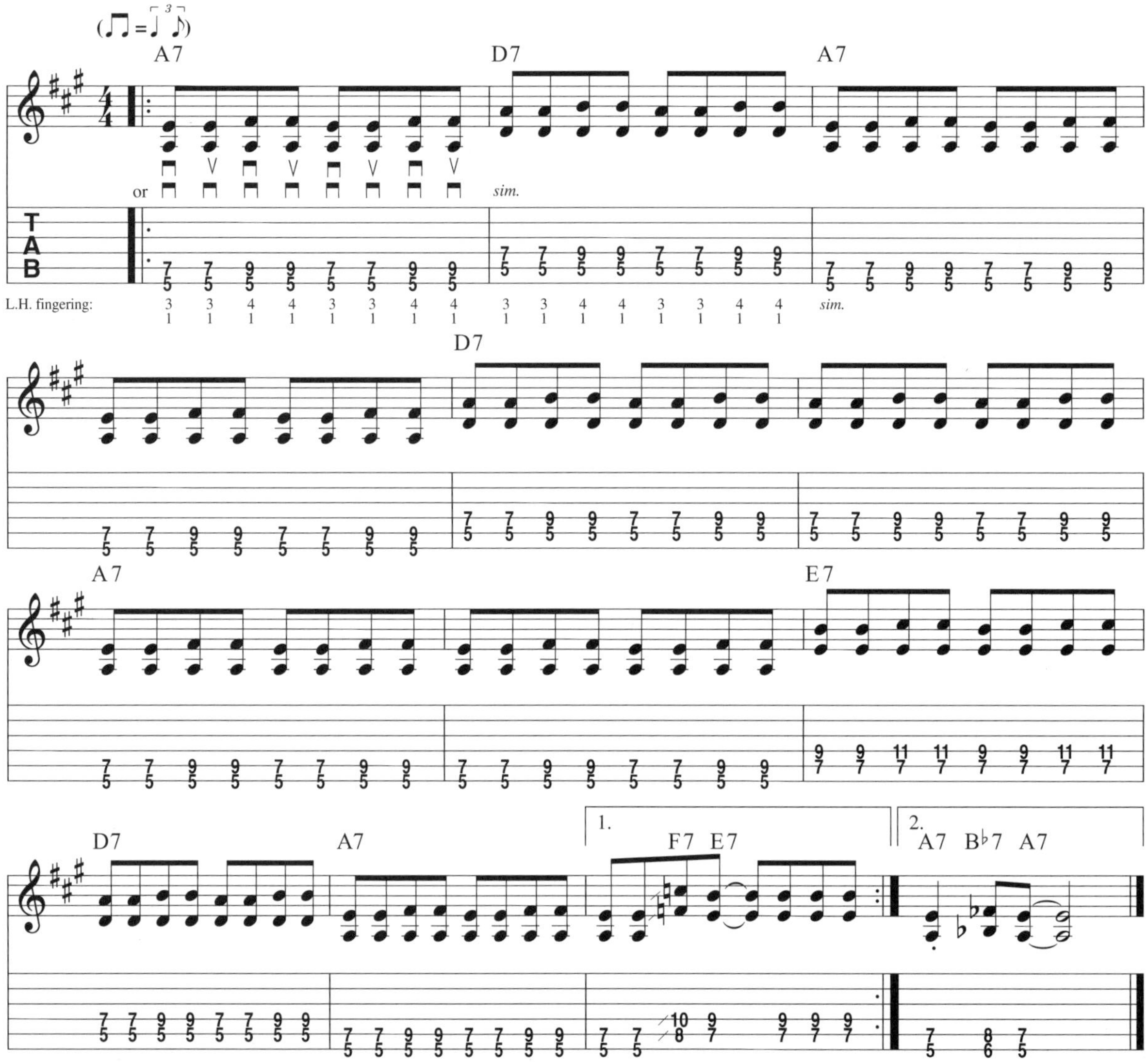

L.H. fingering:

sim.

A7 D7 A7

D7

A7 E7

D7 A7 1. F7 E7 2. A7 B♭7 A7

Initially, it's easy to get lost in the 12-bar form. What you want to do is divide the 12 measures into three four-bar sections. One good way to keep track of these sections is to sing (either out loud or in your head) the lyrics to a blues song. Most blues lyrics come in sets of three; the first two are generally the same, while the third serves as a wrap-up. "Sweet Home Chicago" provides a good example: first phrase: "Come on, baby, don't you wanna go?"; second phrase: "Come on, baby, don't you wanna go?"; third phrase: "Back to that same old place, sweet home Chicago." As these three phrases generally occur in the first two measures of each four-bar section, it makes it easier to keep your place.

Boogie patterns certainly give your pinky a workout, but if you can stand the stretch, try the alternate version on the next page. The patterns for all three of the chords (I, IV, and V) are notated here separately. Simply drop them into their designated slots in the slow-change or quick-change 12-bar blues progressions. (The little dots underneath the notes in the music staff are staccato dots and signify to cut the rhythms short. Do this by lifting your fingers just enough so that the strings come off the frets, but not so much that your fingers come off the strings.)

Track 36
(1:07)

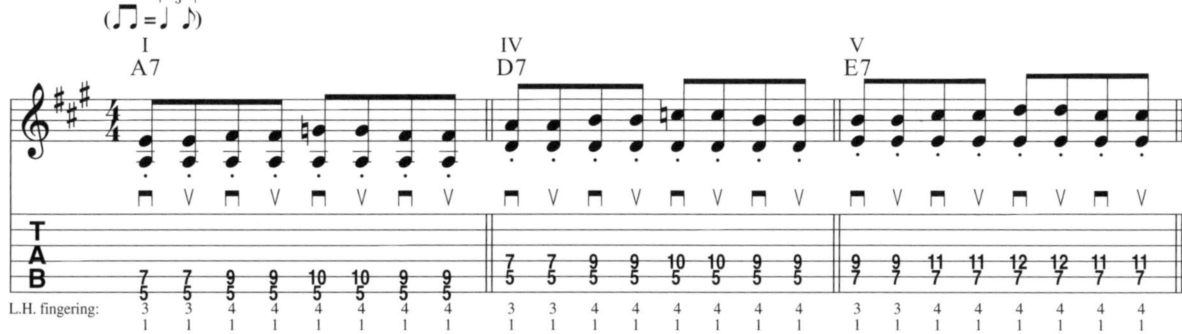

Can't get enough of those boogie patterns? Well, here's a challenging one that will impress any blues aficionado. Again, simply drop each pattern into the corresponding chord slot of either the slow-change or quick-change 12-bar blues.

Track 36
(1:26)

All of the above boogie patterns are movable to any key. Notice that the roots of the I, IV, and V chords form a little three-note box shape at the fifth fret (see below). If you move this box, along with the patterns, down two frets, you can play blues in the key of G. At the eighth fret you have blues in C; and at the 12th fret you can play boogie patterns in E (all shown below). Any key is possible. Practice this transposing method with the basic boogie pattern from earlier in the chapter until you get the hang of it. Then try the more complex versions.

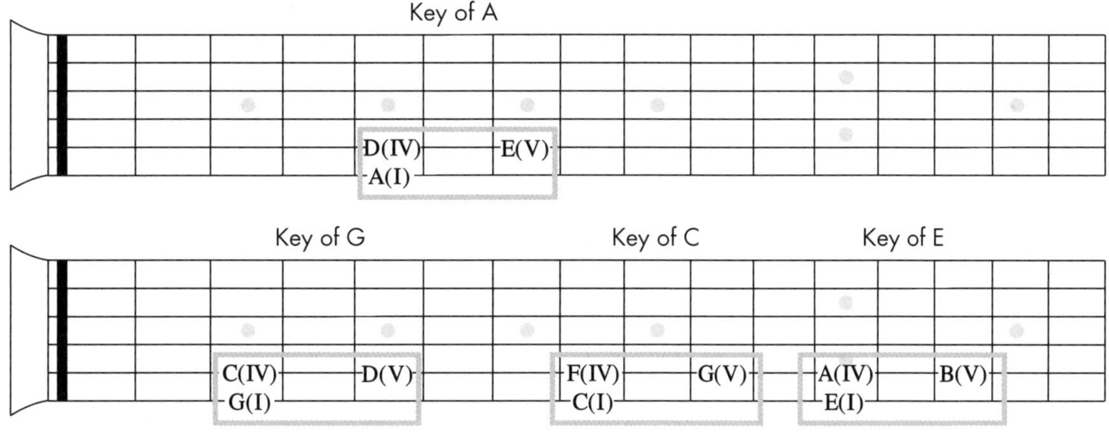

Chords

As we alluded to earlier, in blues music, dominant-seventh chords rule! The following chord frames provide some useful voicings (key of A) that can be plugged into the I–IV–V box pattern we discussed earlier. (The F7 chord is for the ♭VI–V turnaround.) Remember, these voicings are movable to any key. The example below sets these chords in motion in a two-bar rhythm pattern (repeats every two measures).

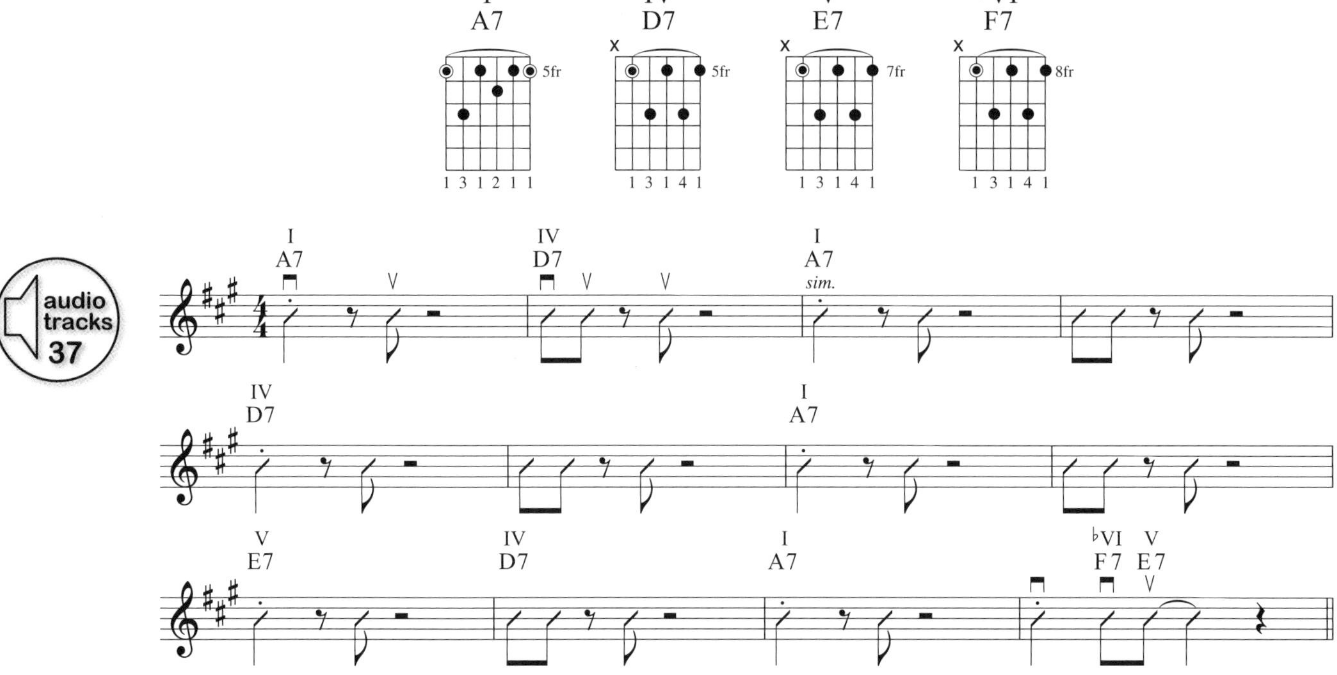

audio tracks 37

Want a hipper sound? Try using the D9, E9, and F9 chords below in place of the D7, E7, and F7 voicings.

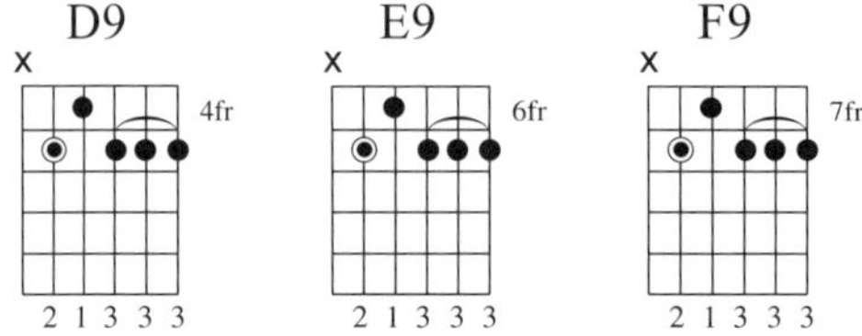

Ninth chords, or *dominant ninth chords*, are dominant-seventh chords with an added ninth. A ninth is the same as a second, only an octave higher.

The next figure features a variety of chords that sound great in a slow blues in the key of A. Practice getting them under your fingers, and then we'll put them to work in a 12-bar blues example.

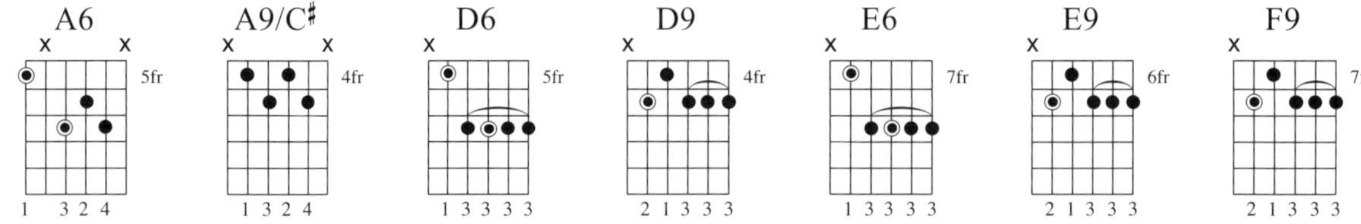

The entire example below is drawn from the chord voicings in the previous figure. Each measure begins with the root of the designated chord, played in two-eighth-note rhythms, followed by a sliding version of the upper part of the chord voicing. Check out *The Allman Brothers Live at Fillmore East* for a heaping helping of these types of sliding voicings.

Track 37
(0:30)

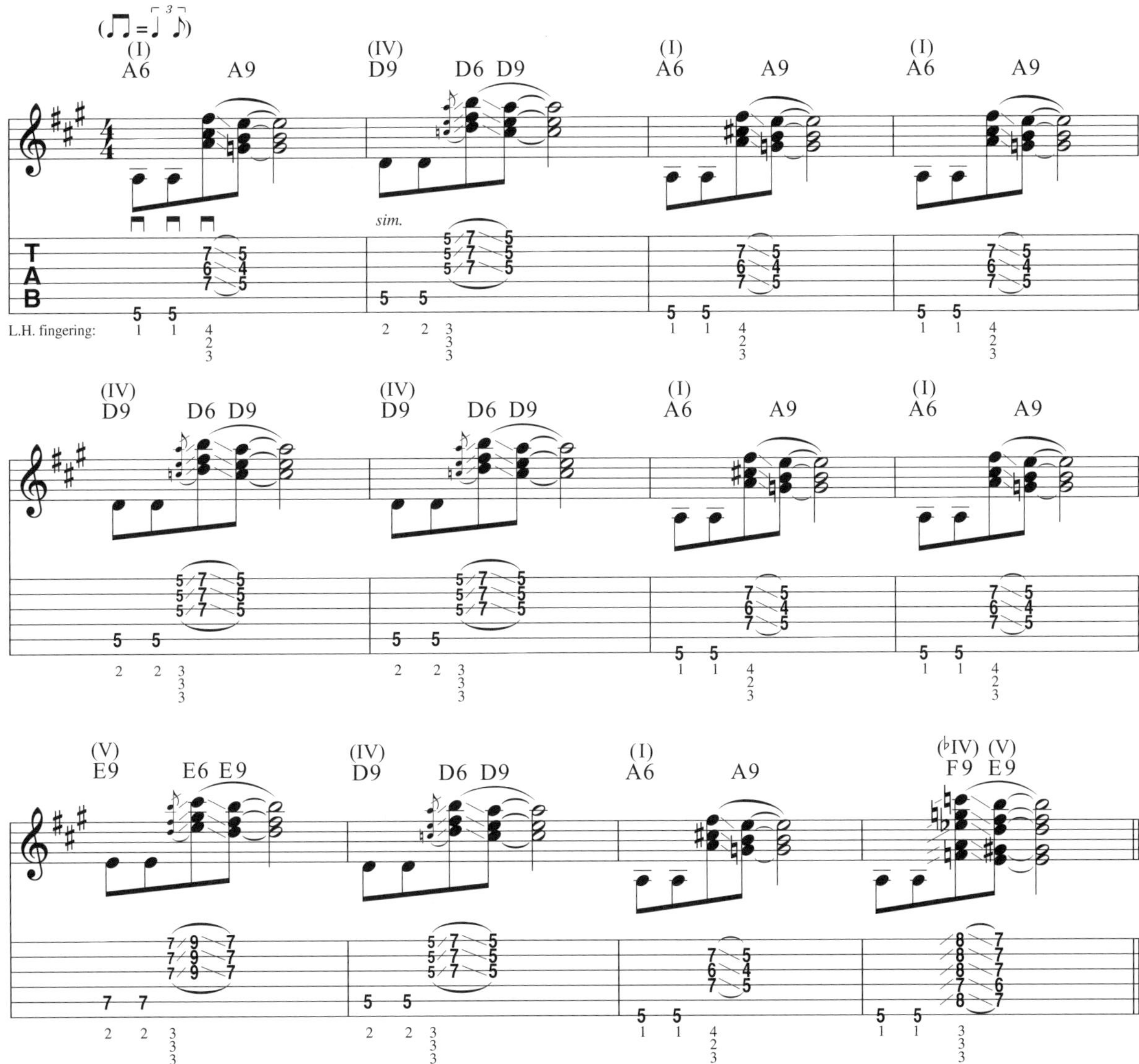

BLUES SOLOING

Now that you know how to comp like a real bluesman, or blueswoman, it's time to try your hand at some blues soloing.

The Blues Scale

The blues is so special, there's even a scale named after it: the blues scale. The *blues scale* is really just the notes of the minor-pentatonic scale (1–♭3–4–5–♭7) with one additional note. This additional note, called the flat fifth (♭5th), is tucked in between the fourth and fifth degrees. The blues scale has been used by just about every bluesman to come down the pike, from Robert Johnson, Muddy Waters, and Eric Clapton to Albert King and Stevie Ray Vaughan. In the next figure, you'll find the "king daddy" of all blues-scale boxes, shown in the key of A (A–C–D–E♭–E–G).

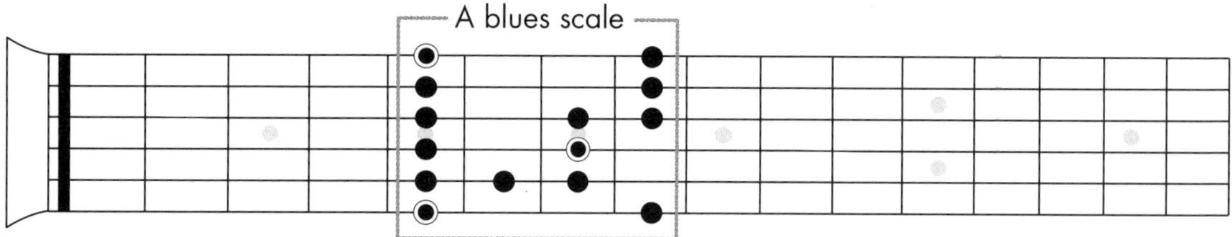

Just like the pentatonic box pattern we talked about in Chapter 12, this blues-scale box is also movable to any key. Lining up the box so that the root is on the third fret of the low E string gives you the G blues scale (G–B♭–C–D♭–D–F); at the eighth fret you get the C blues scale (C–E♭–F–G♭–G–B♭); at the 12th fret you have the E blues scale (E–G–A–B♭–B–D); and so on.

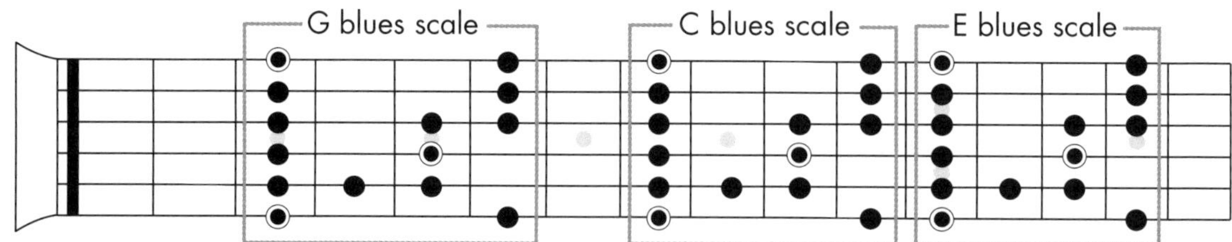

When used properly, the blues scale sounds great over all three main chords of the blues: I, IV, and V. The figure below offers some manageable licks designed for each situation. Have a friend strum the corresponding chord while you play the lick, or you can simply listen to the audio examples to hear how the lick compliments the chord.

Track 37
(1:14)

Little Blues Boxes

Many blues guitarists like to play in small pentatonic box patterns (both minor and major), bending to other notes that lie "outside the box." The adjacent figure contains a variety of these boxes, all in the key of A. The circled notes are the roots (A), while the notes in parentheses designate choice bending notes.

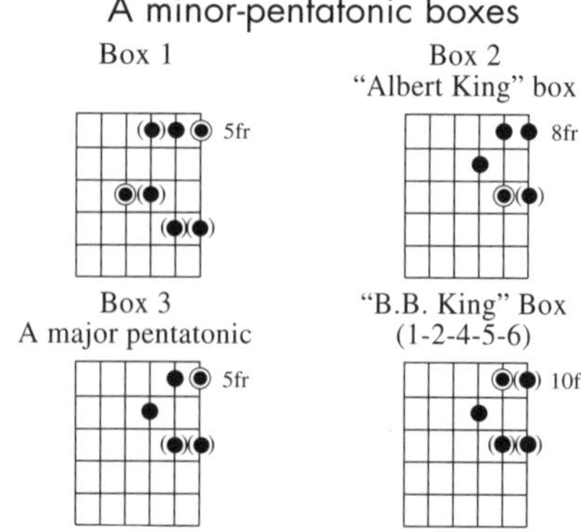

Playing a Blues Solo

Let's put the previous boxes to use in building a blues solo (see below). Again, our format is a quick-change 12-bar blues in A. The solo opens with pickup notes (introduction notes before measure 1) from the A minor-pentatonic box 1. From there, it segues to the "overlapping" A major-pentatonic box 3 for the IV chord (D7). Hear how the notes match the sound of the chord? In bar 3, it goes back to the A minor-pentatonic box 1 for a lick that includes a half-step and a quarter-step bend on the G string. The half-step bend hits the flatted fifth (E♭) of the A blues scale, and the quarter-step bend pushes the C note to the bluesy tonality between the minor and major thirds.

In measures 4–5, the solo zips up to the "Albert King" box (named after the Texas blues guitarist) for more A minor-pentatonic licks. The half-step bend on the high E string hits the flatted fifth of the blues scale. Next up is an extended section in the "B.B. King" box (named after the famous Memphis bluesman). Without bends, this is an ambiguous batch of notes, as it contains no minor or major third. The whole-step bend at the 12th fret of the B string produces the major third (C♯), while a half-step bend creates a minor third (C). In measure 9, be sure to let the notes ring together, and add some vibrato for a cool effect.

The solo returns to the Albert King box at the top of measure 10 for a lick that compliments the one in the previous measure, followed by a bending workout on the high E string. The solo comes full circle, ending with a lick in box 1 and a final A7 chord.

Intros and Turnaround Licks

Let's wrap up the blues soloing section with a look at intros and turnaround licks. The term *intro lick* is short for "introduction lick." Intro licks are important because they set up the song. Here's a popular intro lick that can be used to set up a slow blues in A. Simple but effective, it's an arpeggiated E+ chord (chord name for E augmented: E–G♯–B♯; notice the sharped fifth), followed by a chromatic line to the tonic of the key (A).

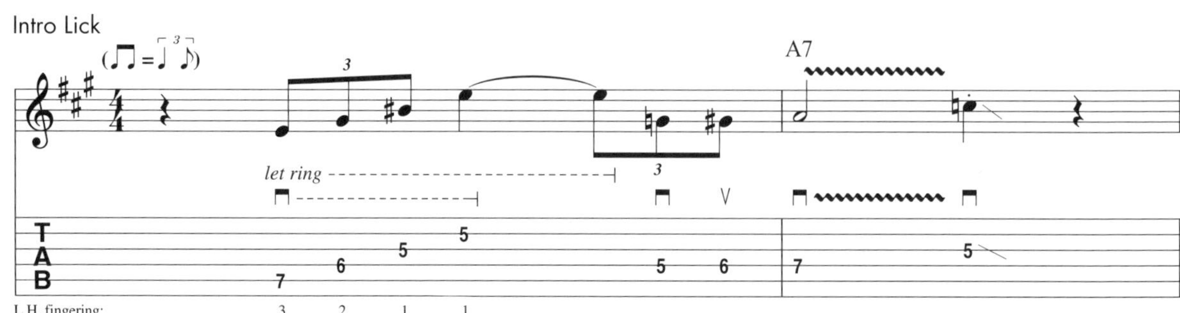

Stevie Ray Vaughan's blazing licks at the start of "Pride and Joy" comprise an intro that won't soon be forgotten. The example below features the four-bar introduction, plus the first two measures of the go-for-broke main riff. Carefully follow the right-hand fingerings, and use an aggressive, alternate-picking attack (down-up-down-up).

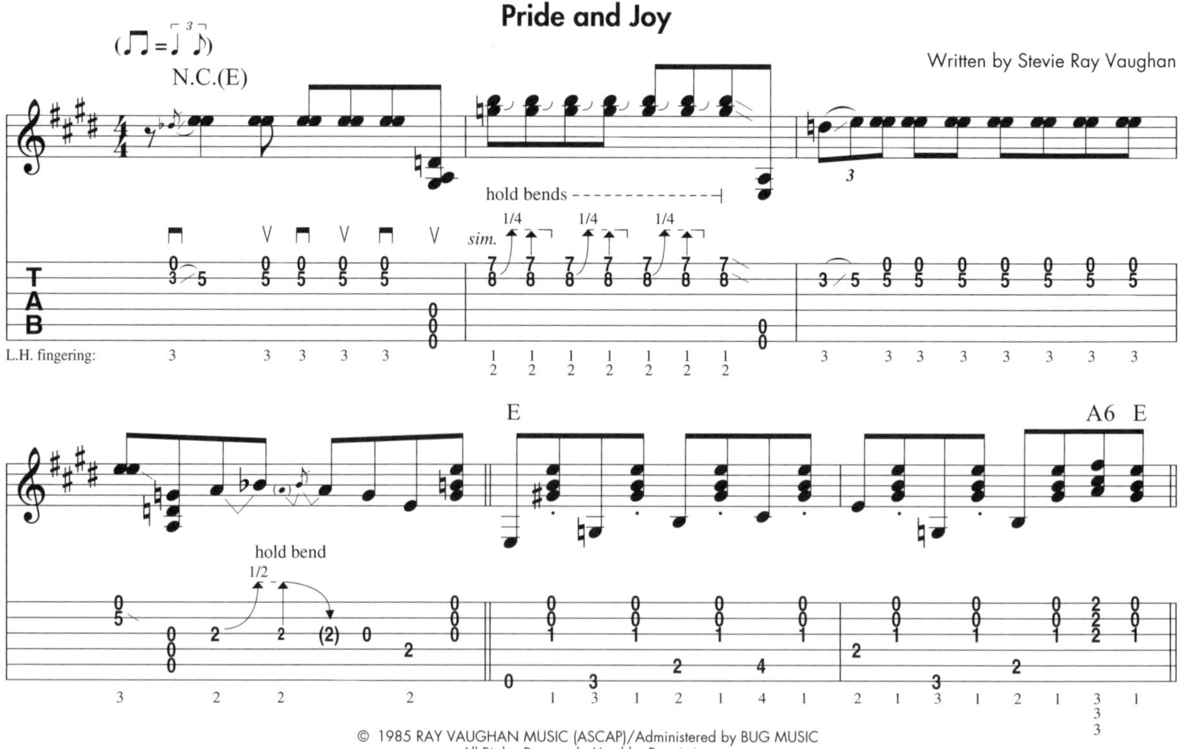

Turnaround licks are what guitarists play in the last two measures of a 12-bar blues. The following examples depict four tried-and-true turnaround licks, all fit for the last two measures of a 12-bar blues in A. The first lick is a single-note turnaround that's drawn from the A blues scale, with a couple of minor-to-major third (C to C♯) hammer-ons. The second lick is the ever-popular sixths-interval (see "Sixths Intervals," Chapter 14) turnaround heard in countless blues songs. Make sure you mute the B string on the downbeat of measure 2. The third lick is an age-old turnaround that features a chromatic line (half-step increments) on the D string with an A-note pedal tone (repeated note) on the high E string. You must be very precise with your picking on this one, as the D and high E strings are quite far apart. The last lick is an easy-going turnaround comprised of descending minor-third intervals played along the G and B strings.

Track 39
(0:13)

Track 39
(0:35)

OTHER BLUES PROGRESSIONS

Although the 12-bar, dominant-seventh progression is the most common form in the blues, there certainly are exceptions. Some 12-bar blues songs are played with a straight-eighth feel. "Mary Had a Little Lamb," by Buddy Guy, is a good example. Then there are some 12-bar blues that are in minor keys. For the most part, minor blues follows the same I–IV–V structure as dominant blues, but the chords are minor in quality (Am–Dm–Em). "Tin Pan Alley," by Stevie Ray Vaughan, is a good example of minor blues. Some minor blues, like "The Thrill Is Gone," by B.B. King (see Chapter 18), use a dominant V chord (F♯7 in the key of B minor), and, sometimes, a ♭VImaj7 (Gmaj7 in the key of B minor).

Another common form in blues is the eight-bar blues. Also based on I, IV, and V changes, eight-bar blues often involves rapid chord changes. Here's an example of a typical eight-bar blues in the key of A.

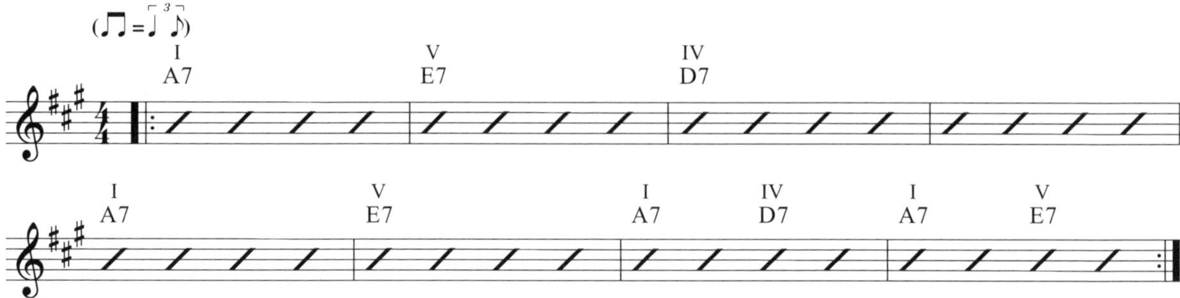

Blues Guitar: A Brief Timeline

Late 1800s

- Blues guitar is born on the back porches and work fields of the post–Civil War Mississippi Delta. In these rural areas, a singer would engage in call-and-response with his guitar. He would sing a line, and the guitar would answer.
- Memphis, Tennessee, eventually becomes the hotbed for blues artists.

Early 1900s

- The blues is first popularized through the publication of "Memphis Blues" and "St. Louis Blues," composed by W.C. Handy. Consequently, blues has a profound influence on jazz, a fledgling music form.

1940–1950

- Many blues musicians migrate to Chicago and Detroit. Players such as Muddy Waters, Elmore James, John Lee Hooker, and Howlin' Wolf help to develop electric blues. T-Bone Walker (Texas) combines jazz-influenced lines with the blues.

1950s

- B.B. King helps define the modern concept of blues lead guitar.

1960s

- Influenced by the roots of electric blues, bands such as John Mayall's Bluesbreakers, the Yardbirds, the Rolling Stones, Cream, Paul Butterfield Blues Band, Fleetwood Mac, and Canned Heat bring the blues to young white audiences. Blues guitarists like Albert King, Freddie King, John Lee Hooker, Buddy Guy, and B.B. King share the bills with popular rock bands of the day.

- The 12-bar blues shuffle is the most common progression in blues.
- Dominant sevenths and dominant ninths are the most popular chords in the blues.
- The blues scale is the minor-pentatonic scale with an added flatted fifth.
- Turnaround licks are played in the last two measures of a 12-bar blues.
- In minor-blues progressions, the I and IV chords are minor; the V chord is sometimes minor and sometimes dominant in quality.

CHAPTER 16
FOLK/COUNTRY

What's Ahead:

- Pick/strum patterns
- Carter strumming
- Fingerstyle
- Travis picking
- Using a capo
- Hot country licks

Since the first cowboy strummed a guitar by the campfire on the lone prairie (circa 1800s), folk music and country music have gone hand-in-hand. Many strumming and picking techniques are just as at home in Woodie Guthrie and Bob Dylan songs ("This Land Is Your Land" and "Blowin' in the Wind," respectively) as they are in Hank Williams and Alan Jackson songs ("Jambalaya" and "Chattahoochee," respectively). That's why we're combining them in this acoustic-oriented chapter. So grab your guit-box and let's get started. Keep your electric handy, though; we'll wrap things up with some hot country licks toward the end.

FOLK AND COUNTRY STRUMMING

Alternating-bass Rhythms

The example below is the standard "boom chick" rhythm used in both country and folk tunes. This style is based on an alternating bass line in which the root and the fifth of the chord are played on beats 1 and 3, while the top part of the chord voicing is played on beats 2 and 4. The bass note provides the "boom;" the chord provides the "chick." Use downstrokes throughout, and let the notes and chords ring together as much as possible.

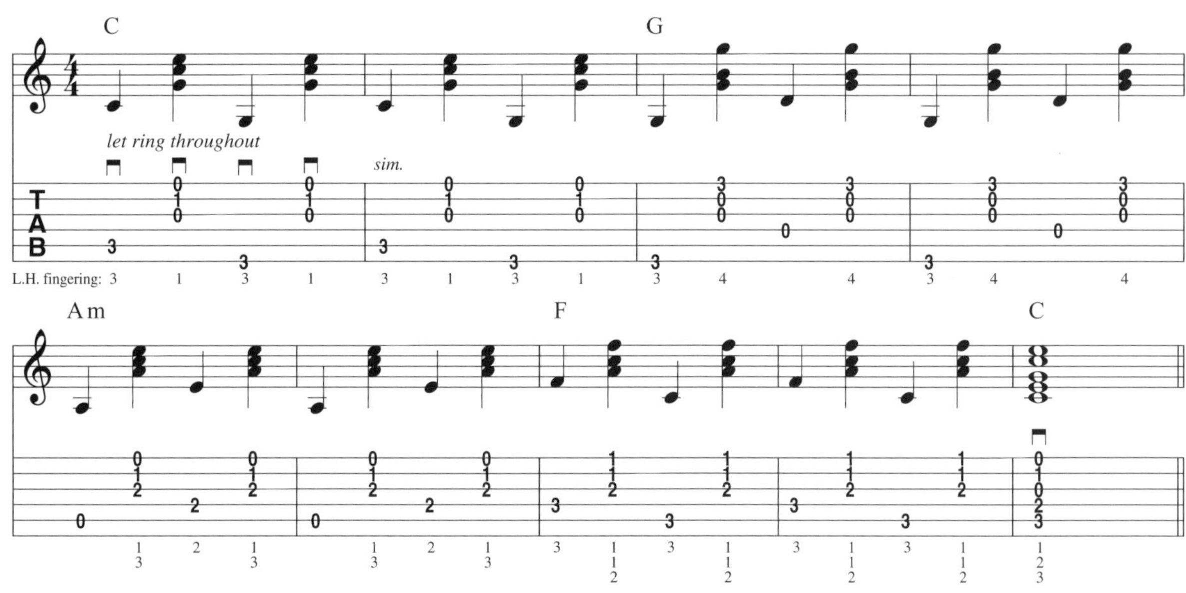

The most difficult part of the "boom chick" rhythm is hitting the bass notes accurately. Start by repeatedly picking the bass notes in the first measure, on beats 1 and 3, leaving out the chords. Don't be afraid to watch your right hand; it'll help you "aim" for the strings. Once you have the bass line down, add the chords to the equation. Keep practicing that first measure until you can play it smoothly, and then work on the rest of the example.

This next example provides more rhythmic flare by adding an eighth-note attack on the chord voicings. This produces the "boom chick-a" rhythm. Pick down for the bass notes and strum down-up for the chords.

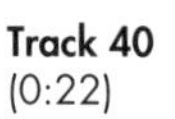

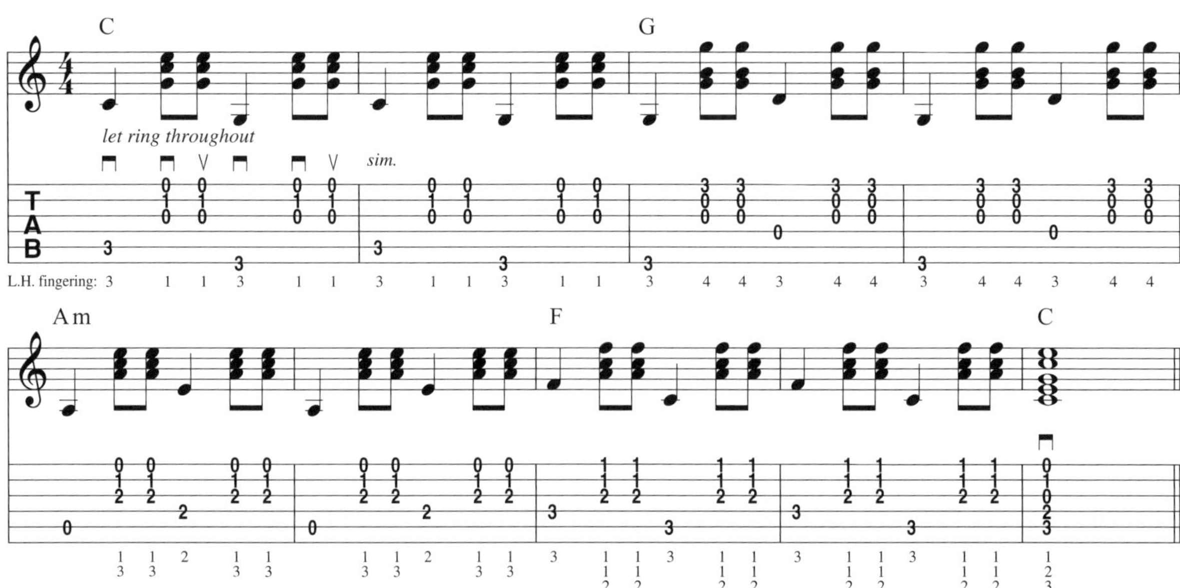

The example below spices things up by adding hammer-ons to beat 3 of each measure. Stay with the same picking/strumming directions from the previous example.

Track 40
(0:45)

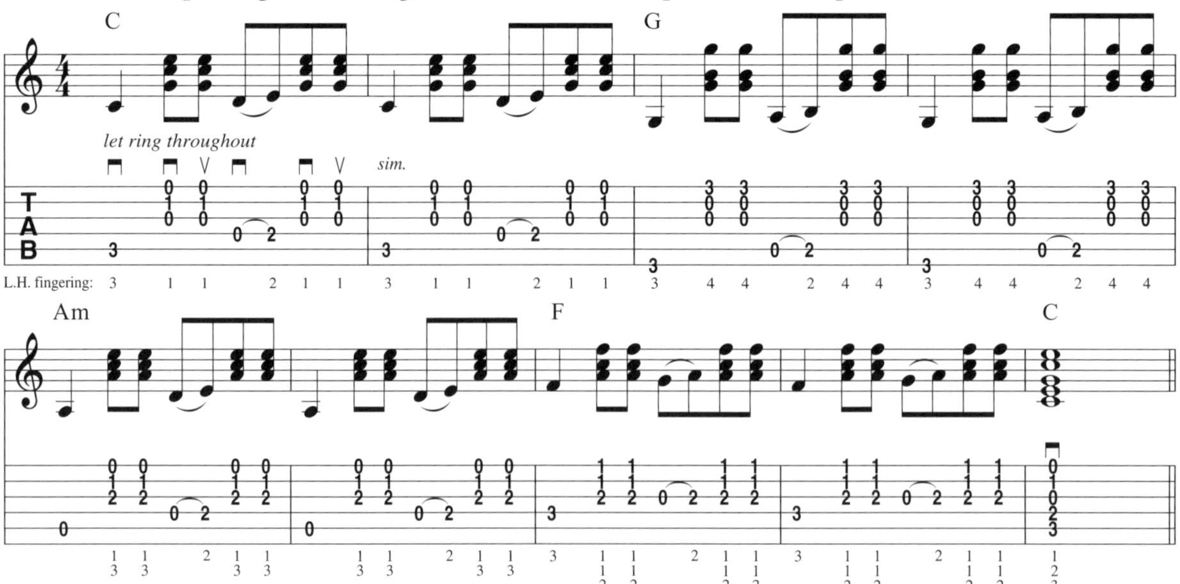

Alternating bass lines don't always stay with the root-fifth pattern; there are several variations. The most common one is the root-third pattern, which is demonstrated in the previous example (C, G, and F chords).

CARTER STRUMMING

Carter strumming (also called "Carter picking") is one of the most famous styles of country rhythm guitar (also employed by many folk guitarists). Named after Maybelle Carter of the Carter Family, an influential group of the '20s and '30s, it combines single-note melodies on the lower strings with strummed chords on the higher strings. This effectively allows one guitar to sound like two instruments simultaneously. This example, which combines the "boom chick-a" patterns with a melody bass line, provides a basic example of Carter strumming. This rhythm style drives country songs such as "I Walk the Line," by Johnny Cash.

Track 40
(1:05)

Maybelle Carter was the mother of June Carter Cash, wife of country music icon Johnny Cash. June was the composer of her husband's signature song, "Ring of Fire."

Next we have a full-blown example of Carter strumming based on, appropriately enough, Maybelle's classic "Wildwood Flower." Mixing bass-line melodies with chord punctuations, it combines all of the techniques from the last four examples. Remember to keep your left-hand fingers in chord position until it's absolutely necessary to move them.

FINGERSTYLE

Fingerstyle is a staple technique in both folk and country. Fingerstyle, if you remember, is when you pluck the strings with your thumb and fingers. If you need a refresher course on right-hand positioning, turn back to "Fingerpicking," in Chapter 4, for a quick review.

Arpeggio Patterns

Arpeggio patterns are very popular in both folk and country. *Arpeggios* are chords played one note at a time. The next example is a *p–i–m–a–m–i* (*p* = thumb; *i* = first finger; *m* = second finger; and *a* = third finger) pattern utilizing Am, C, D, F, and E chords.

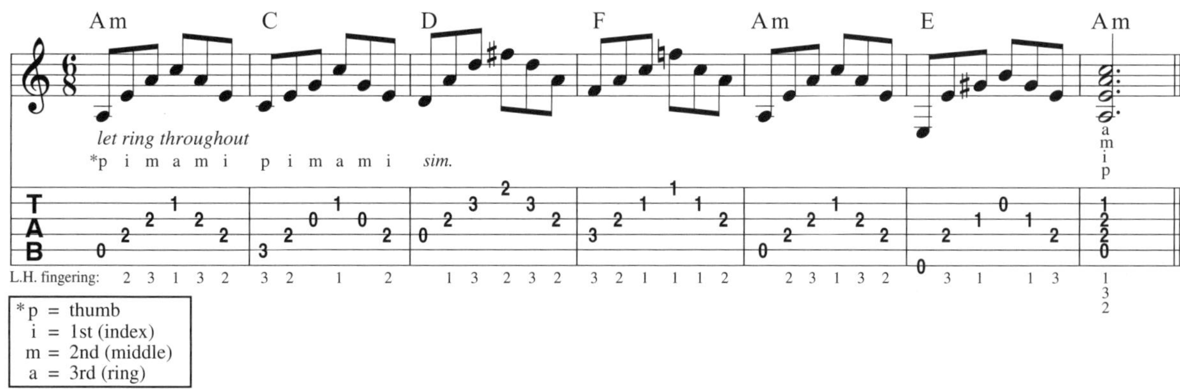

To play chords arpeggio-style, hold down the chord with your left hand, and individually pluck the notes with your right hand, allowing the notes to ring out.

The folky example below features a straight-ahead, *p–i–m–a* arpeggio pattern that works well for standard 4/4 time signatures. Keep your fourth finger planted on the third fret of the B string when you segue from the D/F♯ to G. Remember to let all of the notes ring together.

Track 41
(0:16)

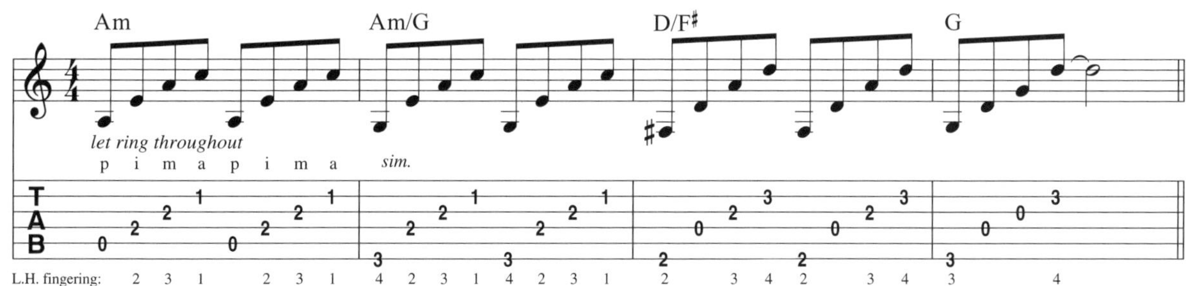

This next example mixes things up a bit with a *p–i–m–i–a–m* pattern. It's perfect for a 3/4 folk ballad or a country waltz.

Track 41
(0:31)

In 3/4 time, there are three beats per measure, with the quarter note receiving the beat.

The intro to "Love Song," by Tesla, is a great 3/4 folk-rock example that combines various arpeggio patterns with a classical feel. The pull-off figure in the first measure is easier to "pull off" than it may seem. The rest flows nicely under the fingers with a Bach-like grandeur.

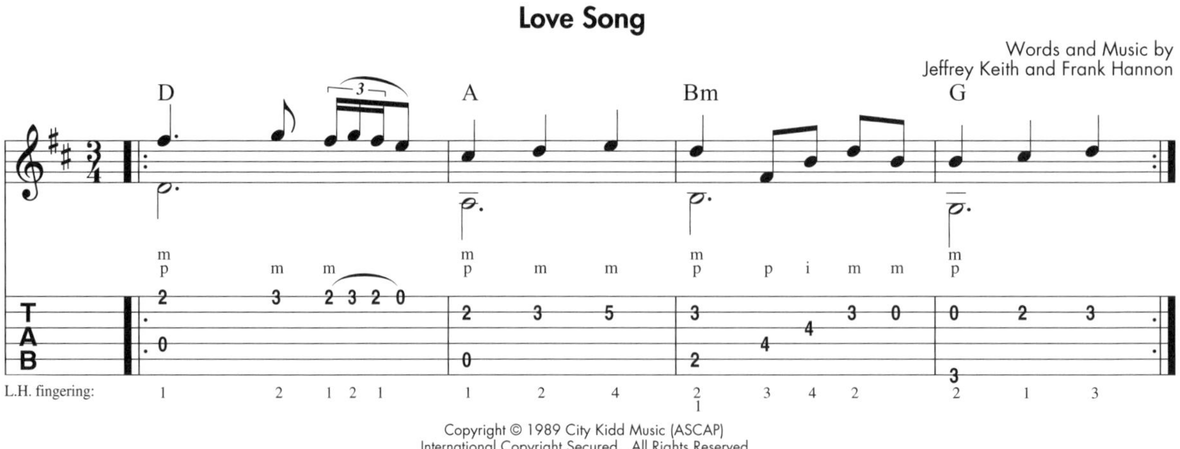

Travis Picking

Travis picking, named after country legend Merle Travis, is another fingerstyle technique common to both country and folk music. Travis picking is based on two main elements: the thumb plays alternating bass lines, usually in quarter-note rhythms, while the fingers pluck the higher strings, mainly on the upbeats. The result is a hypnotic, syncopated rhythm style. Although country artists like Merle Travis and Chet Atkins put the style on the map, it's by no means confined to just country music. Scotty Moore and James Burton, guitarists for Elvis Presley and Ricky Nelson, employed it in their rockabilly rhythms ("Mystery Train" and "Hello Mary Lou," respectively), and many rock and pop guitarists use Travis-picking techniques in their folk-oriented ballads, including Stephen Stills in "Helplessly Hoping," by Crosby, Stills & Nash; Paul Simon in "The Boxer," by Simon and Garfunkel; John Lennon in "Julia," by the Beatles; and Kerry Livgren in "Dust in the Wind," by Kansas (see Chapter 20).

The following examples break down the process into three sections. First, practice just the alternating bass line, using only your thumb. Keep your left-hand second finger planted on the D string. Next, add the open G string between beats 2 and 3, and the first fret of the B string between beats 3 and 4. Let all of the notes ring together. Move on to measure 3 once you have that down. Here you add the third fret of the high E string (G) on the downbeat of beat 1, which you should let ring. Listen to the track to make sure you are playing it correctly.

The following example uses the Travis-picking patterns you just learned in an eight-bar progression featuring C, Am7, and Em7 chords. Go through the example very slowly at first; get a feel for the repetitive patterns. Then play along with the track to check your progress.

Track 42
(0:24)

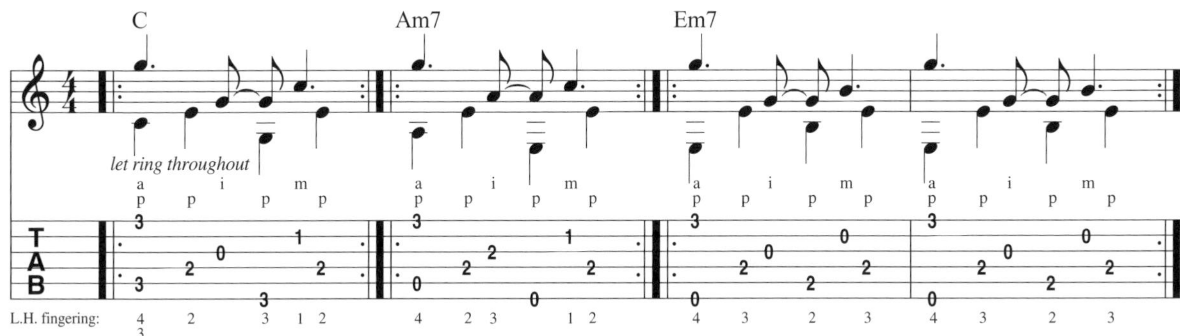

Below is a rockabilly example of Travis picking. The riff is structured from two barre-chord shapes: an E-based G7 chord and an A-based C chord with G in the bass (see "Barre Chords," Chapter 10). First, practice the chords solitarily, and then add the Travis picking. Cut the bass notes short, and don't forget to hammer-on from the third to the fourth fret of the G string.

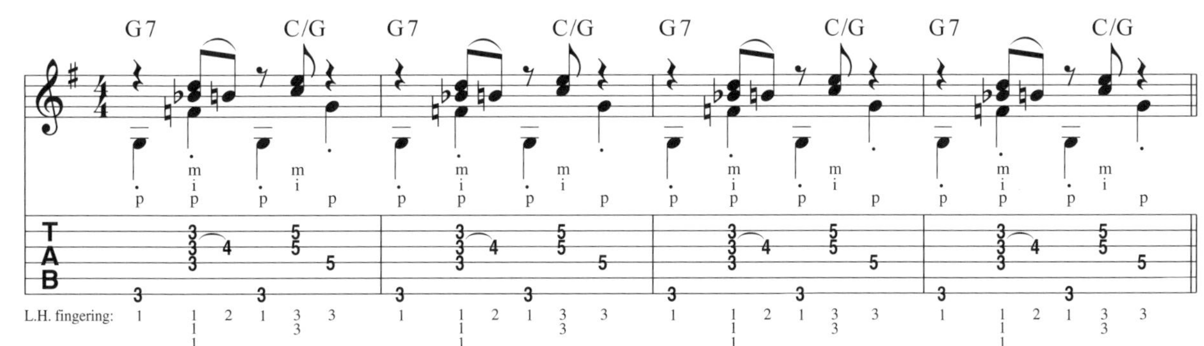

Travis picking doesn't always involve a regimented alternating bass line. For instance, in this '60s folk example the bass notes are only played on beats 1 and 2 (be sure to let them ring).

Track 43
(0:08)

USING A CAPO

A *capo* is a marvelous invention that allows you to play open-position chords in any key! It's a device that clamps, via a spring mechanism or elastic material, to the neck of the guitar, pressing down on all of the strings at a specific fret. This shortens the length of the strings, effectively creating a new nut. With the capo attached to the first fret, all of the open strings sound a half step higher. What good is this, you ask? Well, say you know how to play "House of the Rising Sun," which is in A minor, but the person you're accompanying (or yourself) wants to raise the key a whole step (two half steps) to B minor. Don't worry—there's no reason to fret! (Pun intended.) Simply slap on a capo at the second fret and play it as you normally would. With a capo, you can play the song in any key, using the same open voicings.

The Beatles were quite fond of the capo. One famous example is "Norwegian Wood (This Bird Has Flown)," in which the acoustic guitar is capoed at the second fret. This makes the open D, C, and G/B chords sound a whole step higher (E, D, and A/C♯). Below are the opening measures of the song. The instruction "Capo II," written above the treble clef, indicates to put a capo at the second fret. The tab and music staves read as if the capo were the nut. In other words, "0" means open string; "2" means the second fret above the capo; and so on. Incidentally, this introduction is a form of Carter strumming.

Norwegian Wood
(This Bird Has Flown)

Words and Music by
John Lennon and Paul McCartney

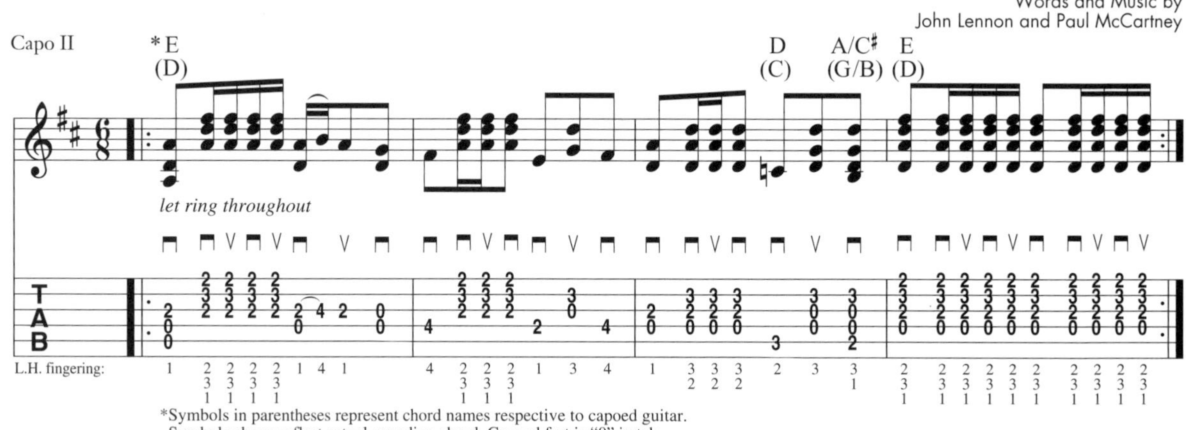

James Taylor also used a capo at the second fret for "You've Got a Friend" (see next page). An excellent fingerstyle guitarist, his playing on this song (and on many others) follows a broken form of Travis picking. Follow the right- and left-hand fingering notations very carefully for this example, making sure to let all of the notes ring as long as possible.

HOT COUNTRY LICKS

All right, grab your electric guitar, or, if you prefer, stay strapped to your acoustic. As promised, we're going to close this chapter with some fancy country licks.

Bluegrass Runs

This first lick is an example of a bluegrass run in G. (Bluegrass is a form of uptempo country/folk music originating in the Appalachians.) Built for speed, it's an open-position lick featuring an abundance of hammer-ons and pull-offs. The second lick is another bluegrass run in G. This one's a little trickier, as there's a lot of string jumping (changing from string to string). Don't worry about playing these examples fast initially; just work out the picking directions, along with the legato moves. Speed will happen naturally as your fingers become more accustomed to the proper moves. Bluegrass runs sound great on acoustic guitar, as well as on electric. Ricky Skaggs, Albert Lee, and Brent Mason are well known for these types of runs.

Hybrid Picking

Hybrid picking is a combination of pick and fingers. With hybrid picking, you hold the pick normally but use your second finger (and sometimes your third) to pluck up on certain strings. The first lick below is a sixths interval lick played exclusively along the G and high E strings. Use your pick to play all of the notes on the G string, and pluck up (in a snapping motion) on the high E-string notes with your second finger.

The second lick is a *banjo roll.* Inspired by country-banjo legend Earl Scruggs, it's an arpeggiated figure played with the pick on the G string, and the second and third fingers on the B and high E strings, respectively. Be sure to let all of the notes ring together.

pl = pick (plectrum)

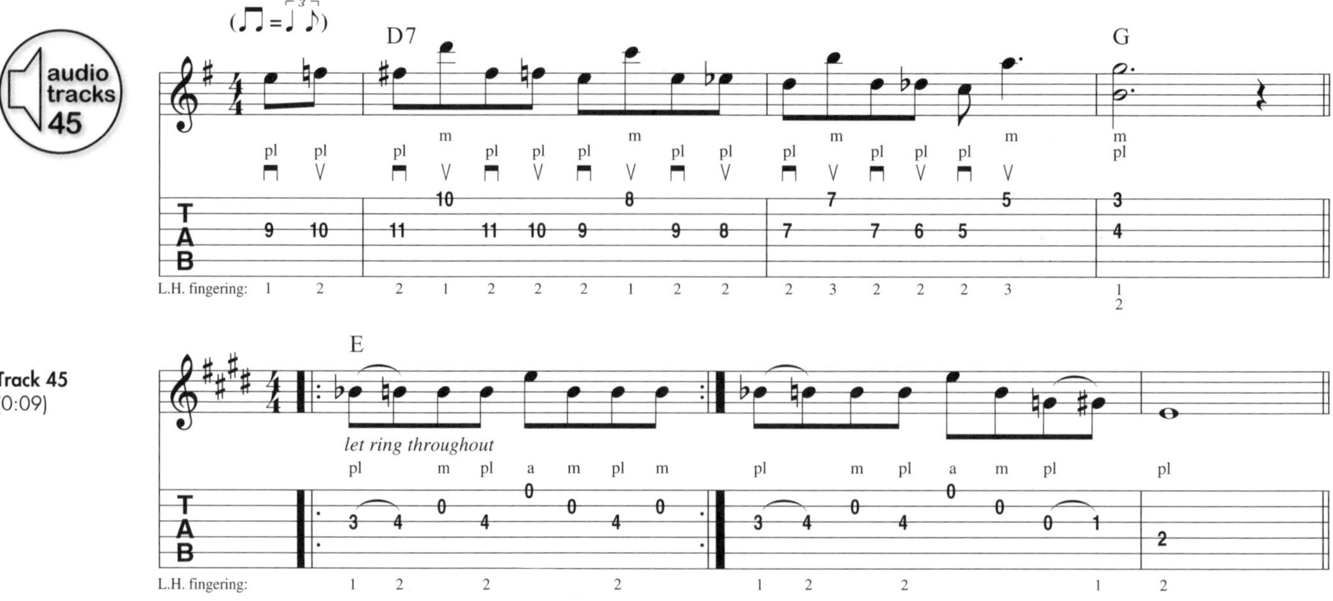

Last, but not least, we have a *pedal-steel lick*. A pedal-steel lick is a fixed-string bend (one note is held stationary while another string is bent) that emulates the sound of the pedal-steel guitar, a stringed instrument containing pedals and levers that raise and lower the pitch of the strings. In the first two measures, bend the B string up a whole step and hold it while you play the note on the high E string, and then hold that note while you release the bend. In the third measure, bar the top two strings at the eighth fret with your third and fourth fingers while you bend the G string up a whole step with your second finger. Don't try this example on an acoustic guitar; you'll either break a string or break your fingers, whichever comes first! Pedal-steel licks are for electric guitars only, preferably strung with light-gauge strings (.008s, .009s, or .010s; see "Putting on New Strings," Chapter 25).

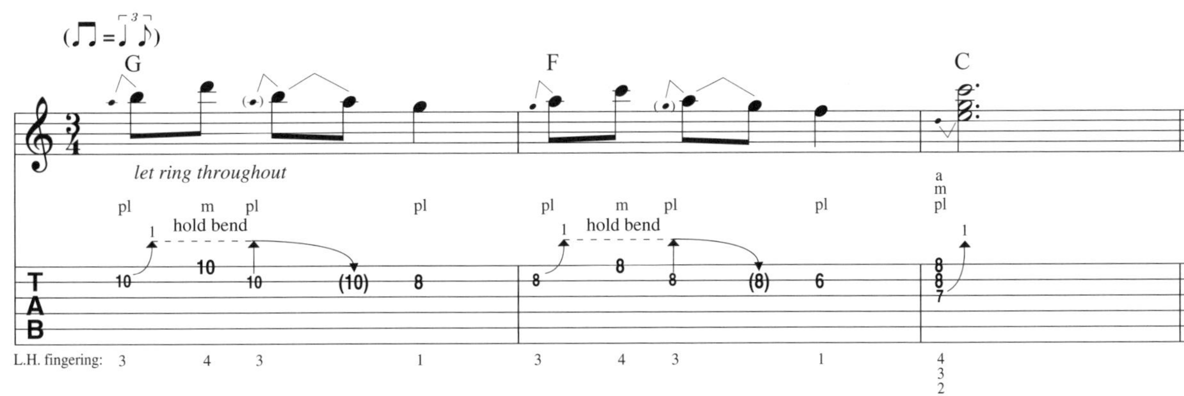

- "Boom chick" and "boom chick-a" rhythms are standard rhythms in both folk and country styles.
- Carter strumming, or Carter picking, combines lower-string melodies with higher-string chords.
- Travis picking combines a driving bass line with syncopated melodies played on the higher strings.
- A capo allows you to play open-position chords in any key.
- Bluegrass runs sound great on acoustic, as well as electric.

SECTION 5

Full-song Transcriptions

CHAPTER 17
"FUN, FUN, FUN"

What's Ahead:

- Palm-muted power chords and boogie patterns
- Combining major- and minor-pentatonic scales
- Double-stop bends

Welcome to the "Songs" section of the book. This is where all of your hard work really pays off. In this section, you'll find the complete lead-guitar parts for five popular songs in different styles: the Beach Boys' early rock 'n' roll hit "Fun, Fun, Fun"; B.B. King's signature blues song, "The Thrill Is Gone"; Deep Purple's '70s rock classic "Smoke on the Water"; Kansas' acoustic folk-rock song "Dust in the Wind"; and Nirvana's grunge anthem "Smells Like Teen Spirit."

The guitar parts are notated on both tab and music staves, along with the vocal melody and lyrics. Each song is also demonstrated by a full band. But don't worry—you won't be on your own. We'll be there every step of the way, leading you through the music.

"Fun, Fun, Fun" was a hit for the Beach Boys in 1964. An uptempo rock 'n' roll outing, it tells the story of a hot-rod cutie racing around town in the Ford Thunderbird (T-Bird) her father gave to her. She lies to her daddy; he takes the keys away; she's rescued by her long-neglected boyfriend; and they drive off into the sunset together. Musically, it exemplifies early rock 'n' roll rhythm and lead guitar techniques.

To play "Fun, Fun, Fun," you'll need to re-familiarize yourself with power chords, root-fifth/root-sixth boogie patterns, major- and minor-pentatonic scale boxes, and bending techniques.

TONE TIPS

Guitar: solidbody electric
Pickup configuration: three single-coils
Pickup selection: middle pickup

Amp: combo
Treble/Middle/Bass: 7/5/5
Gain: clean (1–3)
Effects: reverb (moderate setting)

To play along with the audio, you will need to tune your strings down a half step (low to high: E♭–A♭–D♭–G♭–B♭–E♭).

SONG STRUCTURE

Key: E (B for the solo)

Section	Number of Measures	First Chord	Last Chord
Intro (solo)	12 (plus pick-up measure)	N/A (E)	B7
Verse 1	12	E5	A5
Chorus 1	4	E5	B5
Verse 2	12	E5	A5
Chorus 2	4	E5	F♯5
Solo	8	B5	N/A (B)
Verse 3	12	E5	A5
Chorus 3	8	E5	F♯
Outro	4 (repeat and fade)	B5	A5

THE CHORDS AND RHYTHMS

Although "Fun, Fun, Fun" starts out with a guitar lead, you'll be playing rhythm parts through the majority of the song. In the figure below, you'll find all of the chord voicings that you'll be using in the song. With the exception of the B7 chord, which you play at the end of the intro solo, all of the chords are dyads (two-note chords). The A6 and B6 dyads are used in conjunction with A5 and B5 chords in what is called a root-fifth/root-sixth boogie pattern. You'll be playing the top row of dyads for the verses; the bottom-row dyads are for the chorus and outro sections.

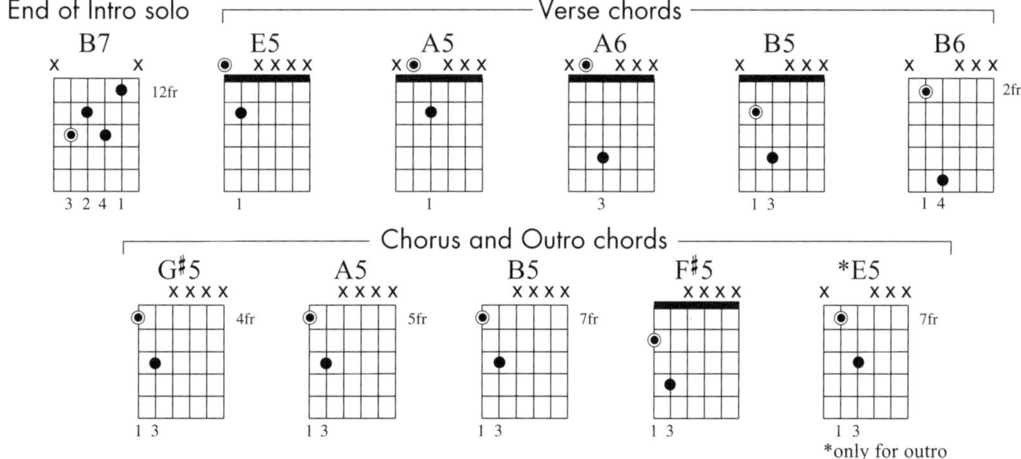

THE VERSES

The verse sections revolve around an open E5 dyad and two boogie patterns involving A5/A6 and B5/B6 interplay. Pick down on all of the rhythms, and use right-hand palm muting.

THE CHORUSES AND OUTRO

The chorus follows an E–G♯m–A–B–E–A–G♯m–B chord progression that's played with power chords, all rooted on the low E string (see above). Again, use all downstrokes and right-hand palm muting. (Chorus 1 and 2 are identical except for the last chord [B5 at the end of chorus 1; F♯5 at the end of chorus 2]. Chorus 3 is played two times and ends on an F♯5 chord.)

The *outro* (ending section) is a four-bar, B5–E5–A5 progression that keeps repeating until it finally fades out. (In live performances, the Beach Boys would end the song on a B chord.) This is the only time in the song in which you don't play an open-position E5 chord. A seventh-position E5 (root on the A string, see above) works best here.

THE SOLOS

You get to have "Fun, Fun, Fun" with this song because there are two solos; one in the intro, and one in the middle of the song. The intro solo is the longest and most involved. It's an excellent representation of the late '50s/early '60s style of rock 'n' roll lead guitar. Heavily influenced by the "Chuck Berry" style, it mixes pentatonic scales with loads of double-stops and bends.

When learning a solo, it's helpful to know the scales and the box patterns from which the licks are drawn. The intro solo draws from both the E minor-pentatonic (E–G–A–B–D) and E major-pentatonic (E–F♯–G♯–B–C♯) scales, on the top four strings in 12th position. The following figure shows the two patterns separately, and in a composite box. This is a tricky solo because there are so many double stops (two notes played simultaneously, on adjacent strings). Go slowly, and work on it one measure at a time. Try to use all downstrokes for extra power. Also, use your third finger for the G-string bends in measures 5–8, and let your second finger help push the string up. For the double-stop bend in measure 10, bar the G and B strings with your third finger, and let your first and second fingers help push up the strings. And don't forget to end your solo with the B7 chord.

Intro solo

E minor pentatonic

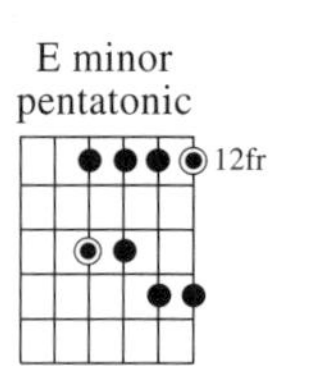

E major pentatonic

12fr

E major and minor composite

12fr

The main solo (after chorus 2) modulates to the key of B. The first four measures draw from the B minor-pentatonic (B–D–E–F♯–A) box shown here. Notice that there's an additional note, the sixth, which is at the ninth fret of the B string. This is the note used in the double-stop bends in measures 3–5. Measures 5–6 jump up to the "Albert King" box, also shown here, for a whole-step bend on the high E string. Use your third finger (with assistance from your first and second fingers) for this bend.

Main solo

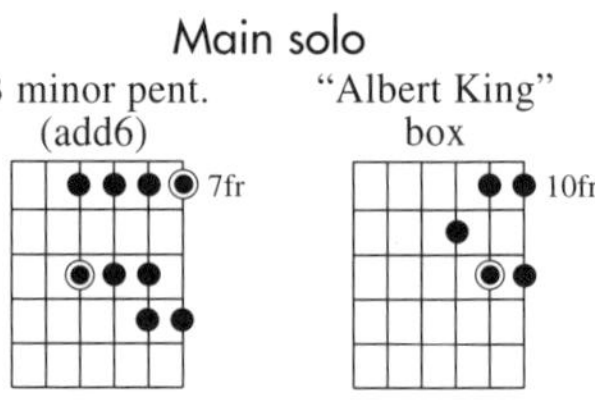

The last two measures involve double-stop moves derived from the F♯ Mixolydian (F♯–G♯–A♯–B–C♯–D♯–E) and B Mixolydian (B–C♯–D♯–E–F♯–G♯–A) boxes shown here. *Mixolydian* is a *mode*, or type of scale derived from the major scale.

F♯ Mixolydian

8fr

B Mixolydian

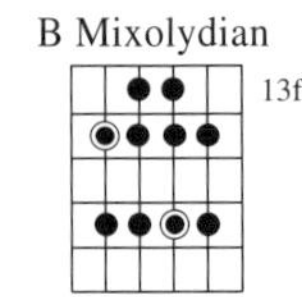

- Tune each of your strings down a half step to play along with the recording.
- Use palm muting for all of the chords.
- E minor and E major pentatonic can be combined to form a composite scale.
- Use your first and second fingers to help the third finger bend the double stops.

Fun, Fun, Fun

Tune down 1/2 step:
(low to high) E♭–A♭–D♭–G♭–B♭–E♭

Words and Music by
Brian Wilson and Mike Love

Intro

Moderately fast ♩ = 168

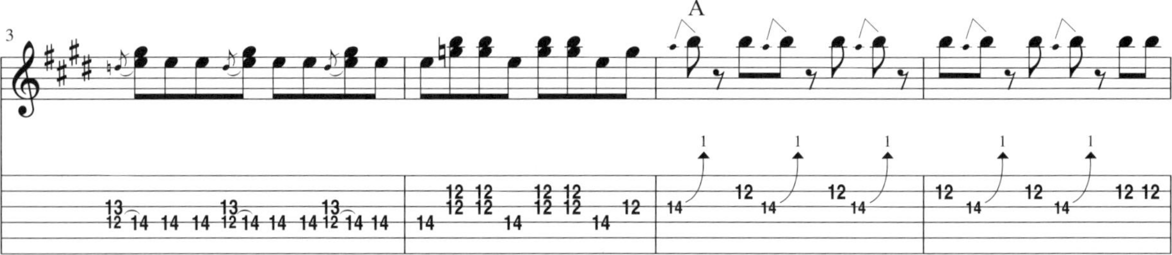

E
B
A
E
B7
1. Well, she
Verse
E
A
got her dad-dy's car and she cruised through the ham-burg-er stand, now.
P.M.
E
Seems she for-got all a-bout the li-brar-y like she told her old man,
P.M.

19
B
E
now.
And with the
ra - di - o blast - in' goes
P.M.
4 4 6 4 4 4 6 4
2 2 2 2 2 2 2 2
2 2 2 2 2 2 2 2
0 0 0 0 0 0 0 0
22
A
cruis - in' just as fast as she can, now.
And she'll have
P.M.
2 2 4 2 2 2 4 2
0 0 0 0 0 0 0 0
25
E
G♯m
fun, fun, fun till her dad - dy takes the T - Bird a - way.
(Fun, fun, fun till her dad - dy takes the T - Bird a way.)
(Fun, fun, fun till her dad - dy takes the T - Bird.
P.M.
2 2 2 2 6 6 6 6
0 0 0 0 4 4 4 4
7 7 7 7 9 9 9 9
5 5 5 5 7 7 7 7

Verse
E A G♯m B E
27
2. Well, the girls can't stand her 'cause she
3. See additional lyrics
Fun, fun, fun till her dad - dy takes the T - Bird a - way.)
P.M.
P.M.
30
A
walks, looks and drives like an ace, now. She makes the
(You walk like an ace, now, you walk like an ace.
P.M.
33
E B
In - dy Five Hun - dred look like a Ro - man char - i - ot race, now.
Oo. You look like an ace, now, you
P.M.

36
E
A lot - ta guys try to catch her but she leads them on a wild goose chase,
look like an ace. Oo. You
P.M.
39
A
To Coda
E
G♯m
now. And she'll have fun, fun, fun till her
(Fun, fun, fun till her
drive like an ace, now, you drive like an ace. Fun, fun, fun till her
P.M.
42
A
B
E
A
G♯m
F♯
dad - dy takes the T - Bird a - way.
dad - dy takes the T - Bird a - way. A - way.)
dad - dy takes the T - Bird. Fun, fun, fun till her dad - dy takes the T - Bird a - way.)
P.M.

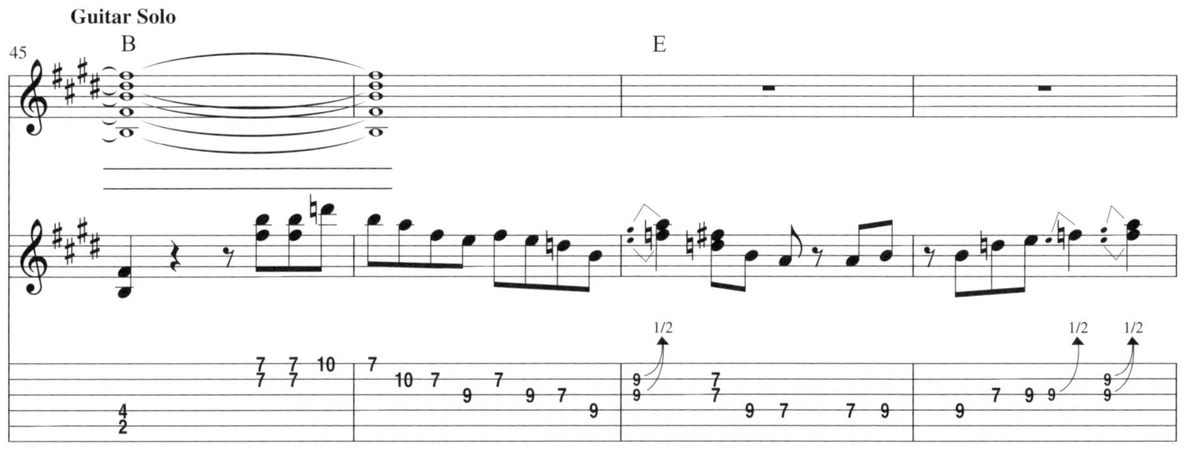
Guitar Solo
45
B
E
1/2
1/2
1/2

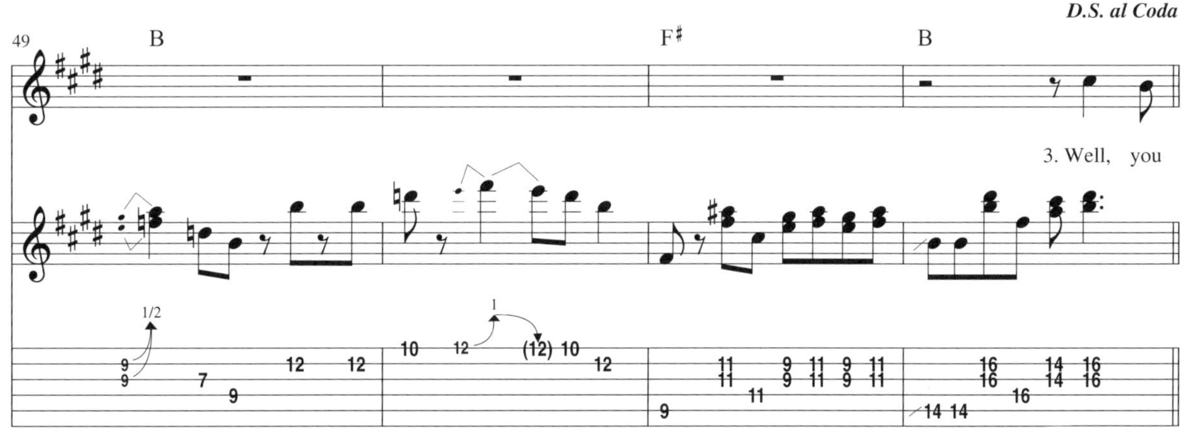
D.S. al Coda
49
B
F♯
B
3. Well, you
1/2
1

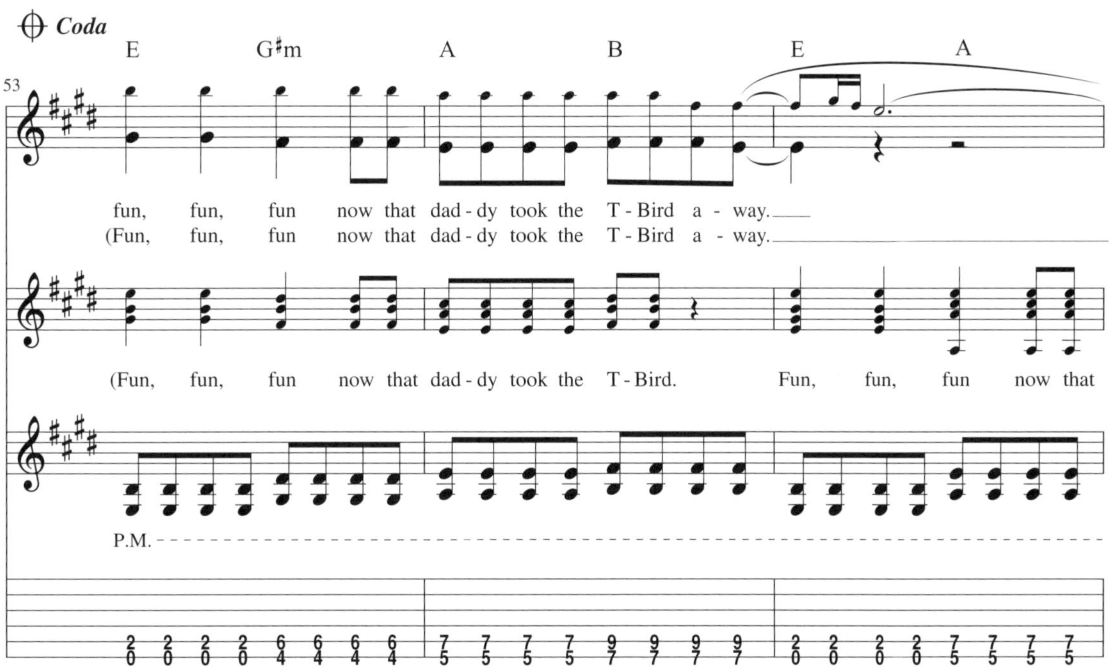
Coda
53
E
G♯m
A
B
E
A
fun, fun, fun now that dad - dy took the T - Bird a - way.
(Fun, fun, fun now that dad - dy took the T - Bird a - way.
(Fun, fun, fun now that dad - dy took the T - Bird. Fun, fun, fun now that
P.M.

56
G♯m B E G♯m A B
fun, fun, fun now that dad - dy took the T - Bird a - way. _
_ And we'll have fun, fun, fun now that dad - dy took the T - Bird a - way.) _
dad - dy took the T - Bird. Fun, fun, fun now that dad - dy took the T - Bird.
P.M.
59
E A G♯m F♯
(Oo,
Fun, fun, fun now that dad - dy took the T - Bird a - way.) _
P.M.

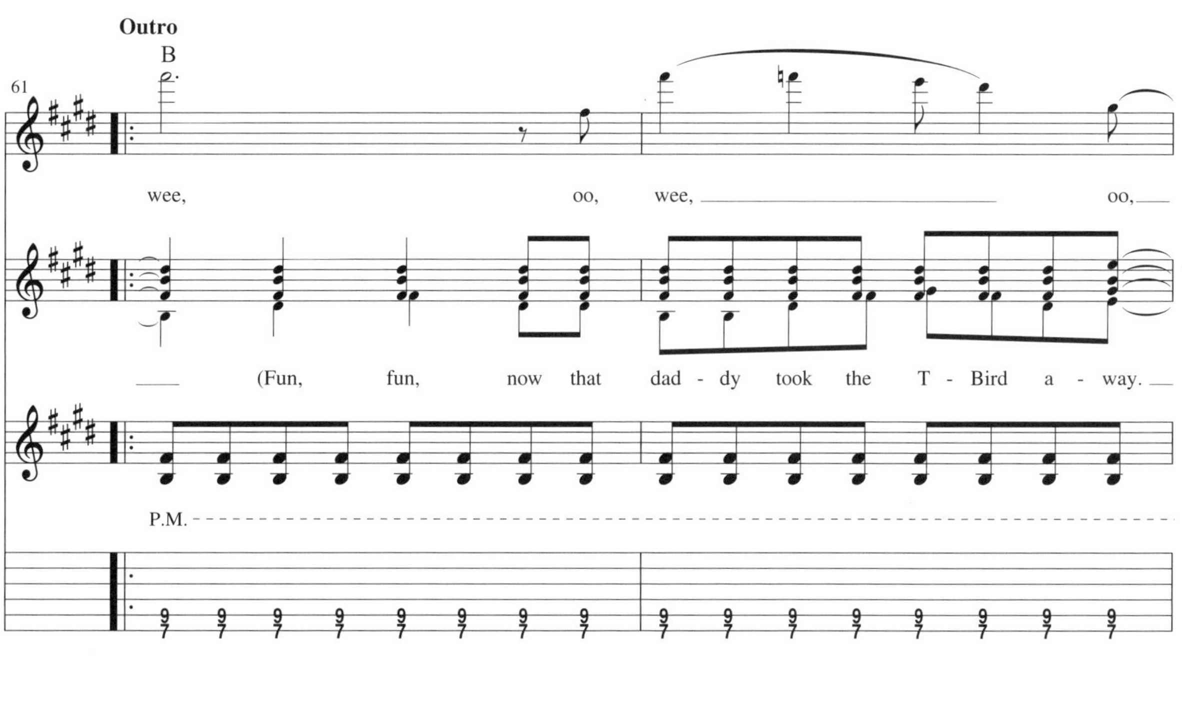

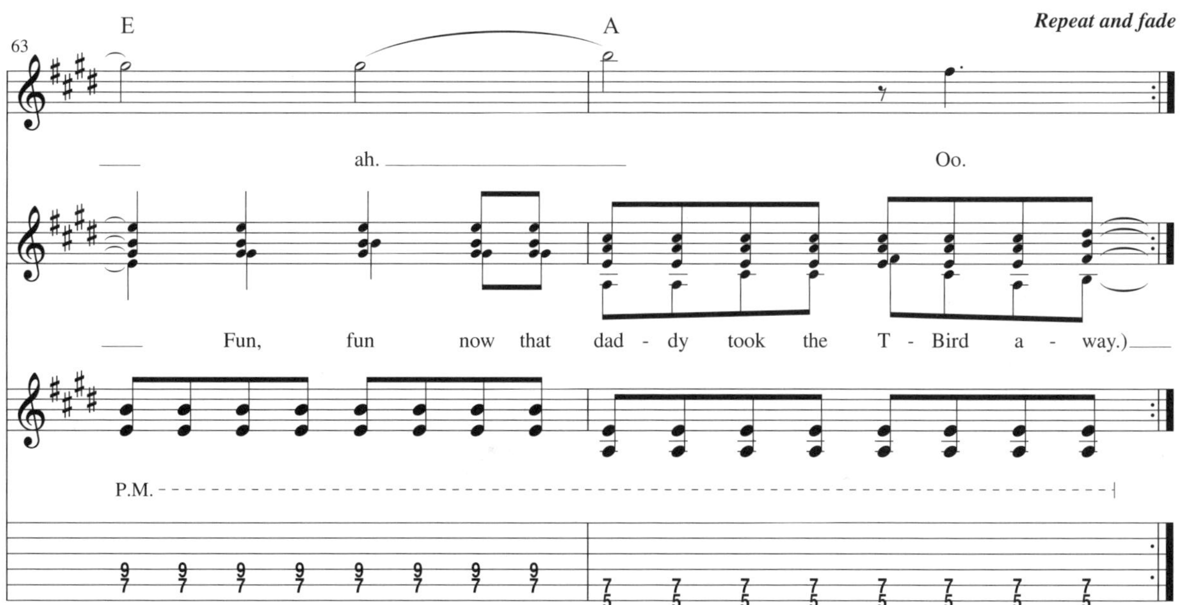

Additional Lyrics

3. Well, you knew all along
   That your dad was gettin' wise to you, now.
   (You shouldn't have lied, now, you shouldn't have lied.)
   And since he took your set of keys
   You've been thinkin' that your fun is all through, now.
   (You shouldn't have lied, now, you shouldn't have lied.)
   But you can come along with me
   'Cause we got a lotta things to do now.
   (You shouldn't have lied, now, you shouldn't have lied.)
   And we'll…

CHAPTER 18
"THE THRILL IS GONE"

What's Ahead:

- B minor-pentatonic soloing
- String-bending and vibrato techniques
- Passing notes
- Dynamics
- How to get away with not having to play a single chord in a song.

B.B. King was "King of the Blues" long before recording his most well-known song, "The Thrill Is Gone." A hit for the king in early 1970, it features his colossal vocal style, and bluer-than-blue, single-note soloing. Following a 12-bar minor blues format, the melancholy lyrics tell the story of a man trying to break free from the love spell cast upon him by his two-timing woman. Guitar players of any caliber can take a lesson from B.B.'s uncanny ability to squeeze a million soul-drenched licks out of a handful of little blues boxes.

To play "The Thrill Is Gone," you'll need to be familiar with minor-pentatonic scale patterns, string-bending techniques, and vibrato.

TONE TIPS

Guitar: hollowbody or solidbody electric
Pickup configuration: twin humbuckers
Pickup selection: middle (both pickups activated)
Amp: combo
Treble/Middle/Bass: 8/5/5
Gain: mild overdrive (5–6)
Effects: reverb (moderate setting)

SONG STRUCTURE

Key: B minor

Section	Number of Measures	First Chord	Last Chord
Intro (solo)	12	N/A (Bm)	N/A (Bm)
Verse 1	12	N/A (Bm)	N/A (Bm)
Verse 2	12	N/A (Bm)	N/A (Bm)
Solo 1	12	N/A (Bm)	N/A (Bm)
Verse 3	12	N/A (Bm)	N/A (Bm)
Verse 4	12	N/A (Bm)	N/A (Bm)
Outro Solo	12 bars over form, plus 34 bars over Bm chord vamp to fade out	N/A (Bm)	N/A (Bm)

THE CHORD PROGRESSION

"The Thrill Is Gone" is based on a 12-bar blues progression in the key of B minor. In minor keys, the I and the IV chords are minor (Bm and Em), while the V is usually dominant (F♯7). In this song, there is also a jazz-influenced ♭VI chord (Gmaj7). The 12-bar progression is repeated throughout the song; the only exception is the outro, which repeats and fades over a i-chord vamp (Bm).

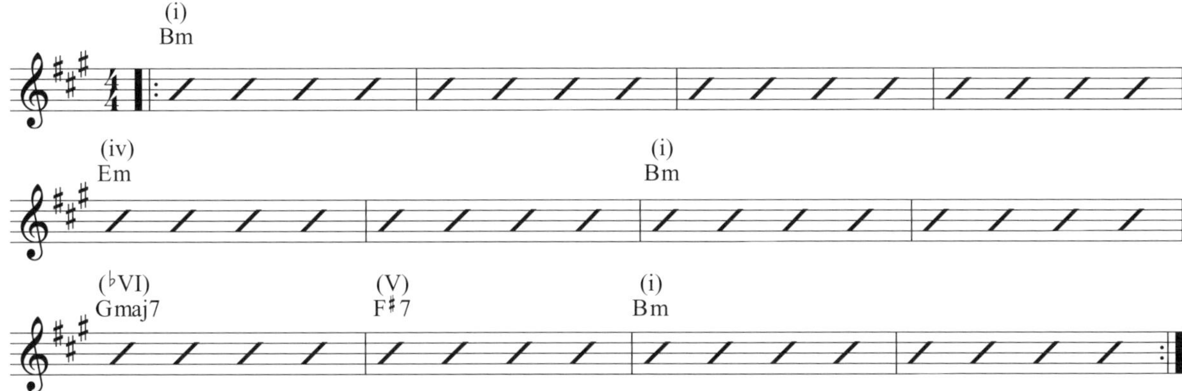

Apparently, B.B. didn't feel much like playing rhythm guitar the day he recorded "The Thrill Is Gone." Instead, he chose to concentrate on his vocals when he wasn't soloing. If you don't plan to sing the song, below are some chord voicings you can play between your solos. (Play them with staccato quarter-note accents on beats 2 and 4 of each measure.) All of the chords are locked in seventh position so you won't have to stare at your guitar. You can be cool like B.B., and keep your eyes closed most of the time.

Suggested chord voicings

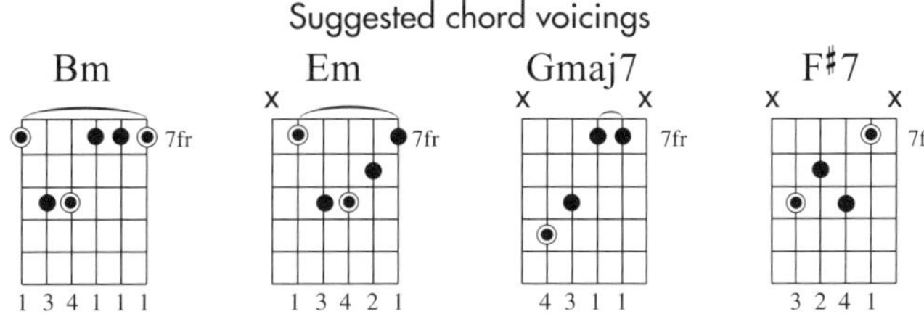

THE SOLOING

With few exceptions, all of the solo phrases in "The Thrill Is Gone" are drawn from the B minor-pentatonic (B–D–E–F♯–A) boxes.

B.B.'s boxes

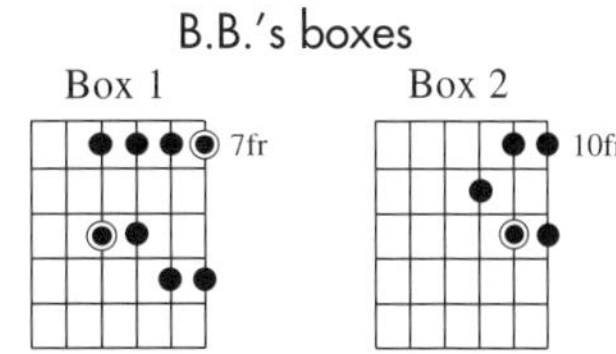

The intro solo jumps back and forth between the two boxes, with a series of licks that are decorated with quarter-, half-, and whole-step bends, and pre-bends. Notice that every sustained note is enhanced with vibrato. Be sure to include the D♯ note in measure 6. That's no mistake; it's a chromatic passing tone (a note that's not in the scale). Also, beware of that whole-step bend on the downbeat of measure 7, which B.B. bends with his first finger. If you lack the strength, go ahead and shift down the neck so you can use your third finger. There's time to sneak back up to tenth position (box 2) to carry on to the end of the intro solo. The intro solo ends on a B/F♯ dyad (seventh fret, on the B and high E strings), about the closest B.B. comes to playing a chord in the entire song.

B.B. King is famous for his aggressive "hummingbird" vibrato. Here's a tip on how to emulate it: While fretting a note, drop your palm from the back of the neck and literally shake your whole hand, flicking the wrist in a rapid, circular motion.

During verse 1, you can lay low, unless you choose to play rhythm. Verse 2 finds you playing fills between the vocal phrases. This is a classic example of the "call-and-response" tactics so prevalent in blues music. The main solo covers similar territory as the intro solo, but watch out for that 19th-fret jump in measure 6.

The outro solo is brimming with more tasty blues licks. You can learn them verbatim, or improvise around them if you choose. That's what the blues masters do; they play from the heart. You've got to include that 19th-fret B note on the high E string, though. That one's a keeper!

Try to use dynamics (fluctuation in volume levels) when you solo. This is a very effective blues nuance. Pick some notes harder than others, and perhaps even raise and lower your pickup volume knobs.

- The chord progression follows a 12-bar minor-blues format.
- Feel free to play chords when you're not soloing.
- Nearly the entire song is played in seventh- and tenth-position B minor-pentatonic scale boxes.
- Use dynamics in your solos.
- Play from the heart.

audio tracks 48

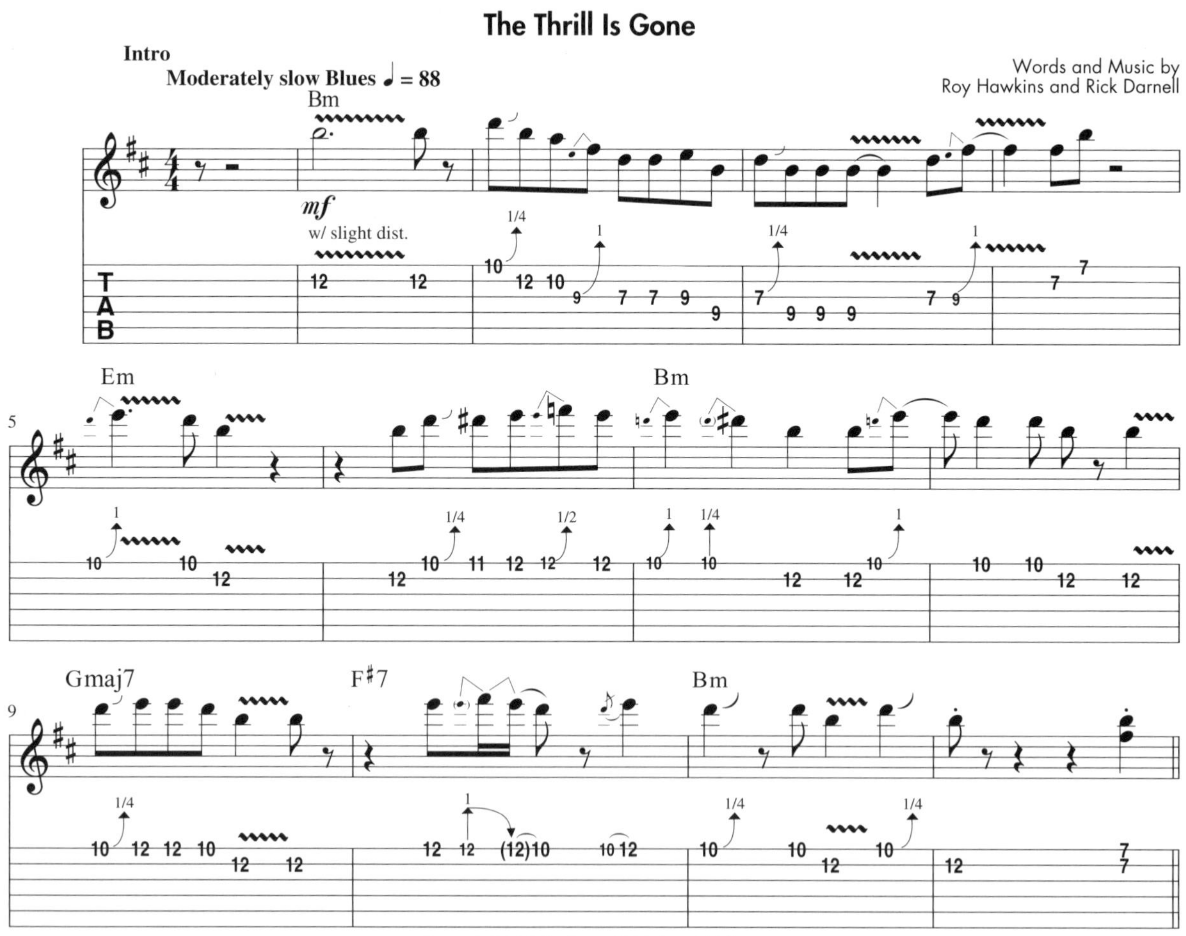

Verse
Gtr. tacet
13
Bm
1. The thrill is gone,
3. See additional lyrics
the thrill is gone a - way.
16
Em
The thrill is gone, ba - by,
the thrill is gone
19
Bm
a - way.
Gmaj7
You know you done me wrong, ba -
22
F♯7
To Coda
Bm
- by, and you'll be sor - ry some day,
mp
9 7
Verse
25
Bm
2. The thrill is gone,
it's gone a - way from me.
7
7
1
7 10 10 10 10
28
Em
The thrill is gone, ba - by,
the thrill has
3
1 1 1 1
10 10 10 10
1 1/4
10 10 12

Bm
Gmaj7
gone a - way from me.
Al - though I'll still live on,
F♯7
Bm
but so lone - ly I'll be.
mf
Guitar Solo
Bm
Em
8va
loco
Gmaj7
F♯7
D.S. al Coda

Coda
Verse
Bm
49
should.
4. You know I'm free, free now, ba - by.
7
7
9
52
Em
Bm
I'm free from your spell.
Whoa, I'm free, free, free now, I'm free from your spell.
3
7
7
9
7
9
57
Gmaj7
F♯7
Bm
And now that it's all o - ver
all I can do is wish you well.
7
7
Outro-Guitar Solo
Bm
62
7
12 12
10
1/4
1
12
10 12
12
10 12
12
1
12
(12) 10
1/4
1
12
10 12
12
(12) 10

Em
Bm
Gmaj7
F♯7
Bm
8va
8va
loco

Additional Lyrics

3. The thrill is gone,
   It's gone away for good.
   Oh, the thrill is gone,
   Baby, it's gone away for good.
   Someday I know I'll be holdin' on, baby,
   Just like I know a good man should.

CHAPTER 19

"SMOKE ON THE WATER"

What's Ahead:

- Inverted–power chord riffs
- Arpeggios
- Playing a solo over the entire neck
- Mixing several scales in one solo

Some songs, like national anthems, make you immediately drop what you're doing and take notice. "Smoke on the Water" is one such song. At the sound of the first power chord, the Average Joe will jump up and perform the mighty riff on an air guitar. Lucky for you, you're equipped with the chops to do it for real.

"Smoke on the Water" was a smash hit for Deep Purple in 1973. A mid-tempo rocker, it boasts one of rock's most enduring riffs, and is bolstered with the simplistic, repeating chorus line. The biographical lyrics describe one fiery night in Montreaux, Switzerland, where the casino in which the band was planning on recording burned to the ground.

To play the rhythm parts in "Smoke on the Water," you must have a handle on inverted power chords and arpeggios. To play the solo, you must know the G minor-pentatonic, G blues, and G minor scales; and also have a firm grip on bending and other legato techniques.

TONE TIPS

Guitar: solidbody electric w/ whammy bar
Pickup configuration: three single-coils
Pickup selection: bridge (riff, verses, choruses); neck (solo)
Amp: Marshall-type w/ 4×12 cabinet
Treble/Middle/Bass: 8/7/7
Gain: medium/heavy overdrive (7–8)
Effects: overdrive boost or distortion pedal for solo

SONG STRUCTURE

Key: G minor

Section	Number of Measures	First Chord	Last Chord
Intro (main riff)	24	G5	G5
Verse 1	16	G5	G5
Chorus 1	6	C5	A♭5
Main riff	8	G5	G5
Verse 2	16	G5	G5
Chorus 2	6	C5	A♭5
Main riff	8	G5	G5
Solo	24	N/A (G5)	G5
Main riff	4	G5	G5
Verse 3	16	G5	G5
Chorus 3	6	C5	A♭5
Main riff	16	G5	G5
Outro-organ solo	12 plus fade	G5	G5

THE MAIN RIFF

Armed with a Stratocaster guitar, a Marshall amplifier, and a handful of inverted power chords, Ritchie Blackmore crafted one of the greatest rock riffs of all time. The really cool thing is it's actually pretty easy to play, too. Four measures in length, it's comprised exclusively of dyads (two-note chords) positioned on the D and G strings, all nice and tidy. Use your first finger to bar the third-fret dyad, and your third finger for the ones at the sixth and fifth frets. Dig in hard with your pick, and use all downstrokes for extra power. Don't overlook the fact that some of the attacks are staccato (short), and some are long.

An inverted power chord is one that has its root on top and its fifth on the bottom.

THE VERSE ARPEGGIOS

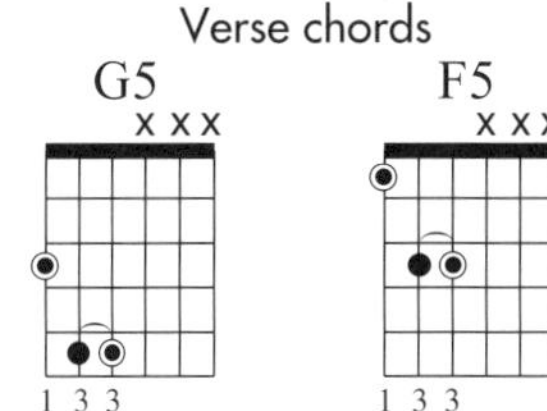

The chords in the verses are played arpeggio-style, or one note at a time, with right-hand palm muting. Check out the adjacent figure for left-hand fingerings. You may want to use an all-downstroke attack, but if that's uncomfortable, try a down-up-down pattern for each grouping.

THE CHORUS CHORDS

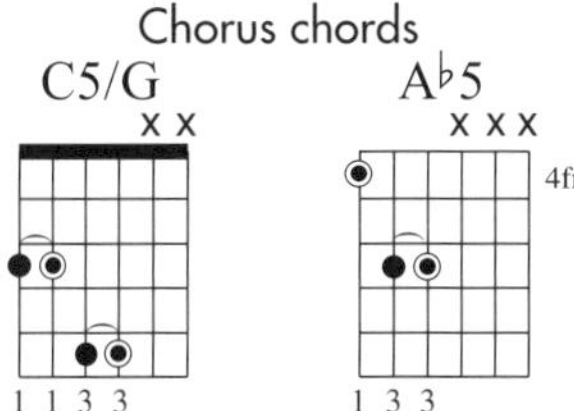

The six-bar chorus begins and ends with two big power chords: C5/G (with an added fifth on the low E string for extra girth) and A♭5. Use the fingerings shown here. Tucked between the power chords is a secondary riff that's similar to the main riff, in that they're both comprised of inverted power chords. Bar the third-fret dyads with your first finger, and the fifth-fret dyads with your third finger. After the brief chorus, don't forget to repeat the main riff before going back to the verse arpeggios.

THE OUTRO RIFFS

The outro section consists of a series of dyads similar to those in the main and secondary riffs. Stay in third position and bar the third-fret dyads with your first finger, and the fifth-fret dyads with your third finger. Grab the one on the fourth fret with your second finger.

THE SOLO

Switch to your neck pickup and step on the distortion pedal—it's solo time! Ritchie Blackmore's 24-measure "bend fest" leaves hardly an area of the fretboard untouched, as it dips and dives from the 15th fret, to open position, and back again. It's easy to get lost in the shuffle; overwhelmed by the constant position-shifting. And not to mention the constant hand-offs of several scales (G minor scale, G minor pentatonic, G Dorian [a mode derived from the major scale], G blues, and C blues). But don't worry—here's how to greatly simplify the process.

The entire solo is mapped out in compact scale boxes on the following page. These will take you, measure by measure, through the whole thing. For example, the first phrase (pick-up notes and the beginning of measure 1) is played in the 12th-position G minor scale box (first scale box). The next phrase drops to the G minor box in eleventh position (second scale box); and so on. If your guitar isn't equipped with a whammy bar, don't worry about the G-string dive in measure 10; just sustain the open G string through beats 3 and 4. The speedy licks in measures 7, 11, and

15 will probably take some extra work. Go through them slowly, working out your picking directions. When in doubt, try alternate picking. Lastly, go easy on those bends. If your hand starts to cramp up, take a break.

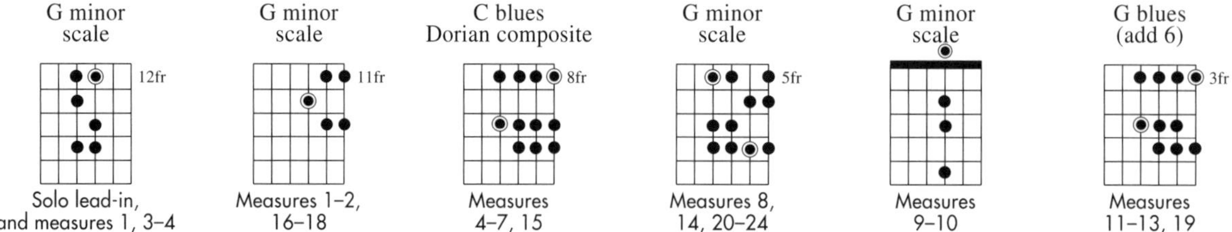

- An inverted power chord has its root on top and its fifth on the bottom.
- Play all of the dyads by barring with your first or third fingers.
- Map out the solo in small box scale patterns.
- Take a break if your hand starts to cramp up from all of those crazy bends.

Smoke on the Water

Words and Music by Ritchie Blackmore, Ian Gillan, Roger Glover, Jon Lord and Ian Paice

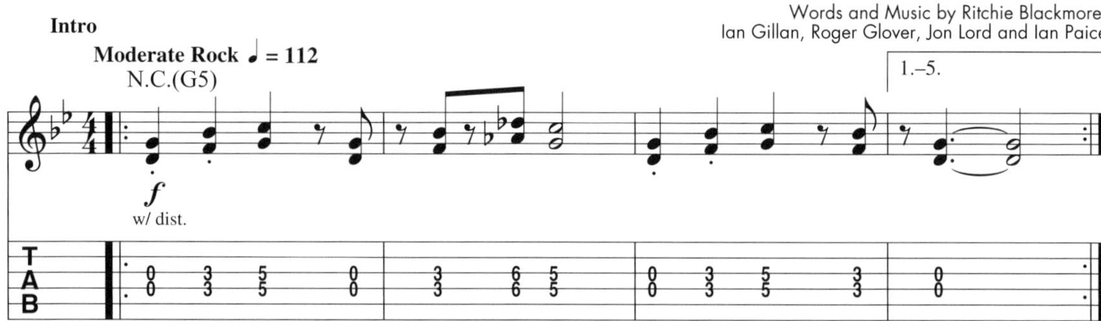

8
F5
G5
Lake Ge - ne - va shore - line
to make rec-ords with the
slight P.M.
slight P.M.
slight P.M.
11
F5
G5
mo - bile,
we did-n't have much time.
slight P.M.
14
F5
But Frank Zap-pa and the Moth - ers
were at the best place a - round.
slight P.M.
slight P.M.
slight P.M.
17
G5
But some stu - pid with a flare gun
slight P.M.
slight P.M.
slight P.M.

Chorus
F5
G5
C5/G
burned the place to the ground.
Smoke on the
slight P.M.
Ab5
G5
C5/G
wa - ter, a fire in the sky.
Smoke on the
To Coda
Ab5
N.C.(G5)
wa - ter.
1.
2.

Guitar Solo

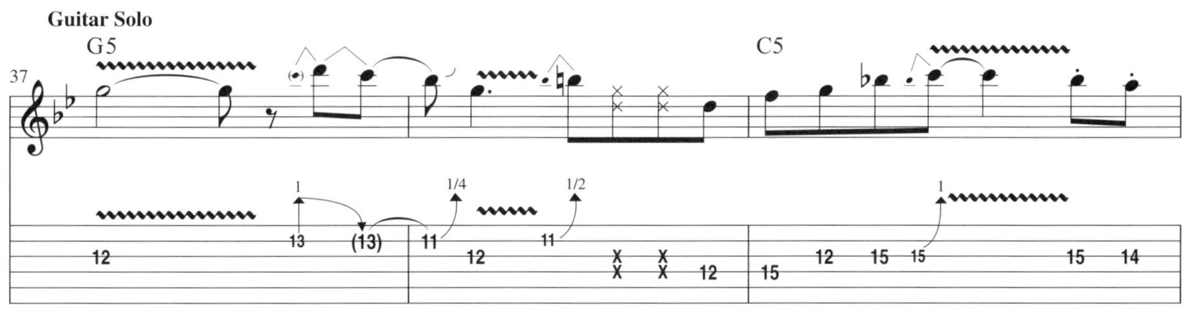
G5
C5
37
1
1/4
1/2
1
12
13
(13)
11
12
11
X
X
X
X
12
15
12
15
15
15
14

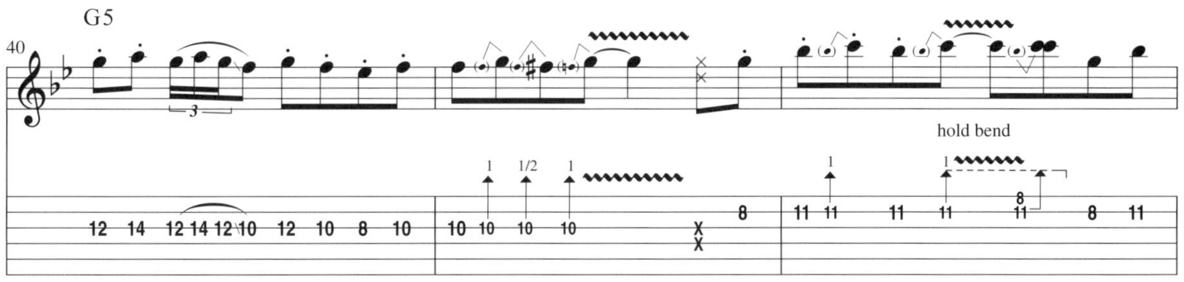
G5
40
3
hold bend
1
1/2
1
1
1
12 14 12 14 12 10 12 10 8 10
10 10 10 10
X
X
8
11 11 11 11 8 11 8 11

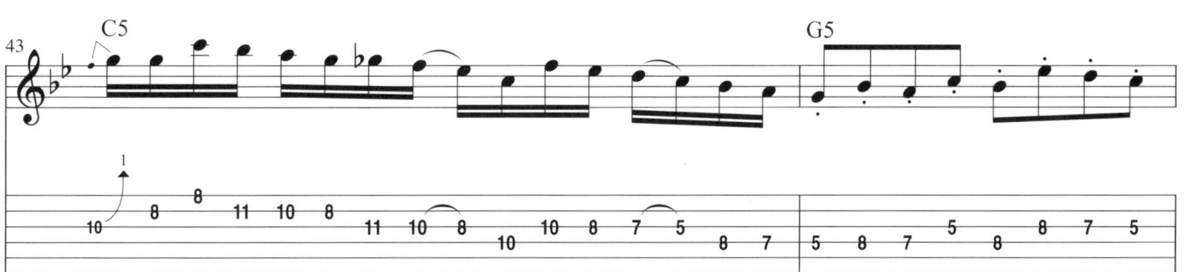
C5
G5
43
1
10 8 8 11 10 8 11 10 8 10 10 8 7 5 8 7
5 8 7 5 8 8 7 5

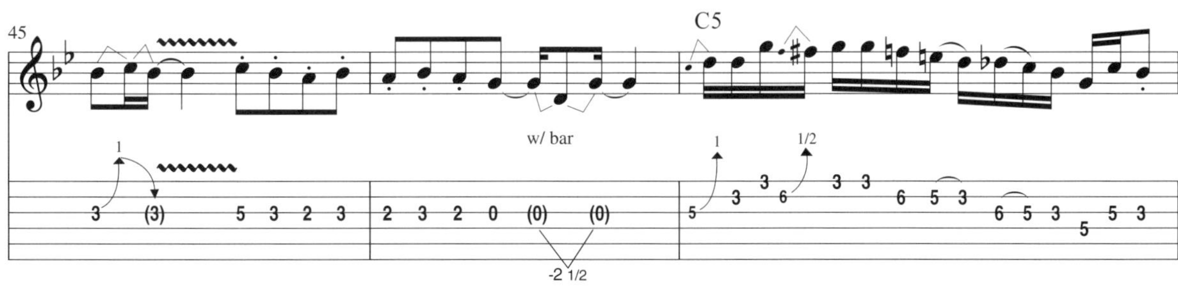
C5
45
w/ bar
1
1
1/2
3 (3) 5 3 2 3
2 3 2 0 (0) (0)
-2 1/2
5 3 3 6 3 3 6 5 3 6 5 3 5 5 3

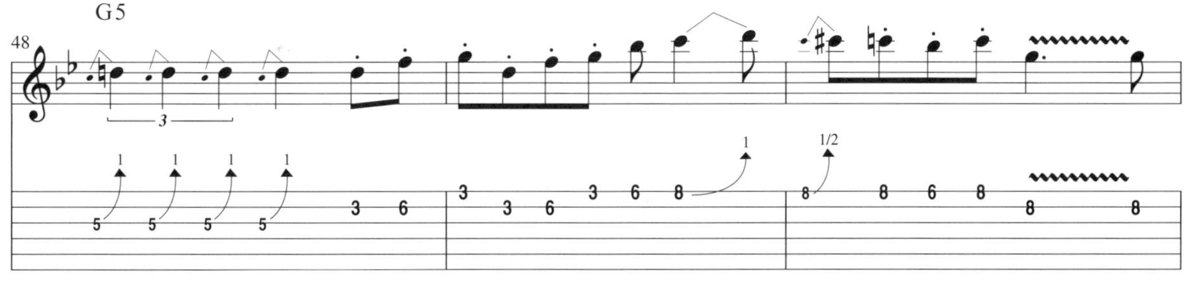
G5
48
3
1
1
1
1
1
1/2
5 5 5 5 3 6
3 3 6 3 6 8
8 8 6 8 8 8

C5
G5
8va
51
1/2
1
11 10 8 8 11 8 8 11 8 8 11 8 10
11 13 13 13
C5
F5
8va
loco
53
1 1 1 1 1
(13) 13 13 13 13 13 13 13 10 13 13
1 1/2 1/4 1/2
5 6 5 (5) 3 5 3 5
N.C.(G5)
56
grad. bend
1
3/4
8 8 6 8 8 (8) 8 8 8 8 8 8 8
58
3
3/4 1/2 1/4
8 8 8 8 8 6 (6) (6)
1
61
D.S. al Coda
0 0 3 3 5 5 0 0 3 3 6 6 5 5 0 0 3 3 5 5 3 3 0 0 5 5

Additional Lyrics

2. They burned down the gambling house,
   It died with an awful sound.
   A Funky Claude was running in and out,
   Pulling kids out the ground.
   When it was all over, we had to find another place.
   But Swiss time was running out;
   It seemed we would lose the race.

3. We ended up at the Grand Hotel,
   It was empty, cold and bare.
   But with the Rolling truck Stones thing just outside,
   Making our music there.
   With a few red lights, a few old beds
   We made a place to sweat.
   No matter what we get out of this,
   I know, I know we'll never forget.

CHAPTER 20
"DUST IN THE WIND"

What's Ahead:

- Open-position chords
- Ringing chords voiced high on the neck
- Travis picking
- How to pronounce weird-looking chords like F6(♯11)/A

"Dust in the Wind," by Kansas, is our featured acoustic-guitar song. A hypnotic and atmospheric pop ballad, with elements of folk and country, it's a perennial classic-rock favorite. Lush-sounding, open-string voicings, all played fingerstyle, mark the perfect balance against the rather despairing lyric content. But, hey, you're here for the guitar parts anyway.

To play "Dust in the Wind," you must be able to play open-position chords, and open-string chords above the third fret. You also need to be familiar with fingerstyle playing and the technique known as "Travis picking."

TONE TIPS

Guitar: steel- or nylon-string acoustic

SONG STRUCTURE

Key: C major and A minor

Section	Number of Measures	First Chord	Last Chord
Intro	8	C	G/B
Verse 1	8	C	Am
Chorus 1	4	D/F♯	G/B
Verse 2	8	C	Am
Chorus 2	7	D/F♯	F6(♯11)/A
Interlude	16	Am(add9)	G/B
Verse 3	8	C	Am
Chorus 3	7	D/F♯	G
Outro	3 (repeat and fade)	Am	Asus4(♭13)

THE FINGERPICKING PATTERN

Before you do anything, you need to engrain the right-hand picking pattern firmly in your mind. It's based on a fingerstyle technique known as "Travis picking," in which the thumb plays alternating bass lines, while the fingers play counter melodies on the higher strings. You can turn back to Chapter 16 for Travis-picking boot camp, or you can march on ahead.

With few exceptions, the fingerpicking pattern established in the opening measure remains constant throughout the song. So let's put that bar together. The following figures separate the complicated moves into three segments. The first segment is the bass line, which you play with your thumb. Anchor your first, second, and third fingers underneath the G, B, and high E strings, respectively, while you practice this measure repeatedly. Pluck in a steady, eighth-note rhythm, and make sure to let the notes ring together. Move on to the next segment when you're ready. This measure adds the open G string to the last sixteenth note of each beat, which you pluck up with your first finger, just after the thumb hits the D string. At this point, it sounds like a horse with a wooden leg, but at least you're getting the moves down. All right, now form an open C chord and have at the final segment. This one has you plucking the B string with your second finger on the downbeat of beats 1 and 3, and on the second sixteenth note of beats 2 and 4. Don't forget to lift your fretting finger off of the B string on beat 3. This creates the Cmaj7 voicing. Spend a serious amount of time on this measure so when it's time to put the other chords in, you won't have to think about the picking pattern; your right hand will be on autopilot.

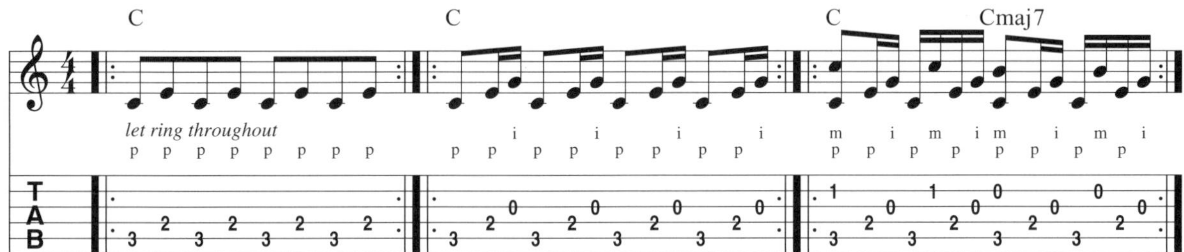

THE VOICINGS

At this point, it may be a good idea to put the fingerpicking aside for a moment and get your left hand familiar with all of the chord voicings used in the song (see below). Here are the chords that appear in the intro and throughout the song.

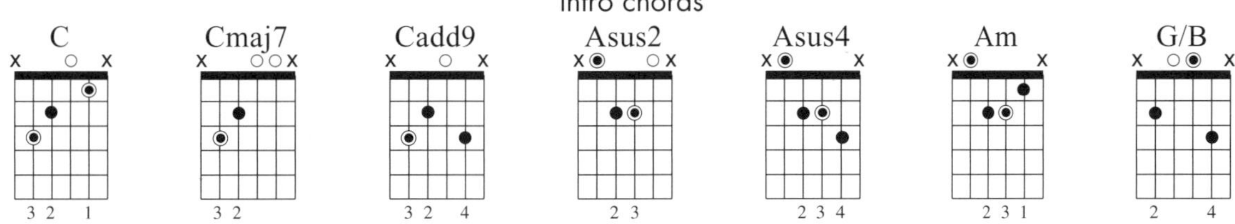

This figure features a few additional chords that pop up in the verse sections.

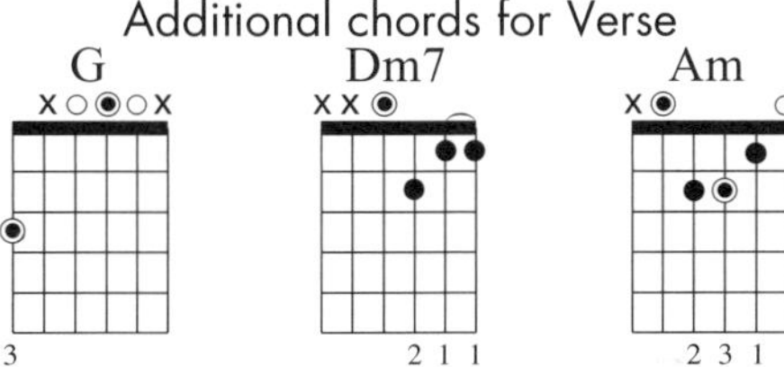

The chords below are used in the chorus and *interlude* (instrumental section of a song that isn't a solo) sections. Of particular interest are the Am(add9), G/A, F(♯11)/A, and F6(♯11)/A (pronounced "F-six-sharp-eleven-over-A").

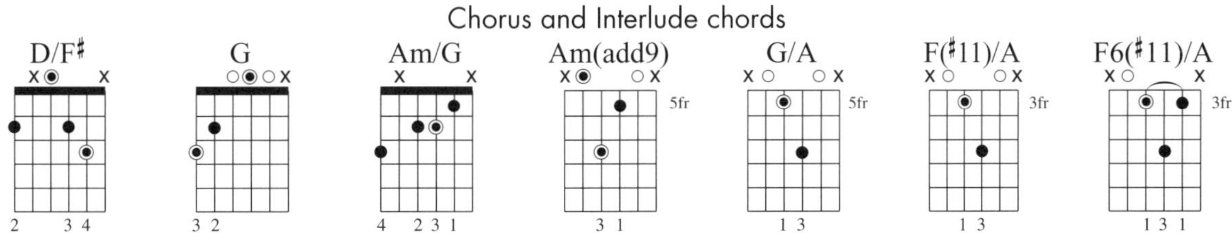

Here are the chords that are used in the outro fade.

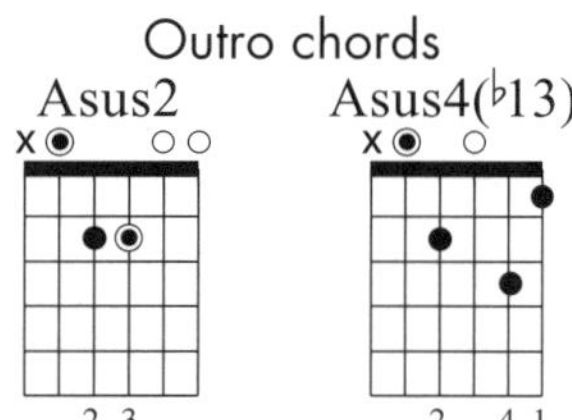

PUTTING IT ALL TOGETHER

Here are a few tips for putting the song together. Practice the intro by itself, very slowly at first, and then get it up to speed gradually. This is the easiest section because every single measure (except the last one) uses the same picking pattern, on the same sets of strings. The verse section gets a little more complicated because the low E and high E strings are thrown into the mix here and there. Isolate this section and play it over and over until you have it down pat. Use the same procedure for the rest of the tune. Once you're able to play each section correctly on their own, string them together, from beginning to end. Good luck!

- You can come up with some interesting voicings by playing open-position chords up the neck.
- Travis picking requires you to play alternating bass notes with your thumb, while simultaneously picking counter melodies with your fingers.
- Playing fingerstyle is much easier on acoustic guitar than on electric.
- Put the song together, section by section, before you attempt to play it all the way through.

Dust in the Wind

Words and Music by
Kerry Livgren

*p = thumb, i = index, m = middle

Cadd9
C
Cmaj7
Cadd9
Am
Asus2
Asus4
Am
G/B
1. I
Verse
C
G/B
Am
close my eyes,
2.,3. See additional lyrics
G
Dm7
Am
G/B
on - ly for a mo - ment, and the mo - ment's gone.

13
C
G/B
Am
All
my
dreams
15
G
Dm7
Am
pass be - fore my eyes, a cu - ri - os - i - ty.
Chorus
17
D/F♯
G
Am
Am/G
To Coda
Dust
in the wind.
19
D/F♯
G
1.
Am
G/B
All they we are is dust in the wind.

2.
Am(add9)
G/A
wind.
F(♯11)/A
F6(♯11)/A
Oh,
ho,
ho.
Interlude
Am(add9)
G/A
F(♯11)/A
F6(♯11)/A
2nd time, D.C. al Coda
Coda
D/F♯
G
Am
Am/G
All we are is dust in the wind.
(All we are is dust in the

Additional Lyrics

2. Same old song.
   Just a drop of water in an endless sea.
   All we do
   Crumbles to the ground though we refuse to see.

3. Now don't hang on,
   Nothing lasts forever but the earth and sky.
   It slips away
   And all your money won't another minute buy.

CHAPTER 21
"SMELLS LIKE TEEN SPIRIT"

What's Ahead:

- Barre chords
- Sixteenth-note rhythms
- Melodic soloing
- Doubling the bass player
- Doing the "effects pedal soft-shoe dance"

In 1991, Seattle band Nirvana officially kicked off the grunge era with the release of "Smells Like Teen Spirit." Few songs epitomize the '90s so effectively as this power-chord rocker. Major staples of modern hard-rock guitar playing are displayed in this song: flailing power chords drenched with super distortion; simple, melodic soloing; creative use of effects; and strange chord progressions. The lyrics are anybody's guess. Either Kurt Cobain was truly a genius poet, or he owned a great rhyming dictionary.

To play "Smells Like Teen Spirit," you must be able to play power chords; sixteenth-note strumming patterns; dyads; single-note melodies with bends, slides, and pull-offs; and be able to turn on and off several effects pedals without looking like a dork.

TONE TIPS

Guitar: solidbody electric
Pickup configuration: humbucking or single-coil
Pickup selection: bridge
Amp: Marshall- or Rectifier-type
Treble/Middle/Bass: 8/4/8
Gain: clean for intro and verses; slight overdrive for pre-choruses
Effects: distortion, chorus, and compression pedals

SONG STRUCTURE

Key: F minor

Section	Number of Measures	First Chord	Last Chord
Intro	16	F5	N/A (D♭5)
Verse 1	8	N/A (F5)	N/A (D♭5)
Pre-Chorus 1	8	N/A (F5)	N/A (F5)
Chorus 1	12	F5	D♭
Bridge 1	4	F5	A♭5
Verse 2	8 (plus 4 intro)	N/A (F5)	N/A (D♭5)
Pre-Chorus 2	8	N/A (F5)	N/A (F5)
Chorus 2	12	F5	D♭
Bridge 2	4	F5	A♭5
Solo	16	N/A (F5)	N/A (D♭5)
Interlude	4	N/A (F5)	N/A (D♭5)
Verse 3	8	N/A (F5)	N/A (D♭5)
Pre-Chorus 3	8	N/A (F5)	N/A (F5)
Chorus 3	12	F5	D♭
Outro	11	F5	F5

STRUMMING THE MAIN RIFF

The main riff is a marriage of power and barre chords, sixteenth-note rhythms, and muted string scratches. The chords are the easy part (see below), it's the rhythm that's gonna getcha!

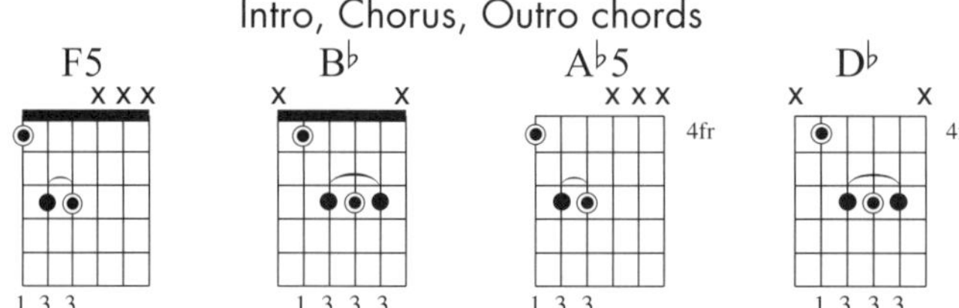

When dealing with sixteenth-note rhythms, it's best to keep your hand swinging in time (down-up-down-up for each one-beat grouping) over the strings, attacking them with the pick when a chord or "scratch" is to be performed. Confused? Well, take a look at this next figure. These are the opening measures of the tune, with strumming notation added below the music staff. The large arrows depict when to attack the strings; the little arrows tell you when to lift your hand away from the strings. The pattern keeps your hand swinging in time to the sixteenth-note pulse. Try it very slowly, one measure at a time. The X's are muted string scratches. They indicate to mute the strings with the fingers of your left hand while you strum the rhythms. This produces a percussive, funky sound. Notice the use of the "secret strum" at the end of each measure (see "The Secret Strum," Chapter 9).

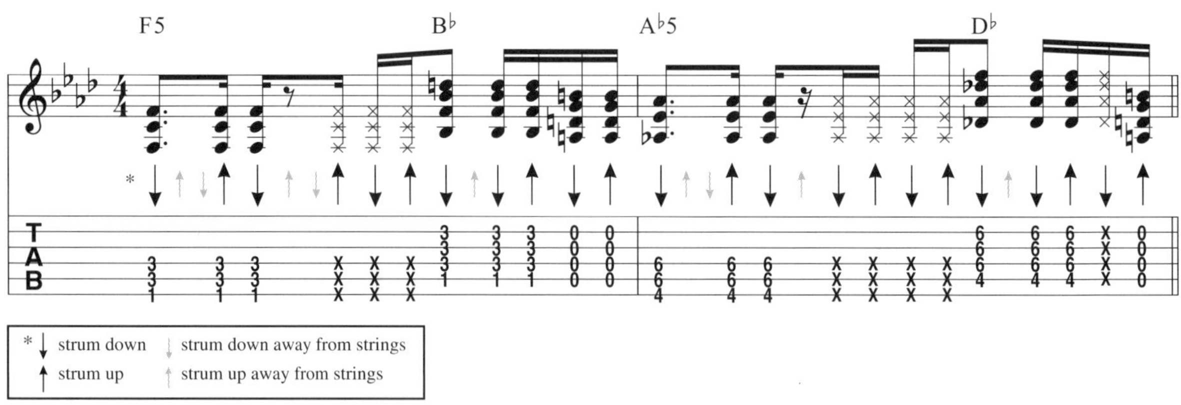

THE SECONDARY RIFFS

"Smells Like Teen Spirit" holds several "secondary" riffs. The first one is the dyad (two-note chord) figure in the verse sections. Use your first finger to bar across the high E and B strings at the first fret. This develops into another riff, involving the same notes but different rhythms, in the *pre-chorus* (section that sets up the chorus). The *bridge* (section that serves as a contrast to the song's other sections) houses the third, and final, secondary riff. This one is actually a series of power chords (see below) interspersed with a quirky bend on the G string, which you can grab with your third finger.

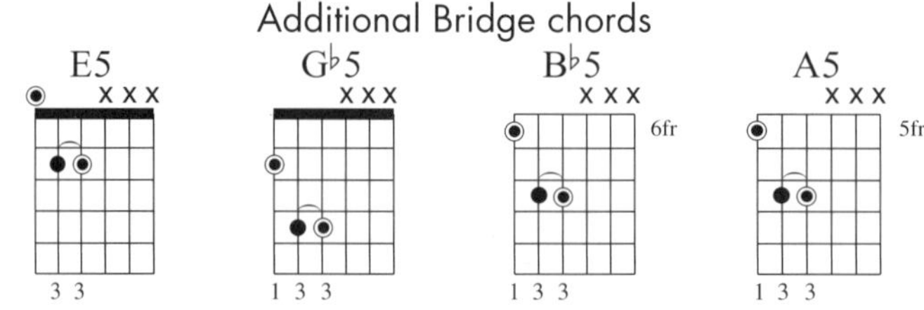

MELODIC SOLOING

Never professing to be a guitar virtuoso, Cobain usually opted for melody as opposed to flash. Such is the case here. The solo is actually the vocal melody of the verse sections, albeit played with a fair amount of legato techniques, such as bends, slides, and pull-offs. What's interesting is that it's played entirely on the D and G strings. Again, we've mapped out the solo for you in small boxes. The instructions below each box signify where the notes are to be played in the solo.

Kurt's solo boxes for F minor scale

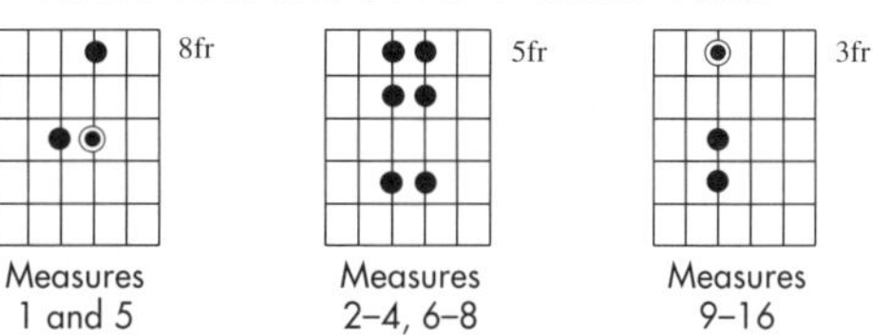

THE EFFECTS-PEDAL SOFT-SHOE DANCE

There's a lot of pedal-stomping involved in "Smells Like Teen Spirit." The "Tone Tips" suggest you use a channel-switching amplifier, with one channel set to a clean tone and the other to a medium overdrive, coupled with a distortion pedal (stompbox). You also need a chorus and a compression pedal (optional). Unless you have a roadie to activate your pedals remotely, you'll need to do some fancy footwork (channel switching and pedals are activated by stepping on footswitches) to change textures. Of course, you could program patches into a multi-effects unit (an all-in-one contraption that produces a variety of sound effects), but let's do it the old-fashioned way. Here's a run down of moves you would have to make to accurately portray the song. ("X" indicates which amp channel is activated and what pedals are on.)

Section	Amplifier Channels		Pedals		
	Clean	Overdrive	Distortion	Chorus	Compression
Intro (bars 1–4)	X				
Intro (bars 5–12)		X	X		
Intro (bars 13–16)	X			X	
Verse	X			X	
Pre-chorus		X			
Chorus		X	X		
Bridge		X	X		
Solo		X	X	X	X

Don't forget—on top of keeping track of all of this, you still have to play the song. Are you sure you want to be a rock-and-roll star? In all seriousness, though, all you really need is a channel-switching amp (or a clean amp and a distortion pedal) and a chorus unit to faithfully represent the tones in the song.

- Keep your arm swinging in time when you play sixteenth-note rhythms.
- When you perform the scratch rhythms, mute the strings with all of your left-hand fingers.
- There are a lot of section changes in this song. Think ahead, and be ready for what's coming next.
- Hire a roadie to turn on and off your effects, so you can just stand there looking cool.

audio tracks 51

Smells Like Teen Spirit

Words and Music by Kurt Cobain,
Krist Novoselic and Dave Grohl

Verse
N.C.(F5)
(B♭5)
(A♭5)
(D♭5)
1. Load up on guns and bring your friends. It's fun to lose
2. See additional lyrics
let ring
and to pre - tend. She's o - ver - bored and self - as - sured.
Oh no, I know a dirt - y word.
Pre-Chorus
Hel - lo, hel - lo,
hel - lo, how low? Hel - lo, hel - lo, hel - lo, how low? Hel - lo, hel - lo,
w/ slight dist.

(A♭5)
(D♭5)
(F5)
(B♭5)
(A♭5)
(D♭5)
24
hel - lo, how low? Hel - lo, hel - lo, hel - lo. With the lights
let ring
w/ dist.
chorus off
Chorus
F5
B♭
A♭5
D♭
27
out it's less dan - g'rous. Here we are
29
now, en - ter - tain us. I feel stu -
31
- pid and con - ta - gious. Here we are

33
F5 B♭ A♭5 D♭
now, en - ter - tain us. A mul - la -
35
F5 B♭ A♭5 D♭
- to, an al - bi - no, a mos - qui -
To Coda
37
F5 B♭ A♭5 D♭
- to, my li - bi - do. Yeah,
Bridge
39
F5 E5 F5 G♭5 N.C. F5 E5 F5 B♭5 A♭5 F5 E5 F5 G♭5 N.C.
yay, yay.

1.
2.
F5
E5
B♭5
A5
A♭5
Guitar Solo
B♭
D♭
w/ chorus & compression
1
1/2

Interlude
N.C.(F5) (B♭5) (A♭5) (D♭5) (F5) (B♭5) (A♭5) (D♭5)
60
compressor off
Verse
N.C.(F5) (B♭5) (A♭5) (D♭5)
64
3. And I for - get just why I taste.
(F5) (B♭5) (A♭5) (D♭5) (F5) (B♭5)
66
Oo, yeah, I guess it makes you smile, I found it hard
D.S. al Coda
(A♭5) (D♭5) (F5) (B♭5) (A♭5) (D♭5)
69
it's hard to find. Oh well, what - ev - er, nev - er mind.

Additional Lyrics

2. I'm worse at what I do best,
And for this gift I feel blessed.
Our little group has always been
And always will until the end.

SECTION 6

Equipment

CHAPTER 22
GUITARS, GUITARS, GUITARS

What's Ahead:

- Acoustic guitars
- Electric guitars
- Special guitars
- Pickups
- Shopping for a guitar

Whether you're in the market for your first guitar, looking to upgrade to a better instrument, planning on buying an amplifier, trying to decide which effects pedals to purchase, or just interested in guitars and accessories in general, this section will help you on your way to making a wise purchase.

Looking for a student-level classical guitar? Interested in a top-of-the-line electric? Thinking of acquiring a good used jazz guitar? In this chapter, we'll look at the most popular types and brands of guitars, from acoustics and electrics, to specialty guitars.

ACOUSTIC GUITARS

Acoustic guitars are generally lumped into three categories: steel-string, nylon-string, and acoustic/electric.

Steel-string Acoustic

The *steel-string* is the most popular acoustic guitar. They have a rich, ringing tone, and are loud enough to accompany a group of singers. Steel-string acoustics are very popular in country, blues, folk, and rock, and can be played with a pick or fingerstyle.

Steel-string acoustics come in different body sizes; the most common being the dreadnought (see photo). Most guitar companies manufacture dreadnought-style acoustics. Popular high-end brands (over $1,500) include Martin, Taylor, Gibson, and Guild, but you can buy a well-constructed dreadnought for $300–$1,000 from companies such as Takamine, Washburn, Yamaha, Ibanez, Fender, and Mitchell. (Many of these companies also produce high-end guitars.) As a general guideline, consider $200–$600 the economy range; $600–$1,500 the mid-range price; and $1,500–$7,000 and up, the professional and high-end range. (The prices in this chapter are based on manufacturer's list price as of this writing. Many music stores offer a substantial discount on guitars; 20–30 percent off of list is not uncommon.)

Dreadnought Steel-string

Dreadnought acoustics are large-body guitars, and may be uncomfortable for people under five-feet, four-inches tall. Many student-model acoustics are smaller in size, but there are also many small-body professional models such as the Taylor Grand Auditorium (see adjacent photo).

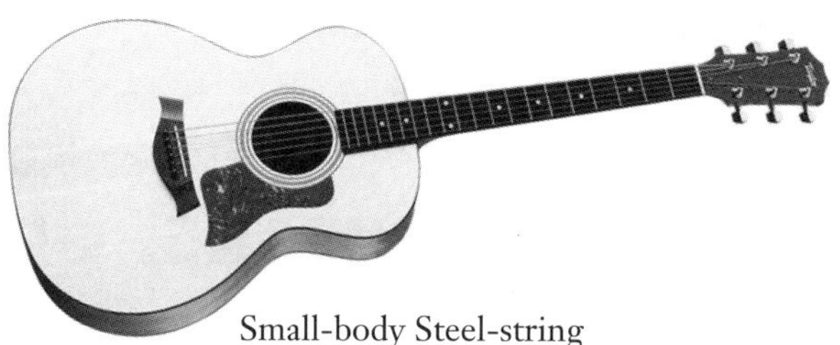

Small-body Steel-string

Price fluctuations for steel-string guitars most often are determined by the types of woods used in the construction of the instrument. For instance, many low-level instruments are made with laminated veneer tops. Instead of using a solid piece of wood, several thin layers of wood are glued together and covered with a veneer top. Besides the level of craftsmanship, other factors that up the ticket price of steel-string acoustics are fancy inlays (position markers), bindings (decorative strips around the sides of the body, the soundhole, and neck), and hardware (tuning pegs).

Nylon-string (Classical)

The *nylon-string*, or classical guitar (see below), is mellower in tone and softer in volume than the steel-string acoustic. It also has less sustain, which means the notes decay quicker. The body of a nylon-string guitar is also smaller in size than most steel-strings. Because of this, and the fact that the strings are easier to press down, some consider the nylon-string a good starter instrument for youngsters. The one drawback is that the neck is much wider than a steel-string, making it harder to play for people with small hands. Also, nylon-string guitars are meant to be played fingerstyle, rather than strummed with a pick, although there are exceptions, particularly in modern jazz. The nylon-string is the essential guitar for classical and flamenco players, but is also popular in styles such as folk, country, and Latin.

Nylon-string

Price ranges for nylon-string guitars are comparable to steel-strings. All of the previously mentioned companies produce nylon- string guitars but you would also want to look into Ramirez (high end), Alvarez, Hernandez, and Cordoba.

Acoustic/Electric

An *acoustic/electric* guitar is an acoustic that is equipped with an inner-microphone or pickup. Although they can be played acoustically, they are meant to be played through an amplifier or sound system (PA). Acoustic/electric guitars have a control board built into their bodies, usually on the top shoulder, where it's visible to the player. This panel usually consists of a volume control and a set of tone-adjusting devices for treble, bass, and middle.

If you're going to be playing an acoustic guitar onstage, with a band, you'll want to think about purchasing an acoustic/electric. (An option is to have a professional repairman install a pickup system into the acoustic guitar you already own.) Most acoustic/electric guitars come with a cutaway body, which is an indentation in the lower shoulder of the guitar (see photo). The cutaway allows easier access to the higher frets. Two major considerations regarding an acoustic/electric: 1) the body size is usually

Acoustic/electric

smaller than that of a standard acoustic guitar; and 2) they are often easier to play. But don't forget—you'll need to purchase an amplifier to enjoy the full benefits of an acoustic/electric.

Although you can find nylon-string acoustic/electrics, the majority are steel-strings. You can expect to see a price tag that is several hundred dollars higher than a comparable acoustic guitar. Taylor, Ovation, Takamine, and Washburn are among the most popular brands of acoustic/electrics, but most companies that manufacture acoustic guitars also offer an acoustic/electric line.

ELECTRIC GUITARS

Electric guitars fall into one of two main categories: solidbody or hollowbody.

Solidbody Electrics

Hands down, the most popular electric guitar is the solidbody. The *solidbody electric* gets its name from the fact that its body is made of solid wood (no hollow cavities). This type of construction helps to increase sustain and resist feedback (whistling or howling sound produced by the pickups at high volume levels). The most famous models include the Fender Stratocaster, Fender Telecaster, and Gibson Les Paul.

Stratocaster Telecaster Les Paul

Strat-style Guitars

The *Fender Stratocaster* is such an influential instrument, there's a category of electrics that bears its name: "Strat-style." There are three main factors that define the Stratocaster: 1) a double-cutaway body design that allows easy access to the higher frets; 2) a "three single-coil" pickup configuration (see Chapter 24); and 3) a whammy-bar assembly.

The Stratocaster is an extremely versatile guitar. It's a must-have instrument for nearly every professional rock, blues, R&B, funk, or country guitarist. The only style it doesn't excel in is jazz. Three famous guitarists forever linked with the Stratocaster are Jimi Hendrix, Stevie Ray Vaughan, and Eric Clapton.

A *Strat-style guitar* is one that resembles the Fender Stratocaster. The main similarities include the body design, the angle of the tuning pegs (all are along the top side of the headstock), and the inclusion of a whammy-bar system. Most Strat-style guitars have three pickups, but many have a humbucking pickup in the bridge position, and sometimes in the neck position. Popular Strat-style guitars include Ibanez, Tom Anderson, Jackson, Charvel, and Kramer.

Fender makes a wide-variety of Stratocaster models in all price ranges, from around $600 to over the $3,000 mark and beyond. Strat-style guitars are comparable in price, but some are a little less expensive.

"Twin-humbucking" Chunk

The *Gibson Les Paul* epitomizes the fat, chunky sound of hard rock. Many a classic-rock riff and solo was played on a Les Paul. It's also a popular choice among blues guitarists, and even some jazz artists. Its only drawback is it lacks the high-end jangle needed for country. The Les Paul is heavy, durable, has a single-cutaway body style, and an arch-top (curved upward). Famous for its "twin-humbucking" pickup configuration (see Chapter 24), the Les Paul is capable of producing seemingly endless sustain. (Nigel from Spinal Tap will attest to that!) Among its most famous players are Jimmy Page, Michael Bloomfield, Slash, Zakk Wylde, and the inventor himself, Les Paul.

The twin-humbucking, heavyweight construction of the Les Paul inspired many popular solidbody designs, among them the Gibson SG, Explorer, and Flying V; the Ibanez Iceman; Paul Reed Smith; and B.C. Rich models.

Les Pauls and other twin-humbucking guitars are a bit pricier than Strat-style solidbodies, but Epiphone offers a variety of Les Paul–style guitars, starting at around $500.

The Telecaster Simplicity

The *Fender Telecaster* is the guitar of choice among country pickers. It's also an excellent rock 'n' roll guitar, ideal for funk and R&B, and great for blues. It only lacks the warmth and low-end needed for jazz.

The Telecaster was the first mass-produced solidbody electric guitar. Its simplistic design and electronics (two single-coil pickups, selector switch, and one volume and one tone knob) are a major part of its allure, along with its famous bite and twang. A few famous players include Keith Richards, James Burton, Andy Summers, Steve Cropper, Chrissie Hynde, and Albert Collins.

Fender offers a variety of Telecaster models, starting from around $350. Mid-level prices are $600–$1,000, and some custom models cost up to $8,000. Many companies make Tele-style guitars, among them G&L and Fernandez.

Vintage Stratocasters, Les Pauls, and Telecasters are highly sought-after instruments; some commanding prices bordering on six figures! The demand has been so great over the past few decades that manufacturers started building replicas, replete with gouge marks and tarnished hardware. Even these substitutes carry a hefty price tag.

Hollowbody Electrics

A *hollowbody electric* has pickups and electronics like a solidbody, but the body has a hollow cavity. Hollowbodies have a warmer, or bassier, sound than solidbodies. They also resonate more than their solidbody counterparts (because the sound circulates in the hollow cavity), and are prone to howling feedback at high volumes.

Some hollowbody electrics are completely hollow inside, like the Gibson ES-175 (see photo). These types of guitars are sometimes called "arch-tops" or "jazz boxes," and, not surprisingly, are the standard choice of jazz guitarists. Other hollowbody electrics, such as the Gibson ES-335 (see photo), have the neck block running through the body, dividing it into two separate cavities. These types of hollowbodies are sometimes called "semi-hollow," and have a thinner body style than jazz boxes. Semi-hollow electrics are also used for jazz, but they're also a favorite

Gibson 175 Gibson 335

among blues players like B.B. King, jazz/pop/rock instrumentalists such as Larry Carlton, and rock players like Chuck Berry, and Alvin Lee of Ten Years After.

Hollowbody electrics (Gibson, Gretsch, Hofner, Ibanez, and Benedetto) are more expensive than solidbodies, with the average starting price above the $2,000 mark. The Epiphone Dot Electric is a lower-price alternative, starting at around $650.

SPECIALTY GUITARS

Most electric and acoustic guitars have six strings, but there are a few popular variations. Let's look at a few.

12-string Guitars

The *12-string guitar* virtually "doubles the pleasure" of a standard six-string. The 12 strings are arranged in six pairs, or courses, so it's almost like playing a regular guitar with big, fat strings. The high E and B string courses are tuned in unison, while the bottom pairs consist of one standard-tuned string and one string tuned an octave higher. The additional high-pitched strings give the 12-string guitar its ringing, jangly character.

Most 12-strings look and handle like their acoustic and electric counterparts, but some come in double-neck form. Jimmy Page's double-neck guitar has a standard six-string neck on the bottom and a 12-string neck on top. Thus, he could segue seamlessly from the mellow 12-string part to the burning six-string solo at the end of "Stairway to Heaven." Listen to "Mr. Tambourine Man," by the Byrds; "Ticket to Ride," by the Beatles; "Hotel California," by the Eagles; and "The Waiting," by Tom Petty and the Heartbreakers for examples of the 12-string guitar.

Seven-string

The *seven-string guitar* is a standard electric guitar with an additional low B string that sits next to the low E. Popular among jazz guitarists as far back as the late '30s (George Van Eps), the seven-string enjoyed a resurgence in the '90s, when guitarists Steve Vai and John Petrucci (Dream Theater) started using it. Soon it became the guitar of choice for low-riffing, hard-rock bands like Korn and Limp Bizkit. Listen to "Freak on a Leash," by Korn, for the ultra-low, grinding sound of the seven-string guitar.

Baritone Guitar

A *baritone guitar* is played exactly like a regular guitar, but the strings are tuned to a much lower register: typically either B–E–A–D–F♯–B or A–D–G–C–E–A, low to high. Country session guitarists have used them for years. The guitar solos in "Witchita Lineman" and "Galveston," by Glen Campbell, exemplify the low, twangy register of the baritone guitar.

PURCHASING A GUITAR

Purchasing a guitar can be an overwhelming experience, especially if you're new to the game. Before you lay your money down, you'll want to get all your ducks in a row.

What Type of Guitar Do I Want?

The first thing you want to do is decide what type of guitar you're looking for. If you're interested in an acoustic, that's fine, but you'll want to buy the one best suited for your playing needs. You may want a steel-string acoustic, or you may want a nylon-string classical guitar. Perhaps your needs will be better suited with an acoustic/electric guitar. The same goes for electric guitars. Some are better suited for jazz, while others are for wailing rock leads. All of these decisions can be based largely on the type of music you play, or want to play. The sections "Acoustic Guitars" and "Electric Guitars," located earlier in this chapter, should help you in the initial decision-making process.

You'll also want to think about your spending limit. This depends on how committed you are, and how thick your billfold happens to be. If money is really tight, you may want to consider a used guitar, or a new one that has been slightly damaged, such as a ding in the paint job. Also, be on the lookout for sales. Once you think you've made up your mind, you're ready for the first step.

Taking the First Step

The first step in a journey is often the hardest one. Here's some advice on how to start your guitar quest:

- Head on down to the music store with the intention of just browsing. (If possible, take a friend along with you who knows about guitars.) Take your time and try to look at all of the guitars in the store. Check out the price tags and ask questions of the salespeople, but don't let them pressure you into a quick purchase. They almost always ask your price range, so have that ready. Also, be prepared to answer questions about your preferred style of music and how long you've been playing. Try to visit a variety of music stores, because some dealers only carry a few different brand names.
- Try out as many different guitars as possible, in all price ranges. This will help you understand the differences between top-of-the-line (expensive) instruments and lower-end models. Depending on your playing experience, you may start to notice variations in playability, sound quality, and craftsmanship. Even if you don't, at least you're gaining the experience of "test driving" various instruments.
- Try to keep an open mind. Don't fall in love with one guitar just because it's your favorite color. And don't overlook some guitars because they aren't your favorite color. That ugly brown guitar may just be the one that screams "Buy me!" if you take it down from the rack and play it.

Eureka—I Found It!

Once you've found that special guitar that "speaks" to you, spend a good amount of time playing it. You may want to go have a bite to eat so you can gain some perspective, and then come back later to play it again. If it still feels just right, you'll want to give it a final check-up. Here are some things to consider:

Appearance: Look over the guitar from front to back, and top to bottom. Are there any dings or scrapes in the paint? Is there any tarnish on the metal parts (frets, pickup covers, bridge, etc.)? Is the color or design something you'll be happy with for years to come?

Neck attachment: If the guitar has a bolt-on neck (the necks of most Fender and Strat-style guitars are attached to the body with a four-bolt system), make sure it is attached firmly and doesn't wiggle. If the guitar has a set-in neck (most acoustics have set-in, or glued-on, necks, as do many electrics, such as Gibson), check to see if there are any visible cracks in the seams. You'll also want to check for any visible separation along the bindings (plastic strips along the guitar's neck and sides) and the neck inlays (position markers).

Neck angle: Make sure the neck isn't curved or warped. Stand the guitar on the floor and look down along the neck, just under the strings. It should appear relatively even with the strings all the way along the length of the neck. If it looks like a roller-coaster track, put the guitar back on the rack. If you're unsure, ask to play a similar guitar that's considerably more expensive. If there's a significant difference in playability, then you'll want to have the guitar looked at by an expert before purchasing it.

Tuners: Check to make sure the tuning pegs are firmly attached to the headstock, and that they don't slip. You can check for slipping by tuning each string a little flat, and then tuning it back up to pitch.

Intonation: When a guitar plays in tune all the way up the neck, it has good intonation. You can test this by hitting a 12th-fret harmonic (see Chapter 2) on the high E string, and then fretting it at the same fret. The pitch should be exactly the same. Do the same test procedure with all of the strings. If you don't trust your ears, you can use an electronic tuner. Again, if you're in doubt, have the guitar checked out by a repairman; preferably not the one who works in the store. You never can tell.

Electronics: If you're buying an electric guitar, don't forget to plug it into an amplifier to make sure that it works properly. Check to see if the pickup selector activates each pickup, and then turn the volume and tone knobs up and down to make sure they're in working order.

Closing the Deal

When you've made up your mind and you're sure you want to buy the guitar, the experience can be somewhat like buying a car. You'll want to prepare yourself to bargain with the salesperson. This is commonplace at most guitar stores, as many salespeople work on commission.

Don't be too anxious to close the deal. Before you shell out your hard-earned dough, make absolutely sure you're not paying too much for the guitar. One way to get an idea of the going rate for a new guitar is to check the internet. A good source that posts both the "deal" price and the manufacturer's suggested "list" price is musiciansfriend.com. As a matter of fact, that would be a good bargaining chip when you speak with a salesperson at the music store. You could say something like, "I can buy a guitar online, just like this one, for $500. Can you beat that?" It may or may not get the results you want, but at least you're not flying blind. Who knows? You may get lucky and get a salesperson who's having a good day. Perhaps he just sold 20-grand worth of gear and he's not too anxious to up his commission with you.

- There are three categories of acoustic guitars: steel-string, nylon-string, and acoustic/electric.
- There are two main categories of electric guitars: solidbody and hollowbody.
- Try out a variety of guitars before you make your final decision.
- Be prepared to bargain with the salesperson when it's time to close the deal.

CHAPTER 23
AMPS

What's Ahead:
- Practice amps
- Performance amps
- Reverb
- Dialing in a sound

Sure, you can play your new electric guitar without an amp—as long as you're alone in a quiet room. But sooner or later, you'll want to be able to crank up the volume and disturb the neighbors. That's when it's time to buy an amplifier. But what type of amp? Poke your head into just about any music store and you'll soon discover that there are all manners of shapes and sizes. Some have only a couple of knobs, while others have all sorts of flashing lights and doohickeys. Don't get flustered—in this chapter we'll help you sort it all out.

HOW DOES AN AMP WORK?

All guitar amplifiers, no matter how sophisticated, are based on the same basic principles: You plug your guitar into them; you turn up the volume; and the sound comes blasting out. From a more scientific standpoint, here's the basic scheme of things, or signal path:

- **Input jack**: Every amp has at least one of these (see below). This is the socket in which you plug your guitar cable. The other end of the cable goes into your guitar output jack, of course.
- **Preamp**: This is the section of the amp that shapes your sound. It contains the input-gain and tone controls. The gain knob, or input volume, boosts the "puny" electrical signal coming from your guitar, and the tone knobs are used to adjust the highs and lows.
- **Power amp**: This is the last stop in the amplifier section. It's where the preamp signal gets a final shot of steroids, making it powerful enough to push the sound out of the speaker, or speakers. Just how much power is sent to the speakers is determined by the setting on the master-volume control, located on the amp's control panel.
- **Speaker**: Technically, the speaker (where the sound comes out) is a separate entity. But since most amplifiers come with at least one speaker (or more) we decided to include it here.

PRACTICE AMPS

Basically, there are two types of guitar amps: performance amps and practice amps. Since you'll be spending a lot of time practicing with your new electric guitar, it only makes sense to buy a practice amplifier, doesn't it? Well, actually it does make sense.

A *practice amp* is a small amplifier (about a foot high) with approximately 10–15 watts (*watt* is the term used to measure the power of an amplifier), and a small speaker (six to eight inches). Loud enough to practice alone or jam with another guitarist, a practice amp doesn't quite cut the mustard when playing with a loud band. The majority of practice amps have solid-state circuitry (solid-state amps are much cheaper than tube amps), and most include a clean and *distortion* setting. (The distortion setting gives you the overdriven, hard-rock sound.) Fender, Marshall, and Crate all make good practice amps for around $150.

Beware of advertisements that offer practice amps for under $50. These are often micro–practice amps that aren't much bigger than your hand. The sound of a micro-amp is weak and distorted.

The earliest guitar amplifiers were manufactured in the 1930s, and were based on the same vacuum-tube technology used for radios and phonographs. These amplifiers were about the same volume as the average practice amp today (5–15 watts). In the 1950s, things got considerably louder. Fender led the pack with combo amps that sported upwards of 50 watts. By the early '60s, twin-speaker amps like the Fender Twin and Vox AC30 were pushing the envelope at upwards of 85 watts.

Just when it seemed things couldn't get any louder, along came the Marshall stack in the mid-'60s. With its 100-watt "head" pushing a tower made from two cabinets, housing four 12-inch speakers each, it blasted the backsides (and the audience's ears) of bands such as Cream and the Jimi Hendrix Experience. The Marshall tone soon became the classic sound of rock guitar. For a brief time, people got on the "transistor" wagon, using solid-state amplifiers. These amps boasted outrageous wattage ratings (200 and above), but they lacked the "warmth" and response of tube amps.

To date, solid-state circuitry has been greatly refined, but tube amps rule the high-end market. Marshall and Fender amps are the main workhorses for rock, blues, and country guitarists.

PERFORMANCE AMPS

A *performance amp* is an amplifier that's loud enough to be heard clearly over a loud drummer. The operative word here is "clearly." In other words, an amplifier with 20 watts may sound loud, but at high volumes it will "break up" and distort. On the other hand, an amplifier with 40 watts will not only be louder, it will stay clean at much higher volumes than the 20-watt amp. Get it? Well, all we're trying to say is, when choosing a performance amp, try to get as many watts as you can for your money.

Performance amps come in two basic varieties: a head with speaker cabinet or a combo. A *combo* amp is a "big brother" version of the practice amp. It's a self-contained unit that houses both the amplifier section and the speaker, or speakers. A Fender Twin Reverb is a combo amp. A *head/cabinet* combination is a two-unit amp, in which the amplifier section is separate from the speaker housing. The amp is the "head," which sits on top of the speaker cabinet. A Marshall "half stack" is a head/cabinet combination.

Combo Amps

Combo

The average combo amp is rated at 40–50 watts, has a 12-inch speaker, and comes with channel-switching capabilities and reverb (see photo). *Channel switching* allows you to switch over from a clean sound to a distorted sound; *reverb*, which stands for "reverberation," is used to create ambience, or depth. (With a low reverb setting, it sounds like you're playing in a large room; higher settings sound like you're playing in a gymnasium.) Consider these to be the *basic* features of a combo amp. You can choose to buy a combo amp with more power (up to 120 watts) and different speaker combinations (two 12s, four 10s, etc.). Additional speakers give you more clarity and better tone. You can also choose between a solid-state or tube combo. Tube amps have better tone, but solid-state amps are less expensive.

Fender, Peavey, Crate, Marshall, and Carvin all feature a wide-variety of combo amps. Solid-state models start at around $500, while tube models begin in the $700 price range. All of these amps are good for blues, rock, or country. For jazz, you're better off with a high-powered combo such as the Polytone Mini Brute II ($850), Roland Jazz Chorus ($1,250), or Fender Twin Reverb ($1,500).

Head/Cabinet Amps

Marshall introduced the "amp-head-sitting-on-top-of-a-speaker-cabinet" design in the mid-'60s, and it has been a mainstay in rock ever since. Why separate the head from the speaker(s)? Well, there are a number of benefits. For one, you can buy a head and choose between several speaker options. For another, it cuts down the overall weight of the amp. (The Fender Twin Reverb combo weighs in at a gut-busting 70 pounds!) And besides, they look cool when you stack the speaker cabinets on top of each other.

Head/Cabinet

The Marshall 100-watt tube head/4×12 cabinet is the classic head/cabinet combination (see photo). "4×12" stands for a speaker cabinet with four 12-inch speakers. This is an incredibly loud amp, and is specially designed with the rock guitarist in mind. Other popular brands are Mesa and Soldano. These are all high-end amps, and are the choice of the pros. You're talking at least $4,000 to wheel one of these beauties out of the front door. If you really have your heart set on a half stack, don't lose heart. Peavey, Randall, and Crate offer solid-state alternatives that start as low as $1,000.

Specialty Amps

Some amplifiers, such as Line 6 and the Fender Cyber series, come with special digital circuitry that allows them to imitate other amplifiers. These cloning amps start at an average price of $500.

Many companies, such as Roland, Fender, and Yamaha, make amplifiers designed especially for acoustic/electric guitars. These amps are usually low on power (average 30 watts), but high in fidelity. Prices start at around $500.

DIALING IN A TONE

"Dialing in a tone" is what you do when you twiddle the knobs on an amp for the purpose of obtaining a preferential sound. There are two basic tone settings: clean and dirty. "Clean" stands for a clean signal with no break-up (distortion), while "dirty" corresponds to a distorted tone. For example, the guitar on "Fun, Fun, Fun" is a clean tone. The guitar on "Smoke on the Water" is distorted. How do you set your amp to get those tones? Let's find out.

The following figure shows the control panel for a very basic amplifier. The first knob is the input volume (some amps label this knob "volume" or "gain"), which adjusts the amount of distortion, from clean to dirty. The middle knobs are the treble and bass controls (some amps label these "hi" and "low"), which work just like your stereo dials. The last knob is the master volume, which controls the overall loudness.

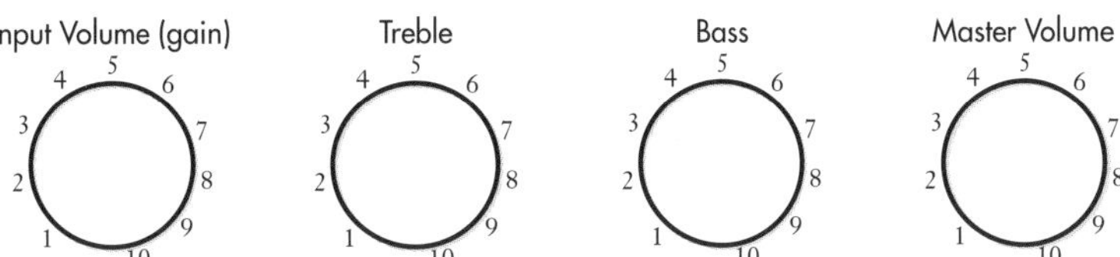

To "dial in" a clean setting, it's a good idea to start by setting the tone knobs halfway. This is known as a "flat" setting. The lower the setting on the input knob, the cleaner your sound will be. "Three" (3) is a good, average setting for clean. Setting the master volume is purely a matter of how loud you want the amp to be. A good place to start is a little over halfway, around "6" (see below). If you select the bridge pickup on your guitar, your tone will be bright. If you select the neck pickup your tone mellows out in comparison. If your overall sound is too "boomy," lower the bass setting on the amp. If you want a brighter sound, raise the treble.

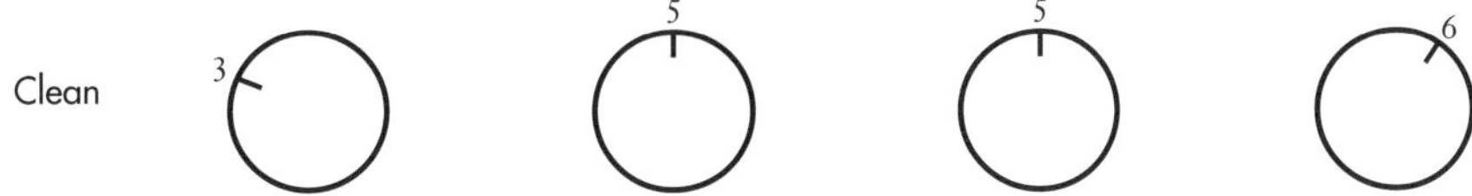

The figure below shows a setting for maximum distortion on the same amp. Notice that the input volume is set to "10" and the master volume is lowered to "3." This produces heavy distortion but keeps the overall volume at a reasonable level.

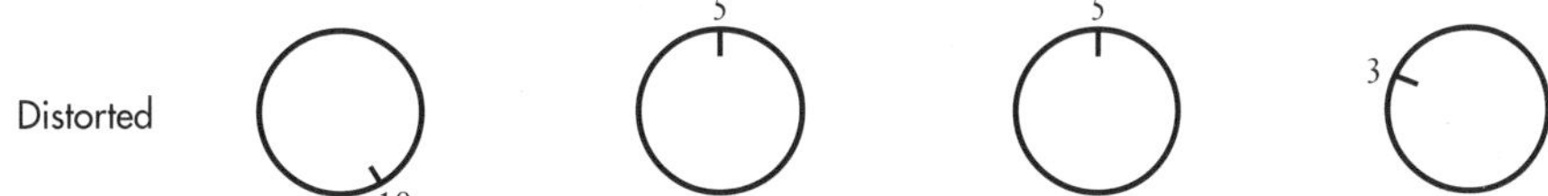

This next figure depicts the control panel of an amp with channel switching. The clean (channel 1) and dirty (channel 2) channels each have their own master volumes (master-volume 1 and 2, respectively). This allows you to dial in the amount of distortion while matching the overall volume of the clean channel. The settings depict a good, average mix. The "middle" knob is an additional tone control, which is featured on many amplifiers. Lowering the setting accentuates the highs and lows (good for heavy metal); raising the setting boosts the midrange of the tonal spectrum (good for blues solos).

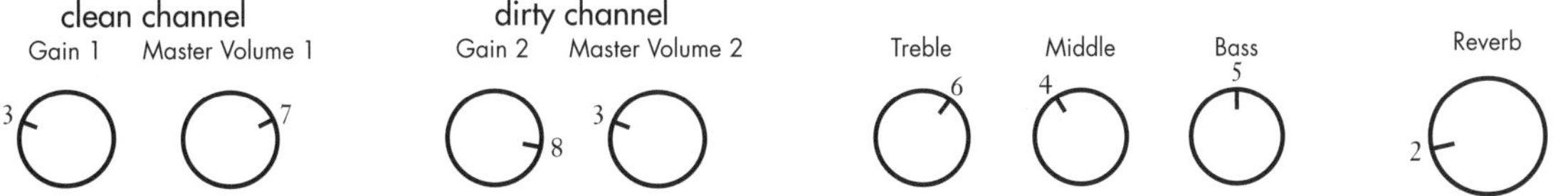

- Practice amps are small, portable, and loud enough to jam with another guitarist.
- Performance amps are louder, bigger, and sound better than practice amps.
- Reverb can make you sound like you're playing in a large concert hall.
- When dialing in a sound, start with the tone controls set at halfway.
- A low setting on the gain knob produces a clean sound; a high setting produces distortion.
- The pickup setting on your guitar also determines the brightness or mellowness of your tone.

CHAPTER 24
ACCESSORIES

What's Ahead:

- Cases
- Pickups
- Strings
- Capos, slides, cords, picks, tuners, and straps

In this chapter, we'll look at all of the extra little goodies available to guitarists; some essential, some recommended, and some just for fun.

JUST IN CASE

If you love your guitar with the same intensity as your first crush, and you live in mortal fear of the slightest ding or gouge, you'll want to get the sturdiest guitar case available. On the other hand, if you just want something in which to carry your axe, you may not be so picky. At any rate, here are a few guitar-case options, along with some price ranges.

Gig Bags

A *gig bag* is sort of like a backpack made to the shape of a guitar (see below). You shove your guitar inside, zip it up, strap it on your shoulders, and away you go. Most gig bags are slightly padded, so they resist bumps and scrapes, but they offer little protection if dropped or shoved into the back of a pickup truck. The advantages are the portability and the price. A cheap gig bag goes for around $30, with the average price ranging from $60 to $100.

Hard-shell Cases

The *hard-shell case* is the industry standard (see below). Hard-shell cases resemble sturdy suitcases. They have latches (some lock), are covered in vinyl or leather, and come with a carrying handle. Some hard-shell cases are a bit flimsy, but others will hold the weight of a child standing on it. The sturdier the case, the higher the price. Expect to pay $100–$150 for a well-made hard-shell case.

Flight Cases

The *flight case* offers maximum protection for your precious instrument (see below). Made from plywood or heavy plastic and covered with metal corners, some close so tight that they protect a guitar from the elements (e.g., heat or rain). If you're going to be traveling on an airplane, you'll want a flight case. The advantages speak for themselves, but the disadvantages are that they're very heavy (usually much heavier than the guitar itself) and expensive. Expect to shell out upwards of $400 for a good flight case.

Hard-shell Case

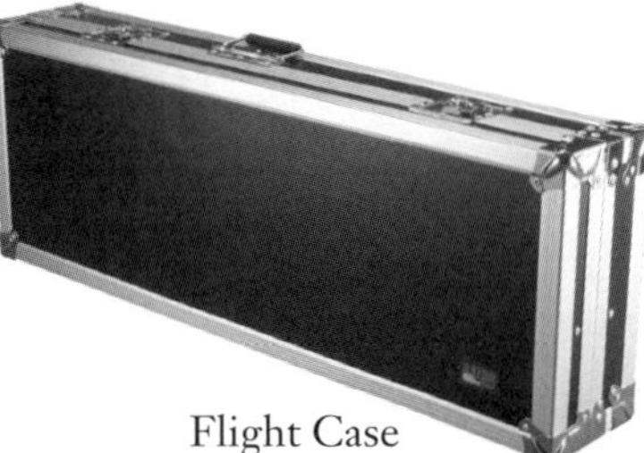

Flight Case

Gig Bag

PICKUPS

It may come as a surprise, but pickups are considered an accessory among guitar aficionados. Many guitarists remove existing pickups and replace them with other types and brands. The reasoning behind this lies in the fact that the pickup is the heart of the guitar and gives the instrument its special character.

Single-coils and Humbuckers

Pickups are generally divided into two groups: *single-coil* and *humbucker* (see below). Single-coil, or single-pole, pickups are the skinny pickups you'll see on most Fender guitars, such as the Stratocaster and the Telecaster. Humbuckers, or twin-pole pickups, are the fatter pickups you'll see on Les Pauls or PRS guitars. Single-coil pickups tend to be brighter and more cutting than humbuckers, which produce a fatter, warmer sound. Humbucking pickups are also more powerful and can push an amp to distortion sooner than single-coils. However, the twin-pole design of the humbucker cancels the electronic hum generated by single-coil pickups. (Hence, the term "bucks the hum.") Popular replacement pickups include Seymour Duncan, DiMarzio, and Fender. The average price for a single-coil is $80; $120 for a humbucker.

Single-coil

Humbucker

If your guitar produces a shrill, high-end feedback whenever you step on the distortion button, you may want to consider purchasing a good replacement pickup. This type of feedback is called *microphonic feedback*, and is a common dilemma of cheaply made pickups.

STRINGS

Strings come in various gauges (sizes), and are made from a few different materials. You can buy them individually (not recommended), or in "six packs." Buying strings by the pack is much cheaper than paying for them individually. (The average price for a set of electric-guitar strings is $8.) Electric-guitar strings are usually made from steel and nickel. Popular brands include Ernie Ball, D'Addario, Fender, GHS, and Dean Markley. String sets are named either by the gauge of the high E string (8s, 9s, 10s, etc., which stand for .008, .009, and .010 millimeters), or in more descriptive terms such as light, medium, and heavy. Light strings are easier to bend, but they also break easier than medium- and heavy-gauge strings. Also, the heavier the string gauge, the better the tone. When you buy strings, make sure they match the gauge that came with your guitar. A qualified repairman can tell you what size to get. Here are the choices:

Name	Gauge
Ultra Light	.008
Super Light	.009
Light	.010
Medium	.012
Heavy	.013

Acoustic-guitar strings are most often made of bronze. Dependable brand names include Martin, D'Addario, and Dean Markley. (Prices start at around $9.) The gauges run heavier for acoustics. Here are your choices:

Name	Gauge
Extra Light	.010
Light	.011
Medium	.012
Heavy	.013

Nylon strings (for classical guitar) usually come in either high or medium tension. Popular brands include La Bella, Adamas, and D'Addario. The average price for a set of nylon strings is $10.

ODDS & ENDS

Here are a few more items to add to the accessories list:

Capos

Back in the "Folk" chapter we talked about using a *capo*, but we didn't talk prices. Capos cost in the neighborhood of $20, but you can get an inexpensive, elastic one for less than $5. Below are a variety of capos. You'll notice they come in all shapes and sizes, but they all get the job done. Be aware that, while most capos fit the majority of electric and steel-string acoustics, many of them won't reach across the wider fretboards of nylon-string (classical) guitars. It would be a good idea to take your guitar with you to the store when you purchase a capo. That way, you can try several on for size.

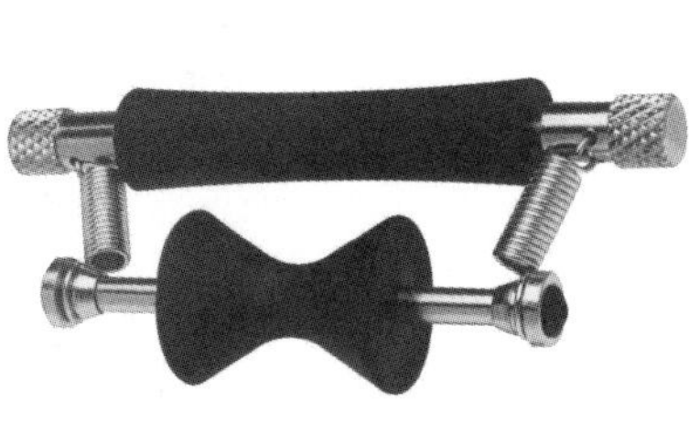

Glider

Partial capo

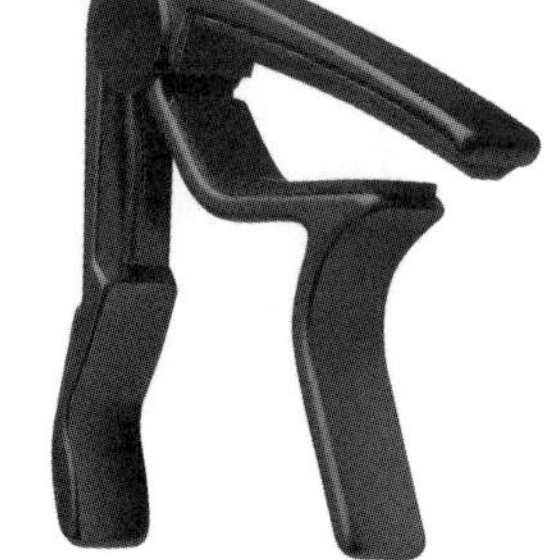

Dunlop

Slides

Slides are used on the fretting hand to literally slide between notes, creating a smooth, legato effect. You'll hear slides used often in blues by players such as Muddy Waters, Duane Allman, and Ry Cooder. Slides come in different sizes, weights, and materials (see below). Lighter slides are made of glass; heavier slides are either nickel or brass. Before purchasing a slide, you'll need to decide which finger to wear it on. Most players wear them on their third or fourth finger. Try several on for size, and choose the one that doesn't fit too tightly or slip off too easily. The average price for a slide is around $8.

Dunlop Hoolahan

Steel Ceramic

Glass

Cables

Guitar cables (or cords) are an absolute necessity for electric guitarists. You'll need at least one to connect your guitar to the amplifier. A few words of advice: Don't buy cheap guitar cables! They wear out quickly, and they have a tendency to be noisy. Ernie Ball, Monster Cable, Fender, ProCo, Hosa, and Spectraflex make reliable cables in most any size, from one foot (for connecting effects pedals) to 25 feet and more. The average price for an 18–20 footer (recommended) is around $22.

Straps

Guitar *straps* come in a variety of materials. Some are made of leather, some are vinyl, and some are of a cloth material. Choosing a strap can be like picking out a pair of shoes; there are scads of colors and widths from which to choose. If you simply want a serviceable strap and don't care about fashion, you can pick up one for around $12. If you want a nice leather one, expect to pay upwards of $60. The main thing is comfort. Don't buy a skinny (less than 2 inches) strap that's going to dig into your shoulder. And make sure it's adjustable, so you can hang your guitar at the height that suits you.

Picks

You would think that a *guitar pick* is just a guitar pick. Not so! There are a multitude of shapes and sizes. Some are flexible (thin), and some are hard as a rock (extra heavy). If you've never used a pick, start with a Fender medium. They're easy to find, and they represent the middle ground of guitar picks. From there, you can decide if you want a thinner pick, a heavier pick, a smaller pick, or a larger pick. Three picks will cost you roughly $1.

Some guitarists use fingerpicks. Fingerpicks attach to the tips of the fingers, similar to backwards fingernails. (The thumbpick attaches to the thumb, at a right angle.) You can pick up a set of fingerpicks for around $5.

Jazz

Thumbpick

Fingerpick

Standard

Standard

Headphone Amps

You'd think that you could plug your guitar straight into a set of headphones and be able to hear yourself, but it doesn't work that way. The electric guitar has a dinky electrical current, and, therefore, needs to be souped-up to power any speaker, no matter how small. If you want to practice in the privacy of your own little headphone world, you can always plug into the "headphone jack" of your practice amp (if you own one). But if you want to wander from room to room, or go outside, or play at the beach, you'll need a *headphone amp*. Two popular models are the Dean "Stack in a Box" ($63) and the Rockman "Guitar Ace" ($99). Both models are small enough, and light enough, to attach to your belt without pulling your trousers down.

Electronic Tuners

The *electronic tuner* is a marvelous invention that allows you to tune up without even hearing yourself. Most tuners run on batteries, and are small enough to pack away in your guitar case. Korg, Boss, and Sabine are among the most popular models. Prices range from $25 to $150. (See Chapter 2 for more on tuning.)

Guitar Stand

Guitar Stands

It's a bad habit to lean your guitar up against the amp, or leave it lying on the couch. Do yourself a favor and invest in a *guitar stand*. Most stands are adjustable and fold down to a compact size for transporting purposes. Prices range from $20 to $40.

String-changing Tools

Allen wrenches: If your guitar is equipped with a whammy-bar unit, chances are you'll need an Allen wrench (L-shaped tool with a hexagonal head, used to turn screws with hexagonal sockets) to remove the strings. Allen wrenches come in all different sizes so make sure yours matches the socket of your Allen screws.

Needle-nose pliers: A pair of pliers (preferably needle-nose) is invaluable for pulling out old strings caught up in the tuning pegs or bridge. You can also use them to pull out your string pegs (acoustic guitars only).

Roadie wrench: This all-in-one tool is like a guitar player's Swiss Army knife. Usually included are a set of Allen wrenches of various sizes, screwdrivers, and wire cutters.

String winder: Use this handy little device to rapidly wind the strings. It not only saves time, it saves your wrist from a world of hurt. Many string winders come with a special notch at one end, which can be used to pull the string pegs from acoustic guitars.

Wire cutter: You'll need a wire cutter to snip the ends of your strings at the headstock. Unless, of course, you like pointed wires dangling like a weapon at the end of your instrument.

- There are three types of guitar cases: gig bags, hard-shell cases, and flight cases.
- Single-coil pickups are brighter than humbuckers, which are fatter and warmer sounding.
- Light-gauge strings are easier to bend than heavy-gauge strings. The downside is that they break easier.
- Heavy-gauge strings have superior tone.
- Never lean your guitar up against the wall. Place it in its case or on a guitar stand.

CHAPTER 25
PUTTING ON NEW STRINGS

What's Ahead:

- Changing strings on acoustic guitars
- Changing strings on a classical guitar
- Changing strings on electric guitars
- Dealing with a whammy-bar system

You may be asking, "Why put off the subject of changing strings until now?" Because, if we introduced it in Section 1 you may have given up on the guitar right then and there and taken up the kazoo or something. Initially, learning to change the strings on your guitar can be a frustrating experience. It can also be painful if you don't exercise some caution. But never fear! We're going to hold your hand all the way through your first string-changing ordeal. On second thought, how can you change your strings if we hold your hand? Never mind. We'll just guide you through, step by step.

CHANGING STRINGS

Before you can slap on new strings, you have to remove the old ones. Until you're really good at changing strings, it's wise to change them individually. (In other words, *don't take the old strings off all at once!*) This especially pertains to electric guitars, as there are more parts that can pop off if you remove all of the strings.

Removing Old Strings

Let's begin with the high E string. Start by detuning the string until it's completely slack. Next, take a needle-nose pliers and detach the string from the tuning peg. Depending on how it was originally put on the guitar, this may take some doing, but if you're patient, you'll get it loose. Be careful not to poke your finger on the tip of the string. Those babies are sharp!

The last step is to free the string from the bridge of the guitar. On a steel-string acoustic, you need to pull the bridge pin (or string peg) out of the bridge to release the string. Depending on the snugness of the peg fitting, you may be able to use just your fingers. If it doesn't pull free, use the special slot in a string winder (see "String-changing Tools," Chapter 24). If you don't own a string winder, you can use pliers, but be careful not to scratch your guitar. If you're removing the string from a classical guitar, simply untie the string at the bridge. Removing the string from the bridge of an electric guitar usually just involves slipping the string through the tailpiece behind the bridge, or through the body of the guitar (Fender guitars).

Now that you've removed your high E string, you're ready to put the new one on.

Be extremely careful when you remove steel strings from the headstock. The ends are as sharp as needles, especially on the high E, B, and G strings.

Stringing-up Acoustics

Here's a step-by-step outline for changing strings on a steel-string acoustic guitar:

Attaching the String to the Bridge

1. Remove the old string from the tuning peg and the bridge.

2. Be sure you have the correct string (check the string's name on its package), and then shove the ball end (not the pointy end) of the string approximately a half inch down into the bridge's peg hole.
3. While holding onto the string with one hand, use your other hand to wedge the bridge pin into the hole. (The string should be positioned on the neck side of the hole, with the peg on the bridge side.) The bridge pin has a little groove in it, which should align with the string.
4. Gently tug up on the string to make sure the ball end is right up against the bottom of the peg. Be careful not to put a kink in the long section of string.

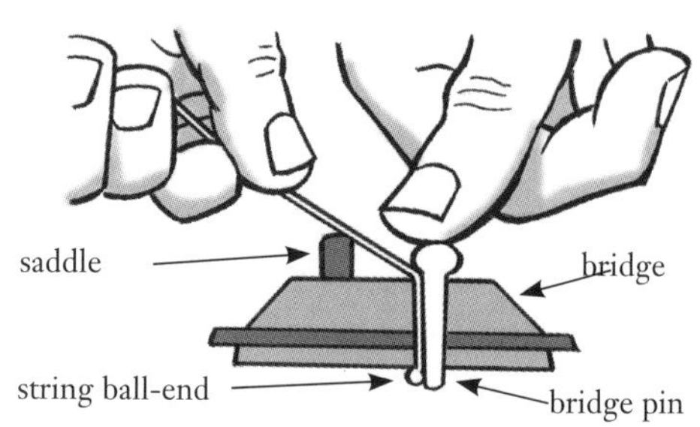

Attaching a String to the Treble Side of the Headstock (High E, B, and G Strings)

1. Now that the string is attached to the bridge, pass the other end through the hole of the corresponding tuning peg on the headstock. Don't pull too tight; you'll want to leave a little slack in the string so that there will be enough length to wind a few times around the tuning post.
2. Bring the end of the string toward the center of the headstock and loop it underneath itself.
3. Bring the end of the string back over itself (toward the headstock) and bend it down so that it makes a kink, or crease, at the junction (see below).
4. Brace yourself—this is the trickiest part. Gently hold the string down between the nut and the tuning peg with your right hand and turn the tuning peg counterclockwise with your left hand. Keep turning until the kink at the string junction is at least halfway around the tuning post. Now you can let go of the string and tune it to pitch.
5. Once you've tuned the string to pitch, pull up on it in several places along the neck. This will stretch it out and take up the loose windings at the tuning peg. You'll have to tune the string again after pulling on it.
6. When you're satisfied that you've stretched out the strings enough, snip off the excess string with wire cutters. Dangling strings are dangerous.

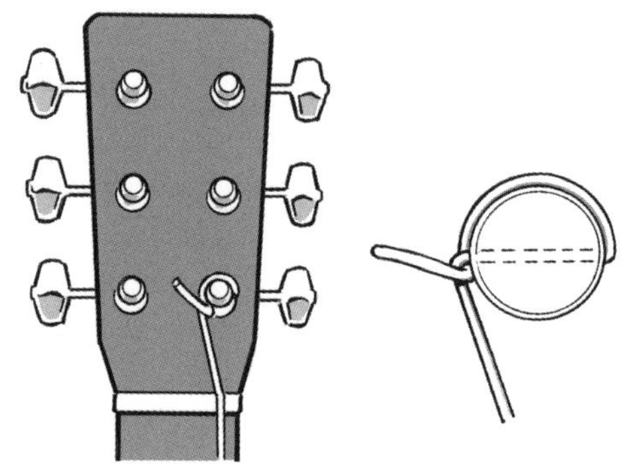

Attaching a String to the Bass Side of the Headstock (Low E, A, and D Strings)

1. Pass the string through the hole of the corresponding tuning peg.
2. Bring the end of the string in, toward the center of the headstock, and loop it underneath itself.
3. Bring the end of the string back over itself, and then bend it down so that it makes a kink at the junction where it folds over on itself.
4. Gently hold the string down between the nut and the tuning peg with your right hand and turn the tuning peg counterclockwise with your left hand. Keep turning until the kink at the string junction is at least halfway around the tuning post. Now you can let go of the string and tune it to pitch.

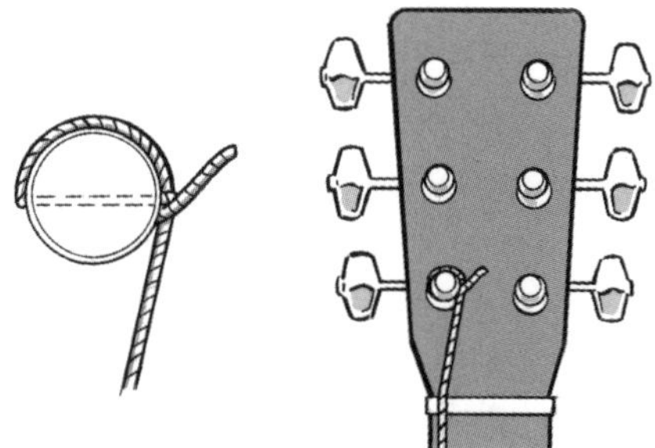

5. Once you've tuned the string to pitch, pull up on it in several places along the neck. This will stretch it out and take up the loose windings at the tuning peg. You'll have to tune the string again after pulling on it.
6. Don't forget to snip off the excess string with wire cutters.

Changing Nylon Strings

You'd think that changing strings on a classical guitar would be the same as on an acoustic guitar. Sorry, but there are some differences. For one thing, nylon strings are tied on at the bridge, instead of held in by pegs. For another, the tuning pegs of a classical guitar attach at a totally different angle than any other guitar.

Attaching the String to the Bridge

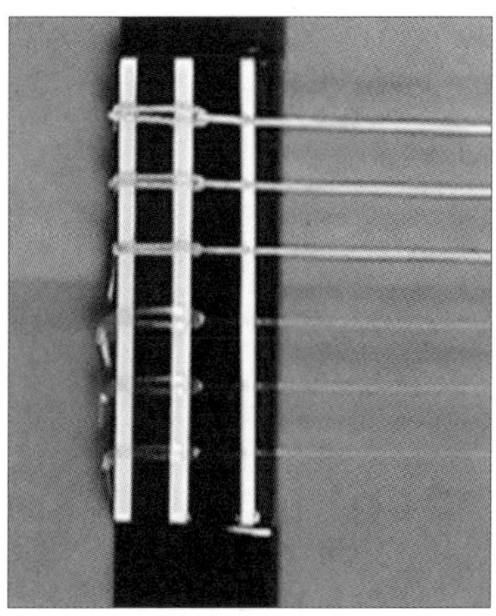

1. Remove the old string from the tuning peg and the bridge.
2. Make sure that you have the correct string, and then pass it through the hole in the bridge (the hole on the soundhole side of the bridge) until approximately two inches are peeking through the other side, toward the bottom of the guitar.
3. Bring the short end of the string over the bridge and loop it underneath itself. Secure it by bringing it back to the bridge and looping in under, over, and under again. The picture here shows the correct end result. If you don't get it right the first time, don't sweat it; just repeat the process.
4. Hold onto the short end of the string while you pull on the other end to take up slack.

Attaching the String to the Tuning Peg

1. Pass the string through the tuning "barrel" (the white roller inside the headstock that is attached to the tuning peg). Bring the end of the string back over the barrel and wrap it around itself two or three times.
2. Hold onto the string with your right hand, and then turn the tuning peg counterclockwise until the string wraps over the "knot" that you just made.
3. Hold the string taut above the fretboard with your right hand and tune the string to pitch.
4. When you're finished, snip off the excess string with wire cutters at the headstock and the bridge.

Re-stringing an Electric Guitar

Here's a step-by-step guide for stringing an electric guitar:

Attaching the String to the Bridge

1. Remove the old string from the tuning peg and the bridge.
2. Make sure that you have the correct string (check the string's name on its package) and then slip it through the bridge (bottom side of guitar) until the ball end fits into its slot. (For Les Paul–type guitars, pass the string through the tailpiece behind the bridge. For Stratocaster- and Telecaster-style guitars, pass the string through the underside of the body.)

Attaching the String to the Tuning Peg

If your guitar has three tuning pegs on either side of the headstock (standard design), follow the steps in "Stringing-up Acoustics" in this chapter. If your guitar has all six tuning pegs on the bass side of the headstock (Stratocaster- and Telecaster-type guitars), follow the instructions for attaching strings on the bass side of the headstock.

Whammy-bar Frustration

If your guitar is equipped with a whammy-bar system, you'll need a set of Allen wrenches to change strings. With a whammy-bar system, it's terribly frustrating to change strings if you remove them all at once. Do yourself a favor—change them one at a time. Here's a step-by-step guide for changing strings on a whammy-bar system:

Removing Old Strings

1. Unlock the nut clamp with an Allen wrench and detune the string.
2. Remove the string from the tuning peg.
3. Unclamp the string at the bridge mechanism with an Allen wrench.

Attaching the String to the Bridge

1. Make sure that you have the correct string, and then snip the ball-end off approximately two inches from the end.
2. Slip the string into the bridge saddle and tighten the clamp with an Allen wrench.

Attaching the String to the Tuning Peg

1. Slip the string through the locking mechanism at the nut.
2. If your guitar has three tuning pegs on either side of the headstock (standard design), follow the steps in "Stringing-up Acoustics" in this chapter. If your guitar has all six tuning pegs on the bass side of the headstock (Stratocaster- and Telecaster-type guitars), follow the instructions for attaching strings on the bass side of the headstock.
3. Once you've tuned to pitch, clamp the locking mechanism at the nut with an Allen wrench.
4. Use the fine tuner located on the whammy-bar mechanism to tune the string to pitch.

- When learning to change strings, remove and replace each string individually.
- Beware of those sharp, nasty little string endings.
- Always double-check to make sure that you're attaching the correct string (e.g., mistaking the B string for the G string).
- Never remove all of the strings at once from a whammy-bar equipped guitar—unless you want to drive yourself crazy.

SECTION 7

Who's Who

CHAPTER 26
TEN GROUNDBREAKING GUITARISTS

What's Ahead:

- Ten influential guitarists

In this section, you'll learn of ten guitarists who changed history. Well, maybe they didn't change history, but they all had a significant role in the evolution of guitar playing.

ANDRES SEGOVIA (1893–1987)

Andres Segovia was not only the father of modern classical guitar; he was the most celebrated guitarist of the 20th century. Interestingly, his parents discouraged his interests in becoming a musician. Unable to secure a teacher, he taught himself. Fortunately, because his first recital (at the age of 15) was so well received, he was encouraged to pursue a career as a concert soloist. His reputation grew and, eventually, he was able to sell out the largest concert halls in the world.

Photo by Palm/Rsch/Redferns

But Segovia is not solely remembered for his superior musicianship. Concerned with the lack of guitar concert repertoire (before Segovia, the guitar was not well respected in the classical realm), he launched a lifetime campaign to persuade prominent composers to write for the instrument. In addition to his ambassadorial endeavors, Segovia's master classes in Italy and Spain drew serious classical students from around the world. Many of his students are famous players today, among them Christopher Parkening and John Williams.

Guitarists of any genre owe a debt of gratitude to this great master. Were it not for Segovia, the guitar may never have had the chance to evolve into the world's most popular musical instrument.

ROBERT JOHNSON (1911–1938)

Robert Johnson may well be the most mysterious figure in guitar history. Legend has it, Johnson was a struggling, mediocre blues guitarist, largely ignored, and sometimes laughed at. Frustrated and angry, he went down to the crossroads at midnight to make a deal with the devil. As you've probably guessed, the devil awarded Johnson with superior guitar chops in exchange for his immortal soul.

Whether the legend is truth or fiction, there's no disputing the fact that Robert Johnson was a blues talent like no other. Though his recordings contain only him singing and playing unaccompanied, at times you'd swear there are two people playing simultaneously. It's Johnson who popularized the classic boogie-bass pattern that has become a staple of the blues. Many classic turnarounds, slide licks, and riffs also point back to his early creations.

Though Johnson achieved great success in his short lifetime, he remained a tortured soul, and constantly complained of nightmares in which "hellhounds were on his trail." This torment came out in his lyrics and in the essence of his music. Whether arranged by Satan himself or just plain bad luck, Johnson didn't get to enjoy his newfound fame for very long. He died at the age of 27, from a lethal dose of poisoned liquor, supposedly administered by a jealous girlfriend.

Photo © 1989 Delta Haze Corporation. All Rights Reserved

Photo by Charles Naden/Frank Driggs Collection

CHARLIE CHRISTIAN (1916–1942)

Somewhere in the heart of virtually every jazz guitarist resides the spirit of Charlie Christian, the undisputed father of electric jazz guitar. In his all-too-brief career (he died of tuberculosis in 1942 at the age of 25), Christian set the standards that have become the very staples of traditional jazz guitar. One of the first guitarists to use an amplifier, Christian played with the fluidity of a horn player. Weaving long, intervallic lines fueled with swung eighth notes, he would enhance them with rhythmic motifs (repeating rhythmic figures) and blues-scale phrases. A two-year stint with Benny Goodman's Sextet afforded the guitarist considerable exposure, and toward the end of his short life he began jamming with future bebop musicians Thelonious Monk and Dizzy Gillespie. Had he lived, there's little doubt he would have become the first great bebop guitarist.

DJANGO REINHARDT (1910–1953)

When you consider the circumstances, it's indeed ironic that a Belgium-born Gypsy named Django Reinhardt would become the most influential acoustic guitarist in jazz history. First, in the '30s, jazz was snobbishly considered an exclusive American art form. Second, there was Reinhardt's severe handicap: the third and fourth fingers of his left hand were scarred and paralyzed, the result of a fire that had swept through his family's caravan when he was a teenager. Persevering, he managed to develop a highly unorthodox technique in which he mostly relied on his first two fingers for normal fretting, occasionally planting his permanently fixed digits on the higher strings to play chord voicings. During the next few years, he laid the groundwork for a playing style that would eventually astound and inspire musicians throughout the world.

Photo provided by Frank Driggs Collection

A true visionary, Reinhardt was churning out blazing melodies and breathtaking improvisations in the mid-'30s, a time when guitar was largely considered a rhythm instrument. Backed by his band, the Quintet of the Hot Club of France, his un-amplified acoustic exploded with personality that reflected his Gypsy soul. Whether putting forth fiery diminished runs, sensitive melodies, furiously tremoloed chromatic passages, or chord-melody flurries, the essence of his music was at once sophisticated and whimsical, intensely romantic, free-spirited, unpredictable, and consistently brilliant.

Photo courtesy of Country Hall of Fame

CHET ATKINS (1924–2001)

Though he was known as "Mr. Guitar" by the rest of the music world, Chet Atkins referred to himself as "C.G.P." (Certified Guitar Player), and rightly so: he had 13 Grammy Awards to back it up. Inspired by Merle Travis' foundational fingerpicking technique, Atkins mixed elements of jazz, classical, and pop to forge a style uniquely his own. A wearer of many hats, Atkins was a solo artist, a session player, a producer, and the vice president of RCA records. Mr. Guitar's contributions to country music are fathomless. He's credited for creating the "Nashville sound," and was instrumental in helping country music cross over from the southern barroom jukeboxes to the pop mainstream.

B.B. KING (1925–2015)

Riley "B.B." King was the undisputed "King of the Blues" and its eldest statesman. Truly a world ambassador for one of America's greatest art forms, B.B. was a living legend and a one-of-a-kind blues guitarist. Many musicians state that they can recognize his playing with one note. Of course, that note would be drenched with B.B.'s trademark "hummingbird" vibrato and played with unparalleled conviction.

B.B.'s illustrious recording career began in 1951 with "Three O' Clock Blues," and continued until his death in 2015. His voluminous catalog is essential listening for anyone even pondering playing a 12-bar blues.

Photo by Marty Temme

CHUCK BERRY (1926–2017)

Bursting onto the scene in 1955 with his first hit "Maybelline," Charles "Chuck" Berry soon became rock's first guitar hero/poet/showman. Drawing from past blues and jazz formulas (blues boogie patterns, major/minor pentatonic soloing), Berry beefed up the tones, sped up the tempo, doubled the notes, and created a template for rock 'n' roll guitar that remains influential to this day.

A true showman (playing guitar behind his back, doing splits, and "duck walking" across the stage), Berry not only carved the cornerstone for rock guitar, he fashioned the flamboyant stage persona that has become the bar by which the performing lead guitarist is often judged.

Photo by Jan Persson/Redferns

ERIC CLAPTON (1945–)

Eric Clapton's career reads like a modern-day version of Homer's *Odyssey*. Through many ups and downs, good times and bad times, he has constantly reinvented himself, consistently rising to each and every occasion.

Born in suburban London, Clapton fell under the spell of American electric blues artists Muddy Waters and B.B. King while still a teenager. Through his kaleidoscope-like career, he has never wandered far from these early blues roots. His first touch with fame came as lead guitarist for the Yardbirds,

Photo by Marty Temme

one of Britain's most popular blues-rock bands in the mid-'60s. When the band became too "commercial" for Clapton's tastes, he joined up with John Mayall's Bluesbreakers for the critically acclaimed Blues Breakers With Eric Clapton. In 1966, he formed the legendary band Cream with Jack Bruce and Ginger Baker. It was during these years that Clapton developed what was to be the rock guitar tone: a Les Paul–style guitar through an overdriven Marshall amp.

Two more landmark groups followed, Blind Faith and Derek and the Dominoes, before Clapton finally went solo in 1974 with 461 Ocean Boulevard. He recorded many hit albums throughout the '70s and '80s, but it was his 1992 live Unplugged release, featuring acoustic versions of "Layla" and "Tears in Heaven," that catapulted him to mega-star status. On 1994's From the Cradle, Clapton returned full circle to his first love, electric blues. To date, he remains one of the most popular recording artists of our time.

JIMI HENDRIX (1942–1970)

Photo by Jan Persson/Redferns

In 1966, Jimi Hendrix appeared like a visitor from another planet, stepped foot on a London stage, and changed the face of rock guitar forever. In the following four years (his brief time in the spotlight), he went on to push the envelope of rock-guitar playing more than any before him or since. With a Fender Stratocaster strapped to his shoulders, various effects pedals at his feet, and Marshall stacks towering behind him, Hendrix captured and harnessed the roaring god of feedback. Not content to merely control it, he would play with it, as if it were a chord voicing he could move around the neck.

But beyond all the psychedelic mayhem, amp humping, and guitar burning, Hendrix played some of the most melodic, rhythmically complex, and harmonically structured solos, riffs, and rhythms in the entire rock idiom.

Photo by Marty Temme

EDDIE VAN HALEN (1955–)

If Eddie Van Halen had been a boxer, his first press release might have read something like this: "In 1978, an unknown L.A. guitarist named Eddie Van Halen bounced out of his corner of the ring to give the rock-guitar world a sucker punch to the side of the head from which it still hasn't recovered." In reality, the sucker punch was his jaw-dropping right hand–tapping solo extravaganza on "Eruption," from his band's self-titled debut album. Any rock guitarist who heard "Eruption," and every other lick on that album, subsequently hit the woodshed (for long practice sessions) for fear of being left behind in what was truly a new era for rock guitar.

CHORD CHART

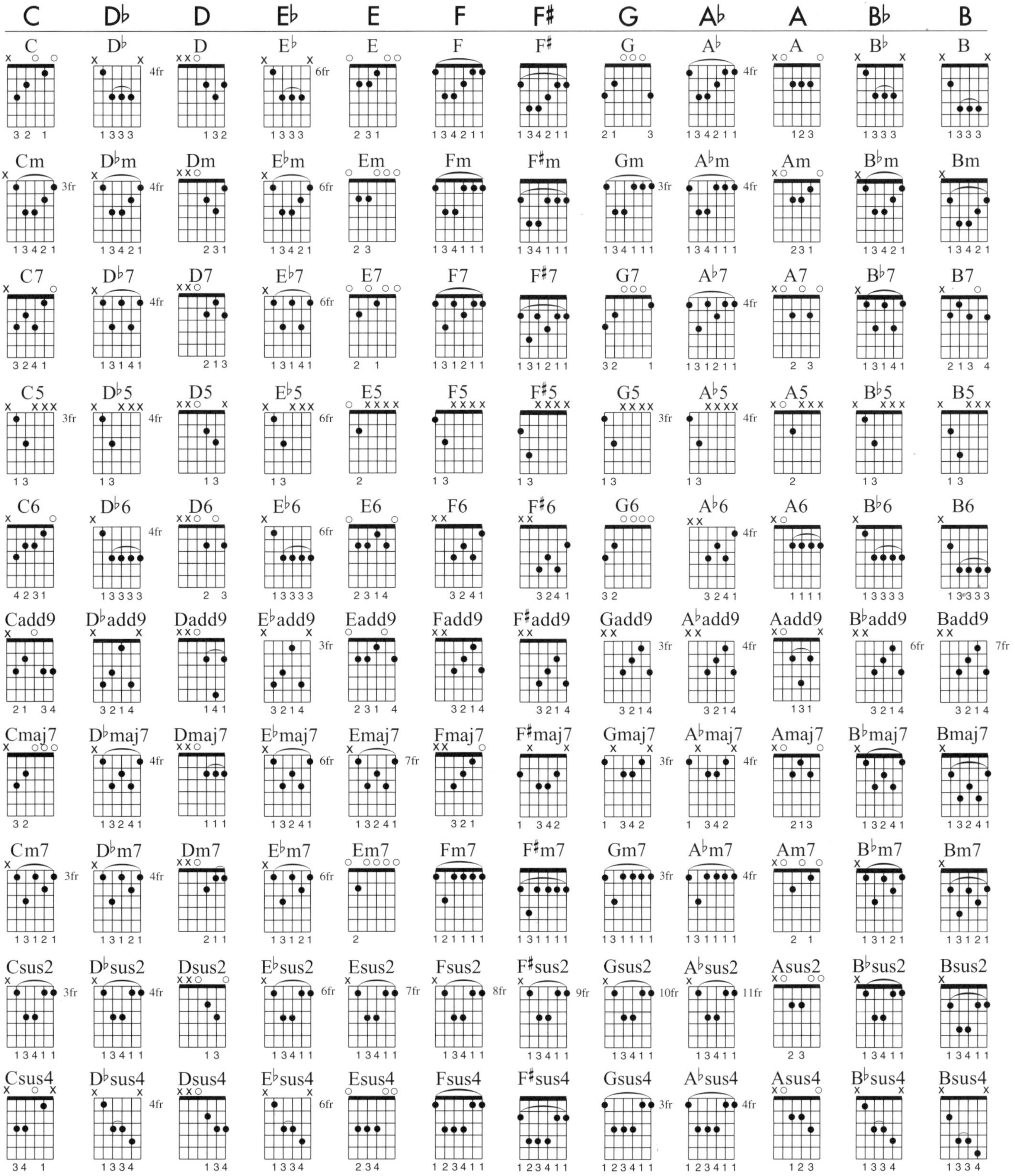

C	D♭	D	E♭	E	F	F♯	G	A♭	A	B♭	B
C 3 2 1	D♭ 4fr 1 3 3 3	D 1 3 2	E♭ 6fr 1 3 3 3	E 2 3 1	F 1 3 4 2 1 1	F♯ 1 3 4 2 1 1	G 2 1 3	A♭ 4fr 1 3 4 2 1 1	A 1 2 3	B♭ 1 3 3 3	B 1 3 3 3
Cm 3fr 1 3 4 2 1	D♭m 4fr 1 3 4 2 1	Dm 2 3 1	E♭m 6fr 1 3 4 2 1	Em 2 3	Fm 1 3 4 1 1 1	F♯m 1 3 4 1 1 1	Gm 3fr 1 3 4 1 1 1	A♭m 4fr 1 3 4 1 1 1	Am 2 3 1	B♭m 1 3 4 2 1	Bm 1 3 4 2 1
C7 3 2 4 1	D♭7 4fr 1 3 1 4 1	D7 2 1 3	E♭7 6fr 1 3 1 4 1	E7 2 1	F7 1 3 1 2 1 1	F♯7 1 3 1 2 1 1	G7 3 2 1	A♭7 4fr 1 3 1 2 1 1	A7 2 3	B♭7 1 3 1 4 1	B7 2 1 3 4
C5 3fr 1 3	D♭5 4fr 1 3	D5 1 3	E♭5 6fr 1 3	E5 2	F5 1 3	F♯5 1 3	G5 3fr 1 3	A♭5 4fr 1 3	A5 2	B♭5 1 3	B5 1 3
C6 4 2 3 1	D♭6 4fr 1 3 3 3 3	D6 2 3	E♭6 6fr 1 3 3 3 3	E6 2 3 1 4	F6 3 2 4 1	F♯6 3 2 4 1	G6 3 2	A♭6 4fr 3 2 4 1	A6 1 1 1 1	B♭6 1 3 3 3 3	B6 1 3 3 3 3
Cadd9 2 1 3 4	D♭add9 3 2 1 4	Dadd9 1 4 1	E♭add9 3fr 3 2 1 4	Eadd9 2 3 1 4	Fadd9 3 2 1 4	F♯add9 3 2 1 4	Gadd9 3fr 3 2 1 4	A♭add9 4fr 3 2 1 4	Aadd9 1 3 1	B♭add9 6fr 3 2 1 4	Badd9 7fr 3 2 1 4
Cmaj7 3 2	D♭maj7 4fr 1 3 2 4 1	Dmaj7 1 1 1	E♭maj7 6fr 1 3 2 4 1	Emaj7 7fr 1 3 2 4 1	Fmaj7 3 2 1	F♯maj7 1 3 4 2	Gmaj7 3fr 1 3 4 2	A♭maj7 4fr 1 3 4 2	Amaj7 2 1 3	B♭maj7 1 3 2 4 1	Bmaj7 1 3 2 4 1
Cm7 3fr 1 3 1 2 1	D♭m7 4fr 1 3 1 2 1	Dm7 2 1 1	E♭m7 6fr 1 3 1 2 1	Em7 2	Fm7 1 2 1 1 1 1	F♯m7 1 3 1 1 1 1	Gm7 3fr 1 3 1 1 1 1	A♭m7 4fr 1 3 1 1 1 1	Am7 2 1	B♭m7 1 3 1 2 1	Bm7 1 3 1 2 1
Csus2 3fr 1 3 4 1 1	D♭sus2 4fr 1 3 4 1 1	Dsus2 1 3	E♭sus2 6fr 1 3 4 1 1	Esus2 7fr 1 3 4 1 1	Fsus2 8fr 1 3 4 1 1	F♯sus2 9fr 1 3 4 1 1	Gsus2 10fr 1 3 4 1 1	A♭sus2 11fr 1 3 4 1 1	Asus2 2 3	B♭sus2 1 3 4 1 1	Bsus2 1 3 4 1 1
Csus4 3 4 1	D♭sus4 4fr 1 3 3 4	Dsus4 1 3 4	E♭sus4 6fr 1 3 3 4	Esus4 2 3 4	Fsus4 1 2 3 4 1 1	F♯sus4 1 2 3 4 1 1	Gsus4 3fr 1 2 3 4 1 1	A♭sus4 4fr 1 2 3 4 1 1	Asus4 1 2 3	B♭sus4 1 3 3 4	Bsus4 1 3 3 4

ABOUT THE AUTHOR

Veteran author, instructor, performing/recording artist Tom Kolb has lived, breathed, and dreamed guitar for over three decades (since the Beatles were still together!). His far-reaching career has found him playing in almost every musical situation imaginable, in virtually every style, from rock concerts to weddings; jazz gigs to folk hootenannies; country bars to Top-40 dance clubs; in addition to TV appearances, radio performances, recording sessions, and live performances (an estimated 6,000-plus of the latter two). Tom is also a celebrated educator: he has taught at world-famous Musicians Institute (G.I.T.) since 1989; holds an Associate Editor position at *Guitar One* magazine, for which he writes a monthly column (Soloing Strategies); has written several method books (*Amazing Phrasing*, *Modes for Guitar*, *Chord Progressions [101 Patterns from Folk to Funk]*, and *Theory for Guitar [Everything You Ever Wanted to Know But Were Afraid to Ask]*); and has been the featured artist in a variety of guitar instructional DVD/videos, including *50 Licks Rock Style*, *Fender Stratocaster Greats*, *Modes for the Lead Guitarist*, the *Starter Series*, *Best of Lennon and McCartney for Electric Guitar*, *Famous Rock Guitar Riffs and Solos*, *'60s Psychedelic Guitar*, *Advanced Chords and Rhythms*, and the *Hal Leonard Guitar Method*. All books and videos are available through Hal Leonard.

ACKNOWLEDGMENTS

I'd like to thank my wife, Hedy, and daughter, Flynnie, for their unconditional love and support, especially through the tumult of writing this book; my Dad, for driving me around to all those gigs way back when; all at Hal Leonard; Musicians Institute; *Guitar One*; and all my students past, present, and future, without whom I would lack a good amount of the drive to keep growing as a musician.

MUSICIANS

Tracks 1–46:

Tom Kolb: guitars, keyboards, and drum programming
Dan Brownfield: bass and assistant engineering
(Drum loops used: Backbeat, by Spectrasonics)

Tracks 47–51:

Doug Boduch: guitar
Tom McGirr: bass
Warren Wiegratz: keyboards
Scott Schroedl: drums
Jake Johnson: tracking, mixing, and mastering